“Keith Raffel is a writer of wide range and deep insights whose topics resonate with the authority of his diverse life experiences and strong, uncompromising voice. His engaging, thought-provoking commentary has become a critical component in the Daily Herald's diverse lineup of syndicated columnists.”
Jim Slusher
Managing Editor, Daily Herald (Suburban Chicago)

“Stop. Read. Think. How fortunate we are to have Keith Raffel to provide context, both historical and political, on the vital issues of the day. His thoughts spur us to formulate our own opinions, a much-needed effort in the fraught world that we live in.”
Judy Perry Martinez
President of the American Bar Association 2019-20

"This collection of Keith Raffel’s columns is a must-read and will be something you can go back to often for insight and reflection. His achievements aside, his writing is very accessible and reflects a palpable curiosity along with humor, candor, love of country and effective translation of complex current events through unpretentious observation, historical parallels, anecdotes and salient quotations from diverse sources including philosophers, historians and the Marx Brothers movie "Duck Soup." Even in the rare instance where one may not agree fully or always with his interesting take on things, his thoughts will stay with you, inform you and may change your mind! Do yourself a favor, read this and follow the work of Mr. Raffel. It is a jewel and packs the punch of art and truth."
Ty Cobb
Prominent Washington, D.C., lawyer and former White House Special Counsel

The Raffel Ticket

Betting on America

The Raffel Ticket

Betting on America

Keith Raffel

Creators Publishing
Hermosa Beach, CA

THE RAFFEL TICKET: BETTING ON AMERICA

Cover by Coral Black
Author photo: Doug Peck

CREATORS PUBLISHING
737 3rd St
Hermosa Beach, CA 90254
310-337-7003

ISBN (print): 978-1-962693-24-0
ISBN (ebook): 978-1-962693-25-7

First Edition
Printed in the United States of America
1 3 5 7 9 10 8 6 4 2

Contents

Introduction

Each week, I sit down and write an essay of around 800 words to scratch a recurring mental itch. Now, to my amazement, I've accumulated well over a hundred of them. Sitting here now in front of my keyboard, I wonder how the heck that happened. The underlying explanation has to be my discomfort, my anger, my frustration with the world we live in. I love my family, adore my friends, delight in my students and cherish what America stands for, but I am far from happy with a planet where hunger, violence, poverty, callousness, authoritarianism, racism, antisemitism, sexism, inequality and unfairness flourish.

As a first resort, I tried to escape from this world. Writing my novels transported me to fictional realms, where justice (usually) triumphed and I had (some) control over what happened. But in the end, writing fiction just wasn't enough.

The ancient sage Tarfon_said: "The work is plentiful. ... It is not your duty to finish the work, but neither are you at liberty to neglect it." Calling from across two millennia, Tarfon reminded me that even though the world will never be perfect, I had an obligation to do more about improving it. It was time do some writing cemented in the real world, not the imaginary one dwelling inside my head. I started submitting occasional opinion pieces to newspapers, magazines and websites, which addressed topics such as gun deaths, the wisdom of women voters, rampant careerism among students, Trump's pro-Russian past and the importance of studying the humanities. Then I decided I wanted to do more still, something more regularly. I bundled up those dozen or so columns published over seven years and sent them to Creators Syndicate. They offered me the opportunity to write a column every week, and this book is the result — so far.

Friends asked how I was going to come up with enough ideas to write a short essay every seven days. Credit — or blame — Trump and his cronies, their Democratic opposition, the Supreme Court, Hamas, American education and Silicon Valley for ensuring there's never a shortage. I have a file of over 100 pages on my laptop titled "Column Ideas." It continues to grow. After two years of column-writing, I have a rhythm. On Tuesdays I compose a first draft, often pretty rough. On Wednesdays I edit and polish the piece and submit it by 1:30 in the afternoon.

The writing process helps me grapple with how I feel about the problems of the world. In essence, I am thinking with my fingertips. As the brilliant novelist and essayist Joan Didion explained, "I write entirely to find out what I'm thinking, what I'm looking at, what I see and what it means." Me, too. And without those two days of articulating my concerns and frustrations, of ranting, I think I would burst. Now that I've started, I can't shut up. So, each week's column might provide therapy for me, but what is it doing to make the world a better place? Has it stopped gun deaths, terrorism in the Middle East, government roundups on American streets, corruption at the highest levels?

The German philosopher Friedrich Nietzsche wrote, "Beware of spitting against the wind!" Sometimes it feels as though that's exactly what I'm doing each week. Little frustrates me more than ignorance of the past. Americans, including those who live in the White House and work on Capitol Hill, don't seem to know much about historical events such as the American failure to conquer Canada in the War of 1812, the role the Smoot-Hawley tariffs played in causing the Great Depression, the American roundup of citizens during World War II, the Civil Rights Movement of the 1960s, Nixon's Watergate coverup and the Arab rejections of a Palestinian state in 1937, 1948, 2000 and 2008. As the Roman philosopher and orator Cicero said, "To be ignorant of what occurred before you were born is to remain always a child."

I do take some solace when I see my columns shared on social media and read responses to them in letters to the editor. It doesn't matter much whether the column is praised or criticized as "intellectually embarrassing" as a recent one was by a reader. What matters is that the columns are reaching people and maybe even making them think.

Thank you for reading what I write. We form a partnership. Without you, I would indeed just be spitting into the wind.

— *Keith Raffel*

Fox News and Liberal College Fail to Answer to Higher Authority

April 19, 2023

In abruptly settling a lawsuit on Tuesday, Fox News admitted to airing falsehoods about the 2020 presidential election. There was much less coverage of Marymount University's decision earlier this year to do away with nine undergraduate majors. Two disparate, unconnected stories? No, I don't think so. Underneath lurks a disturbing similarity that exposes the cracking foundations of two of our nation's vital institutions.

Guests and hosts on Fox News supported claims that voting machines covertly transferred votes from Donald Trump to Joe Biden in the aftermath of the 2020 presidential election. Fox star Tucker Carlson tried to squelch a reporter's tweet that there was no voter fraud in Arizona involving the manufacturer of the voting machines. In a text, he urged: "Please get her fired. Seriously...." Why? Not for bad or untrue reporting but because her story was "measurably hurting the company. The stock price is down."

In February, the trustees of Marymount University, the Catholic liberal arts school in Virginia, unanimously voted to do away with undergraduate majors in disciplines including history, English, theology and religious studies, philosophy, art and mathematics. A college spokesperson indicated this was done to improve its finances and increase enrollment.

In the case of Fox, money trumped the network's promise to provide the "most watched, most trusted" news. With Marymount, money overrode the goal to provide an education "grounded in the liberal arts ... that values diversity and focuses on the education of the whole person."

The Nobel Prize-winning economist Milton Friedman said, "There is one and only one social responsibility of business — to use its resources and engage in activities designed to increase its profit." I understand that. I myself founded a Silicon Valley internet company. But are there not businesses like the kosher hot dog brand Hebrew National that "answer to a higher authority"?

In the very first provision of our Constitution's Bill of Rights, freedom of the press is guaranteed. Why this special treatment? As former President Herbert Hoover explained, "Self-government can succeed only through an instructed electorate." The Washington Post's motto says it this way — "Democracy dies in darkness." Lies do not instruct nor enlighten. So don't Fox's Tucker Carlson and his colleagues have a moral, if not legal, obligation to instruct and not deceive the electorate? Isn't being a source of news critical to democracy, and therefore different from a business that manufactures computers or builds roads? In a time when newspapers are going under at a disturbing rate, one can understand the pressure to turn out profits, but a news network still has a special role in a democracy.

Marymount University said it was cutting programs that were "no longer serving Marymount students" in order to invest in programs that give the school a competitive advantage. The competitive advantage is doing an especially good job in preparing students for well-paying positions in "the fulfilling, in-demand careers of the future." Yes, students do have loans to pay off, and the university can do no good if no students apply. But take a step back and think about what's happening. A liberal arts university is eliminating art as a major. A Catholic university is eliminating theology and religious studies as a major. Pope Benedict said: "A good school provides a rounded education for the whole person. And a good Catholic school, over and above this, should help all its students to become saints." Shouldn't any liberal arts college measure the success of its students by values imparted as well as by dollars earned?

Those reporting and those teaching should not be just holding down a job. They should be supporting the pillars of democracy, our freedom, now and in the future. And if news sources and universities are motivated only by money, I fear what the future holds for our democracy and for today's students.

Poll of Young Americans Gives Reasons for Despair ... and Hope

April 26, 2023

A generational shift at the top of America's political system is inevitable before the end of the decade. After all, Joe Biden is 80, Donald Trump is 76 and 16 members of the Senate are 75 or older. The so-called Gen Z will play an important role in how that shift evolves.

Does that scare you? Me, I don't know whether to be more frightened or more hopeful. The results of the Harvard Youth Poll of 18- to 29-year-old Americans, released this week, can be read to support either reaction.

So just who are these young Americans who will determine what kind of country we'll be living in before too long? It's a generation where almost half of its members have felt "down, depressed, or hopeless" in the two weeks prior to being polled. And in the same period, almost a quarter figured they would be better off dead or thought of hurting themselves.

Who can blame them? Look at the world they're being handed, one where existential threats — climate change, pandemics, artificial intelligence and nuclear war — loom. Half of the females polled fear sexual assault, 2 in 5 respondents fear being caught in a mass shooting, while nearly one-third fear being left homeless.

It sure doesn't sound like fun to be a young American in the 2020s. "From fears of mass shootings to concerns of one day becoming homeless, the current state of Gen Z could perhaps best be summarized in one word: anxious," said Ethan Jasny, the student director of the poll. (Disclosure: Ethan, an undergraduate, and I, a resident scholar, regularly discuss politics over meals in the dorm where we both live.)

And yet, and yet, there are grounds to hope this generation will nudge our country to a fairer, healthier, safer society.

In the last 10 years, the number of 18- to 29-year-olds who believe government should guarantee a basic right to health insurance has risen from 42% to 65%. For a guarantee to food and shelter the number has climbed to 62%. And the multitude of droughts, heat spells, hurricanes and floods has apparently convinced 50% of the cohort to demand the government do more about climate change even at the expense of economic growth (up from 29%).

Almost three-quarters of the cohort support psychological exams for gun purchasers including a majority of Democrats (88%), Republicans (59%) and independents (71%). A 2-1 majority (58% to 29%) want to see a ban on assault weapons.

What then is the best way for the country's 18- to 29-year-olds to make what they want move from wish to reality? It's sure not Aladdin rubbing a lamp! John Lewis, the giant of the Civil Rights Movement, wisely said, "The vote ... is the most powerful nonviolent tool we have in a democratic society, and we must use it."

Alas, in the 2022 midterm elections, not even a quarter (23%) of 18- to 29-year-olds voted. Still, there are promising signs. While the 23% turnout in 2022 is dismal, it is still up from the typical 20% of the 1990s. And those who agreed with the statement "my rights are under attack in America today" were 9% more likely to vote. Hopeful? Maybe, but still over half of these young Americans worried about their rights do not bother to vote.

So there are trends that are promising on the one hand and disappointingly weak on the other. Being passive-aggressive — complaining about the wrongheadedness of elected officials and the ineffectiveness of government while not voting — is no path to change. It's a shortcut to anxiety and even more useless than rubbing a lamp.

The key question then for a young American today is whether they are going to sink into a mire of anxiety or participate in the political process to make for a better world. Of course, 18- to 29-year-olds can and should work for candidates, contribute to campaigns, post lawn signs and — why not? — even run for office. But the first two steps must be to register to vote and then to cast a ballot.

Today's young Americans can come together to make the choices that determine the future of our country. For their sake and for the sake of the country, I sure hope they choose to do so in rapidly increasing numbers.

Apathy or Applause Among Voters for Trump's Relations with Women?

May 3, 2023

As evidence mounts that Donald Trump raped E. Jean Carroll in a department store dressing room, so his lead mounts in the race for the 2024 Republican nomination for president.

The jury has not yet issued a verdict in the New York courtroom where Carroll, a journalist and long-time columnist for Elle Magazine, is suing Trump for sexual assault. Still, witnesses under oath supported her claims in a New York courtroom this week.

In CBS polling done after the trial had begun, Trump climbed to a 36-point lead over runner-up Florida Gov. Ron DeSantis. That's up from a 13% average advantage in mid-January polls.

There are two logical reasons why Trump could be widening his lead in the nomination contest despite the trial and despite another case where Trump has been indicted for paying hush money to cover up a sexual encounter. First, because any negatives surrounding the accusations don't count much in the opinion of potential supporters compared to Trump's appeal over DeSantis and other candidates. Second, because the accusations do count, but to actually *increase* Trump's appeal.

Under the first scenario, many GOP voters believe that anything Trump might do or say, whether legal or illegal, matters far less than the essence of what he stands for. They see him as their champion in a fight against an undeserving "other" that includes immigrants, coastal elites, liberals, Muslims, people of color, the Washington establishment, corrupt vote counters and feminist women. Why settle for any pale imitation?

Or could it be that the charges directed at Trump actually add to his brand and allure? Are MAGA voters flocking to him over

DeSantis and others because of his swagger and machismo? Do they get vicarious satisfaction from Trump's upsetting norms set by the elite? After all, Trump won the 2016 election after he was broadcast boasting that he "could do anything" including grab the genitals of desirable women. This persona would logically appeal more to men than women. A fact supporting this reasoning is that Trump carried the male vote in 2020 and lost the women's vote to President Joe Biden by 13%.

Why choose between the two hypotheses? Let's just say Trump is climbing in the polls because he's a more compelling champion than other GOP candidates *and* because of the appeal of his persona to supporters' wish fulfillment.

Back in 1979, Suzannah Lessard wrote an article disclosing Sen. Edward Kennedy's proclivity for sexual trysts — behavior that was problematic but not illegal. So controversial was the piece that the New Republic refused to run it, but the Washington Monthly did. The author believed the people's need to know outweighed any privacy interest of a presidential candidate when it came to sex: "the character of a president has enormous significance because of his great personal power and the sensitive ways in which he can use it." Lessard argued that in Kennedy's case, journalists should lay out what they know, so voters can decide what to do about it at the ballot box. She herself was bothered because "this type of behavior ... suggests an old-fashioned, male chauvinist, exploitative view of women as primarily objects of pleasure."

About Kennedy, she concluded, "The fact that (his affairs have) been overlooked must be a sign of how much we want to believe in him." Sound familiar?

But Lessard said let the voters decide, and they did. They did not support Kennedy over incumbent president Jimmy Carter in the 1980 primaries. Rather than face the voters, the married Sen. Gary Hart dropped out of the 1988 presidential race when he was caught having an affair with Donna Rice, and the married New York Gov.

Eliot Spitzer resigned when he was caught visiting prostitutes in 2008.

On the other hand, during his 2016 campaign, Trump declared, "I could stand in the middle of Fifth Avenue and shoot somebody, and I wouldn't lose any voters, OK?" There's no evidence that he's committed murder, but a civil jury in 2023 could well decide he committed rape and even so won't lose — and might gain — voters in the upcoming Republican primaries.

Lessard wrote her controversial article four decades ago, so voters could decide what Kennedy's sexual behavior said about him. We already know what Trump's sexual conduct says about him. The question is what does the reaction of us American voters say about ourselves?

Did The United States Make a Wrong Turn in 1776?

May 10, 2023

Were Washington, Hamilton and Jefferson wrong? Would we be better off today if King George III had continued his rule over the 13 colonies and the American War of Independence had never been fought?

No, I'm not raising the question out of envy for the pageantry surrounding the recent coronation of King George's descendant Charles III. However, the celebration did spur me to do a little research. It turns out that constitutional monarchies fare pretty well in side-by-side comparisons with the U.S.-style government headed by a president. Is that heresy? Maybe, but facts are facts.

In the mind of most any American, having a monarch inherit a throne seems anti-democratic. However, a minute or two of web browsing took me to The Economist's democracy index, which ranks countries based on free elections, voter security, independence from foreign interference, and the ability of government officials to implement policies. Eight of the top 15 countries are monarchies. The former British colonies of New Zealand (2nd), Canada (12th) and Australia (15th) — now all independent monarchies where Charles reigns as king — finish well ahead of the United States down in 30th place.

Of course, that can't be much of a wonder. After the election of 2020, the American president schemed to remain in power even after suffering a defeat at the polls. In contrast, there's been no recent threat to the transfer of power in those three former British colonies. How would insurrectionists in New Zealand overthrow their king anyway? He lives in London some 11,000 miles away.

U.S. voters support Roe v. Wade by 59% to 40%. How democratic is it to have had a right to abortion first found and then retracted by an unelected Supreme Court? Abortion is legal in New Zealand under the Abortion Legislation Act 2020 passed by its legislature. Abortion is legal under Australian and Canadian parliamentary laws as well.

So maybe, even while living in a more democratic country, the subjects of constitutional monarchies are oppressed and miserable? No, darn it! Their inhabitants are happier. The United States comes in 15th place in a happiness poll published in March by the U.N., but of the 14 nations ahead, eight are monarchies, again including the former British colonies of Australia, Canada and New Zealand.

OK, OK, but what about the American Dream, which holds that even the least-privileged can rise to the top through hard work and moxie? By definition, a monarchy has built-in barriers to social mobility: a king or queen, who claims the throne by birth, not effort, tops the social pyramid. How come then the U.S. sits in 27th place in the Global Social Mobility Index? Eleven of the countries ranking ahead of us are constitutional monarchies, again including Canada, Australia and New Zealand.

I'm a guy who believes in measurements. If constitutional monarchies are more democratic with happier people and more social mobility, what do they have that we don't? For one thing, there can be no question of succession. Charles was fated to inherit the throne from his mum and become king of Great Britain, Australia, Canada and New Zealand from the day he was born. No violent insurrection was about to take that away. Of course, no matter how legitimate Charles may be, he's not politically or constitutionally powerful. The last British king who believed in his divine right to rule, the first King Charles, lost his head in 1649. For the last century, it's been pretty clear that Parliament rules and the monarch reigns.

Charles' sister Princess Anne recently said, "I would just underline that the monarchy provides, with the constitution, a degree of long-term stability that is actually quite hard to come by any other way."

Is she right? Would the United States be in better shape today if we'd evolved from the original 13 colonies into a constitutional monarchy?

My own answer is no. I've lived in the U.K. and have two Canadian grandparents. From what I've seen, the dynamism and diversity of this country is missing where Charles reigns. Still, keeping up with Australia, Canada and New Zealand is something we should aspire to. Competing with China is not all that's important. Just parroting that the United States is the greatest country in the world does nothing to make us more democratic, happier or more socially mobile.

And finally, here's a postscript addressed to the pluralities in Australia and Canada and substantial minority in New Zealand who want their nations to replace King Charles with elected presidents. The United States evolved differently than you did after the end of British colonial rule, but there's lots to value in your form of government. Be careful what you wish for.

Trump and I Both Tell Lies for a Living

May 17, 2023

I tell lies for a living. Well, what do you expect? I write fiction.

No one calls me out when my novels describe events that didn't really happen. In fact, the more believable I make these lies, the more positive the reviews.

The best fiction authors then convince their fans to suspend disbelief. Donald Trump has clearly mastered this skill. The former president maintains the 2020 election was rigged against him and that he in fact won. Sixty-three percent of Republicans and Republican-leaning independents believe him. It doesn't matter that state and federal judges have dismissed over 50 cases alleging electoral fraud. It doesn't matter that The Associated Press' review of voting in six battleground states found nothing that would overturn the reported results.

On Jan. 6, 2021, the Capitol was overrun by those who bought into Trump's story that he had won the election. More than 600 insurrectionists have been convicted for their role in the attack. Leaders of both the Proud Boys and the Oath Keepers have been found guilty by juries for "specifically conspiring to oppose by force the lawful transfer of presidential power." The House Jan. 6 committee played tapes where we heard the trespassers chanting, "Hang Mike Pence." Body cameras worn by Capitol police show over a thousand assaults on officers, including a vicious beating with a flagpole. Trump's story as told to CNN's Kaitlan Collins on May 11? Those who'd overrun the Capitol "were there with love in their heart ... it was a beautiful day."

A dozen years ago, I sat in my local cafe and wrote a novel where Russians conspire to sway a presidential election. The result was my 2011 thriller "Drop By Drop." It was meant to be fiction, not predictive. In real life, a report of the Senate Intelligence Committee on the 2016 presidential election found "irrefutable evidence of Russian meddling," according to its acting chair, Republican Marco Rubio. In Trump's account, stories of Russian interference were part of a "hoax" perpetrated by Democrats.

Is Trump then a liar? Creating fiction is an essential element of who he is. He's the author of his own narrative. In the story he tells of America's great past, coal fueled a mighty industrial machine, the beauty of Confederate statues stood erect in American cities and crime posed little danger. He spun his tale credibly enough to win a presidential election. In his four White House years, he made 30,573 fictional — false or misleading — statements, according to The Washington Post.

Tens of millions of Americans have spent time in the world of wizards and giants created by J.K. Rowling in her Harry Potter series. President Trump can be viewed as a comparably talented storyteller with over 40% of American adults willing to support him in the polls. I only wish my novels had the same reach.

Does his storytelling stem from delusion or deceit? We can't know, not really. But it doesn't matter. He lives in the world he has constructed. As Tony Schwartz, the ghostwriter of Trump's "The Art of the Deal," said, "More than anyone else I have ever met, Trump has the ability to convince himself that whatever he is saying at any given moment is true, or sort of true, or at least *ought* to be true."

In the world of Donald Trump, the Chinese cheat us, the Mexicans infiltrate us, the Muslims terrorize us, the NATO nations exploit us and the journalists deceive us. It's a place where he graduated with honors from the University of Pennsylvania's Wharton School, where he can have any woman he wants, where the 2020 election was rigged and where the Jan. 6 attack on the Capitol was "a beautiful day."

Trump, the master storyteller, lives in an alternative world where only he, the hero, can provide a happy ending. If only that world really existed. But alas, it is fiction.

Hey, Mr. Chief Justice, Game Over!

May 24, 2023

Chief Justice John Roberts has long proclaimed his commitment to the Supreme Court's institutional legitimacy and to interpreting the Constitution based on precedent and nonpartisanship. He's failed. It's time for him to go.

Of course, there's no chance the chief justice is about to be fired. That would require a majority of the House of Representatives to impeach and two-thirds of the Senate to convict on the basis of "high crimes and misdemeanors." And Roberts is no criminal. A couple of friends we have in common tell me he's a good guy. He's just a failure in leading the court.

I started a company in Silicon Valley. When presenting to investors and the board, I told them what my goals and deliverables were. If I fell way short of what was promised, I'd expect to be fired or to quit. Since Roberts can't be fired, he should resign.

When it comes to institutional legitimacy, faith in the Supreme Court has plummeted to its lowest point since Roberts became chief justice in 2005. In an April NPR/PBS NewsHour/Marist poll, 62% of respondents said they have not very much or no confidence in the court. That number is up from 38% five years ago.

The scent of corruption seems to be wafting through the Supreme Court chambers as well. Justice Clarence Thomas has accepted luxury vacations, lavish gifts, tuition money for his great nephew and free rent for his mother from billionaire Harlan Crow. This was despite the fact that Crow's interests as a real estate developer and investor have had business before the court. On top of that, Thomas failed to disclose the earnings of his wife who vigorously supported the false claim that Donald Trump had won the

2020 presidential election. Has Roberts addressed these wounds to the court's reputation? No, not specifically. Has he supported a code of ethics for Supreme Court justices? No, not specifically. He did say earlier this week, "I want to assure people that I'm committed to making certain that we as a court adhere to the highest standards of conduct." But the time has passed for such vague words. Justice Thomas has made him look foolish and inept.

In fact, questions about spousal moneymaking have tainted the chief justice himself. Roberts's wife reportedly generated $10.3 million in commissions from law firms over an eight-year period for placing new hires. A Supreme Court spokeswoman said that a judge "need not recuse merely because" their spouse recruited for law firms who had issues before the court. Maybe that's the letter of the law, but it sure looks corrupt and further undermines the court's legitimacy.

At his confirmation hearing, Roberts made a metaphorical promise to "call balls and strikes, and not to pitch or bat." He was promising to be like a baseball umpire who ensures rules are followed but is not a participant in the political game.

In 2013's decision in Shelby County v. Holder, Roberts wrote an opinion that threw out a key section of the Voting Rights Act of 1965. Here he did not merely call balls and strikes, he struck out the batter. With four colleagues, he usurped Congress' role by taking on a legislative function. In the five years after the ruling, nearly a thousand polling places were closed, many in predominantly African American precincts. In 2019, two professors wrote in an American Economic Association paper: "Although only a few years have elapsed since the Shelby County decision, we are already starting to observe erosions in black Americans' socioeconomic status. ... Our findings suggest that perhaps Chief Justice Roberts should be slightly less optimistic about the state of democratic equality in the South."

The court's judgment in the 2010 Citizens United case allowed unlimited independent campaign spending by corporations and thereby inflated the influence of big money in politics. Over a hundred years ago, Theodore Roosevelt argued, "All contributions by corporations to any political committee or for any political purpose should be forbidden by law." It didn't matter what Roosevelt thought or Congress legislated — Roberts' Supreme Court decided the issue.

In the case of Dobbs v. Jackson, he sided with the majority to overturn the half-century old precedent set down in Roe v. Wade that gave women the right to control their own bodies in the early months of pregnancy.

At his confirmation hearing, Roberts promised, "I will be vigilant to protect the independence and integrity of the Supreme Court, and I will work to ensure that it upholds the rule of law and safeguards those liberties that make this land one of endless possibilities for all Americans."

No, Mr. Chief Justice. You have lost the faith of the American people in the court you lead. You have failed to maintain the court's integrity. You have failed to safeguard American liberties. Three strikes and you're out! Get off the bench.

If Screenwriters Should Make More Money, Shouldn't Book Writers, Too?

May 31, 2023

Members of the Writers Guild of America, those people who write streaming series like Bridgerton, Ted Lasso and Game of Thrones, are on strike. Here's one big reason: The writers want to be paid more when more people view what they have written.

Way back when, soon after publication of my first novel, I checked the online catalog of the Palo Alto City Library and saw that over 80 patrons had reserved it. What was my reaction? "Go without a few lattes, you penny pinchers, and buy the darn thing — it's only $13.95."

Maybe we book writers should go on strike, too, just like the screenwriters. We certainly could use a few extra cents each time one of our books is checked out of the library. Sure, the net worth of J.K. Rowling or James Patterson might be close to a billion dollars. But let's get real. A survey of full-time U.S. authors showed they earned a median income of $23,329 in 2022 with only about half coming from book royalties.

Legislators in 34 countries have taken a step toward increasing pay for authors with something called a "public lending right." In the U.K., for example, each time a book is checked out of a public library, the author receives around 38 cents paid for by the national government. You think that might bankrupt His Majesty's Treasury? The PLR scheme is not designed to make Jo Rowling (no, it doesn't apply to Americans) even richer. Authors under the U.K. plan are limited to payments of around $8,000 per year. Under our northern neighbor's PLR program, more than 18,000 Canadian authors are compensated annually with payments ranging from $50 to $4,500 a year. Not a lot, but those sums will make a difference to many new writers. Computerized checkouts ease gathering the information on which books are checked out.

I'm not suggesting a subsidy here. It's payment for services provided. Writers *should* be paid when their books are read. That's fairness, not a subsidy. Abraham Lincoln said, "All I have learned, I learned from books." Let's keep the authors of those books compensated and writing.

The U.S. government will run a deficit of $1.6 trillion (!) this fiscal year, and adding billions to it would be a distasteful prospect. No fear. The annual cost of a PLR program is about $8 million in the U.K. and $17 million in Germany. On a pro rata basis, it would cost less than $100 million in the U.S. It might then add 0.0063% to the deficit, truly no more than rounding error.

So let's get this straight. Libraries buy books. The national government pays writers a small sum each time a book is checked out. Writers make a little extra money from people reading their books. (Writers making money? Call the police!) A great idea? I think so. And not that expensive either, especially considering the benefits. As John F. Kennedy said, "If this nation is to be wise as well as strong, if we are to achieve our destiny, then we need more new ideas for more wise men reading more good books in more public libraries."

I am rooting for those writers who believe they should earn more money when viewers watch their shows via a streaming service. I'm rooting even harder for writers to make more money when readers read their books checked out of the library.

In 1983, Maryland's Republican Senator Charles Mathias introduced Senate Bill 2192 to establish a commission to evaluate a system "for compensating authors for the public lending of their books." Forty years of waiting is long enough. Why not write your senators and representatives about a public lending right for American authors? It's a small price to pay for a more literate society.

What If Day Care Workers and Business School Professors Swapped Salaries?

June 7, 2023

The pay scale for educators is topsy-turvy in this country. Business school professors are paid over four times more than day care workers. Based on the value of their work, it should be the other way around.

Say what? Let me explain my reasoning.

At birth, an infant's brain has about 100 billion neurons. That's about a million times more processors than in a supercomputer. But in a supercomputer, the processors are all linked. When a baby is born, the neurons are not.

What's required, then, to form the super-duper computer we call the human brain is making connections among those neurons. How do we get that to happen? By stimulation in the first three years of life, by the interaction between infants and adults in simple activities such as talking, playing, reading, rocking and singing. And who's doing that stimulation and building the foundation for lifelong learning? Parents, certainly, but around half of all American children are enrolled in day care with paid staff.

In the early years of life, with sufficient stimulation, about a million new connections are made every second. Limited stimulation means fewer connections and less potential for learning. Day care workers, then, play a vital role in unleashing the power of a child's brain. Speaking in business school terms, day care workers have the potential for an awful lot of "value add."

Judith Graham, a human development specialist at the University of Maine, summarizes the research this way: "Early childhood is the time to build either a strong and supportive, or fragile and unreliable foundation." Thus, in the first year of life, babies can make the connections needed to respond to any language, but that capacity is narrowed by the sounds and words they hear. By age 5, a child's brain has reached 90% of its adult size.

If the foundation isn't made in those first years, a baby starts out at a disadvantage. How many potential great inventors, novelists, artists and researchers never fulfill their destiny? For that matter, deprived kids have lower chances of going to college and getting a highly paid job. Good day care is a good investment, too. According to an article by professors Garett Jones and W. Joel Schneider, raising children's IQ by a single point raises their living standards by 6.1%.

Let's compare the value added by a business school professor to that of a day care worker. A business school professor is at best polishing the jewel first discovered and tended by the early childhood educators who came before them. The fact their students can come up with successful marketing programs, understand a profit-and-loss statement and run a successful startup is in no small part due to the foundations built by early child care.

In the United States, an average day care worker is paid $28,520 per year. An average business school professor makes a median salary of $130,498. One professor at a well-known university tells me that B-school professors can easily earn double or triple that from consulting done for outside businesses. I doubt day care workers are offered the same opportunity.

In fact, low wages undermine the quality of early learning programs. A report from the U.S. Department of Health and Human Services acknowledges that "high-quality providers and educators are the single most important factors" in high-quality early education, but goes on to say "too many individuals within the early learning workforce earn low wages — sometimes at or near the Federal poverty line." Unsurprisingly, the report finds that where providers earn higher wages, the children "spend more time engaged in positive interactions and developmentally appropriate activities with peers and teachers, which contributes to healthy development."

My daughter lives in upstate New York. Her son's day care provider recently cut back its hours by more than 20% due to a staffing shortage. I'll bet if the day care workers there were paid what business school professors earn, the problem finding high-quality staff would disappear.

The entire situation is ass-backward. Day care does a bad job and half of all American kids suffer. Business school professors do a bad job and what happens? An old boss of mine who founded a Fortune 500 company thought B-school taught the wrong values to its students, but we'll put his argument aside for another time. Suffice it to say that without the foundation to express oneself well and to form meaningful personal relationships, an MBA isn't worth much.

What if the best and brightest were attracted to working in day care? What if they earned $130K per year? Any business school professor would tell you it would be a good investment.

President Biden's and My 40-Year-Old Fingerprints Are All Over Trump Indictment

June 14, 2023

Did President Joe Biden indeed set things in motion for the indictment of his predecessor? Yes, he did — over four decades ago — and I was an accomplice.

Please let me explain.

In the late 1970s, then-Senator Biden was chair of the Senate Intelligence Committee's Subcommittee on Secrecy and Disclosure. Back then, accused spies and rogue agents could cast a broad net in demanding that classified documents and testimony be used for their defense. Even if the documents and testimony were found inadmissible after review by the judge, damage to the national security would be done once they were revealed in the public trial guaranteed by the Constitution.

According to a 1978 subcommittee report, "So long as there is a real threat that prosecution of the defendant may reveal sensitive information in the course of a trial, he or she may engage in this 'gray mail' to avoid prosecution." The report goes on to describe how spies, murderers and drug dealers all used graymail to escape prosecution. For example, in 1973, an intelligence source in Thailand was indicted for illegally importing over 60 pounds of opium into the United States. The prosecution was dropped because the CIA feared that its clandestine operations in Southeast Asia would be exposed at trial. The Biden subcommittee concluded that legislation was needed "to facilitate the enforcement of espionage statutes and thereby protect our national secrets without jeopardizing constitutional principles."

So what was my role in all this? I joined the staff of the Senate Intelligence Committee as a 26-year-old newly minted lawyer in 1977. By the next year, the other two counsels to the committee had left as had the chief author of the subcommittee report. So suddenly there I was, the senior counsel on the committee working to write and pass the recommended legislation. Under Sen. Biden's direction, I worked to hammer out a bill in negotiations with congressional staffs, the Justice Department, the CIA, the American Civil Liberties Union and others. The senator introduced the Classified Information Procedures Act on July 11, 1979. It passed both houses of Congress and was signed into law by President Jimmy Carter on Oct. 15, 1980.

It's as if Sen. Biden anticipated the former president's misdeeds four decades before they were allegedly committed. Of the 37 counts in last week's indictment of the former president, 31 were for violations of section 793 of title 18 for willful retention of national defense information. In 1978, the subcommittee report had pointed out the dilemma the prosecutors would face in 2023: "In a prosecution under section 793 of title 18, it is necessary to prove that the information passed will actually damage the national security or be of aid to a foreign government." That of course means "it becomes necessary to explain to the jury, and therefore to the public and to the intended recipient, the significance of the information passed." In other words, trying the case undercuts the rationale of the statute which, after all, is to keep national defense information secret!

Under the Classified Information Procedures Act, Donald Trump's defense must alert the government to classified information it plans to introduce in open court before the trial begins. Once the government sees what the defense will introduce, it can decide whether to contest the introduction of anything classified. Moreover, any appeals as to admissibility and relevance can be made pretrial. Without knowing what secrets might be revealed in open court, chances are good that, as with the Thai drug smuggler, the government would have feared proceeding to trial, and hence there would have been no indictment. The prospect of a former commander in chief sitting on the witness stand spouting every secret he knew, whether relevant or not, could not be risked. The safety of the country — and its military personnel and human intelligence sources — would be paramount.

President Biden has publicly declared he's been hands-off in the investigation and indictment of his predecessor. Hands-off now, but his 40-year-old fingerprints are all over the case.

And he's not the only one who appears to have anticipated the indictment. In 2018, then-President Trump pronounced that giving former executive branch officials access to "our Nation's most sensitive secrets long after their time in Government has ended ... is particularly inappropriate when former officials have transitioned into highly partisan positions." That same year, he even signed a bill extending the penalty for "unauthorized removal and retention of classified documents or material" from one to five years. Whoops!

Trump Campaigning for Get Out of Jail Free Card

June 28, 2023

The prospect of a trial by jury in the Southern District of Florida looms over Donald Trump. He has been indicted for illegal possession of national defense documents and obstructing federal attempts to regain them. The former president's attorney general William Barr told Fox News that Trump was "toast" if even half of the 37 counts in the indictment are true.

Not so fast. Trump does seem to recognize he is unlikely to be acquitted on all counts by a South Florida jury. So he is seeking a not-guilty ruling from an altogether different jury.

In a Florida courtroom, Trump would face evidence of flagrant lawbreaking backed by photographs, texts and witnesses galore. He has appeared to admit his own guilt. In an interview on Fox, he claimed to have been too busy to return the classified materials in his possession. And in a recording disclosed by CNN, he sure seemed to acknowledge possession of a classified document dealing with potential U.S. action against Iran.

What's at stake for Trump in the trial? When a former National Security Agency contractor stole a "breathtaking" amount of top-secret information, he received a prison sentence of nine years. If the court metes out the same sentence to 77-year-old Trump (37 counts!), he could die in prison. Moreover, the DOJ guidelines say a judge can consider "whether the defendant has expressed regret for the crime" in handing down any sentence. Trump most certainly has not. Instead, after his booking, he denounced the indictments as no more than "a boxes hoax."

So Trump is following his usual path — when he can't win, he changes the rules. He will take his case and seek amnesty from a jury consisting not of 12 people "good and true" but from a jury of around 150 million likely voters. If they elect him president in November 2024, he can simply instruct the Justice Department to drop any and all counts against him once he takes office. Even if already found guilty in a trial court, he can order the Justice Department not to oppose his appeals.

But wait a minute. The judge scheduled the trial to begin in August, the month after next. Isn't that plenty of time for a verdict before the presidential election? No. The prosecution has already asked for a delay until December because the case involves classified information. Defense attorneys will need to obtain the requisite clearances. Motions on the admissibility of that information will involve the Classified Information Procedures Act, which the prosecution acknowledges "will inject additional time into the leadup to trial." That understates matters. A case under CIPA rules will be filled with as many delays, motions and appeals as the Trump defense team can come up with. (Note: I was an author of the CIPA legislation when counsel to the Senate Intelligence Committee.)

So, as the Justice Department seeks a win in federal court, Trump seeks a win at the ballot box. If the odds are stacked against him in the courtroom, are his odds better at the ballot box? According to a recent NBC poll conducted *after* Trump's indictment, he extended his lead from 15% to 29% over the second-place candidate for the Republican nomination. The same poll found that in a head-to-head match against President Joe Biden, Trump trails by only four points — within the margin of error. Remember, too, that he lost to Hillary Clinton by 2% and still carried the Electoral College. No wonder he likes the odds better at the ballot box.

What about the case Trump faces in New York for hiding a payoff to alleged sexual partner Stormy Daniels and the likely case in Atlanta for illegal interference in the 2020 presidential election? Because these are state cases, a victorious presidential campaign would also provide Trump with a get out of jail free card. A 1997

Supreme Court decision implies a state criminal prosecution of a sitting president would raise federalism concerns. In a recent interview, University of Virginia law school professor Saikrishna B. Prakash explained the Justice Department believes a state cannot put a serving president in jail because the Constitution would not allow a state prosecutor "to incapacitate the chief executive."

In sum, Trump's defense against the 37-count indictment is two-pronged — delay in the courtroom and attack on the campaign trail. "We're warriors in a righteous campaign," Trump told the crowd at the Faith and Freedom Coalition last Saturday. "Every time the radical left Democrats, Marxist, communists and fascists indict me, I consider it a great badge of courage." In an appearance in Michigan the next day, he declared, "They wanna take away my freedom because I will never let them take away your freedom." For Trump, the great advantage of a political campaign over a courtroom trial is that contrary evidence can be ignored.

Back on June 22, 2016, in a New York City campaign speech, candidate Trump proclaimed, "The voters are the jury. Their ballots are the verdict." He's acting on that belief still.

How Many Did Supreme Court Sentence to Death in Recent Term?

July 5, 2023

The Supreme Court's ethics-tainted term ended last week. Plenty has been written on the court's momentous decisions involving election law, presidential power, gay rights, affirmative action and free speech. However, little attention has been paid to the number of deaths that will inevitably result from this term's majority opinions.

Two months ago, Chief Justice John Roberts said, "The hardest decision I had to make was whether to erect fences and barricades around the Supreme Court." Really? At the beginning of the term in October, Roberts and five other justices refused to hear the appeal of Andre Thomas. Thomas, a mentally ill Black man, was convicted of killing his white wife and biracial son by an all-white jury that contained three members who admitted their opposition to interracial marriage and procreation. Allowing the State of Texas to execute him by lethal injection would keep me awake many, many more nights than erecting temporary fencing that has already been removed.

Andre Thomas' capital case continues a recent trend. As Justice Sonia Sotomayor wrote back in 2021, "Over the past six months, this Court has repeatedly sidestepped its usual deliberative processes, often at the Government's request, allowing it to push forward with an unprecedented, breakneck timetable of executions." The Supreme Court is this nation's court of last resort. Doesn't a decision to ignore justice and let a man die by lethal injection make the court majority in Thomas' case complicit in his death?

The May decision in Sackett v. Environmental Protection Agency will inevitably result in the death of not one person, but a multitude. A 5-4 majority of the court agreed to cut back on the protection of wetlands by the Clean Water Act. Justice Brett Kavanaugh argued against the majority's reasoning, stating it would have "significant repercussions for water quality and flood control throughout the United States." Justice Elena Kagan agreed, noting that "wetlands play a crucial part in flood control (if anything, more needed now than when the statute was enacted)." Two former EPA commissioners, one appointed by President Bill Clinton, the other by President George H.W. Bush, wrote in a brief to the court that "wetlands have long been recognized as vital to protecting a range of important values essential to Congress's clean water directives, including ... water storage to mitigate effects of floods and droughts."

A single acre of wetlands can store 1 million to 1.5 million gallons of floodwater. By allowing more wetlands to be drained, the Sackett decision will lead to more floods like the 2017 one in Houston where 65 people died from freshwater flooding. As the two EPA commissioners noted, "in Houston, there have been five 500 year flood events in the past 6-7 years." In other words, more deaths by water are coming and coming soon.

In addition to preventing flooding, U.S. wetlands store 11.5 billion metric tons of soil carbon. As wetlands disappear, carbon is released into the atmosphere, dirties the air and accelerates climate change. The danger is clear. In the wake of last year's court decision in West Virginia v. EPA that restricted the EPA's ability to regulate carbon emissions by power plants, Francesca Dominici, professor of biostatistics, population and data science at Harvard, said, "the dirtier air will make us sicker — and many Americans will die earlier as a result." A study published by GeoHealth found there were approximately 12,000 heat-related premature deaths annually in the U.S. from 2010 to 2020. By 2100, the number of deaths increase by 97,000 in a high-warming scenario that is made more likely by the court decisions in West Virginia v. EPA and Sackett v. EPA.

There were other cases in the past two decades that led to an increase in American deaths. Last year's Dobbs decision struck down a federal right to abortion. A University of Colorado study shows that abortion bans increase maternal mortality by 24%. Decided early in Chief Justice Roberts's term, the 2008 District of Columbia v. Heller case struck down most prohibitions on gun ownership. In its wake, the number of firearm deaths in the United States has increased from 31,593 in the year of the decision to 48,830 in 2021.

The infamous Soviet dictator Joseph Stalin once said: "The death of one man is a tragedy. The death of a million is a statistic." The majority of this Supreme Court showed no signs of finding a death sentence imposed by a biased jury on one man — Andre Thomas, who allegedly suffered acute psychosis from a lifelong mental illness — to be a tragedy. Are numerous deaths stemming from dirty air, climate change, abortion bans and gun proliferation indeed a mere statistic scarcely considered in majority decisions?

Attributing direct responsibility to the court majority for the coming deaths of so many Americans may be a legal stretch. Still, my verdict is guilty.

Time To End Affirmative Action for Males in College Admissions?

July 12, 2023

Last month in the case Students for Fair Admissions v. Harvard, the U.S. Supreme Court outlawed use of race as a factor in college admissions decisions. Isn't it time, then, to prohibit the use of gender as well?

Statistics indicate that males are given preference for admission to the most selective colleges. Here are a few examples:

— In the spring of 2023, the nationwide rate of college enrollment was 58% female and 42% male. And yet in the eight elite colleges of the Ivy League, which include Harvard, the average enrollment of males is 48%, six points higher.

— At Dartmouth, another member of the Ivy League, men formed the majority of undergraduates.

— According to the student newspaper at Brown, also an Ivy League school, 6.7% of male applicants were accepted there in 2021-22, compared to 4.1% of the females. In other words, a male applicant had a 1 in 15 chance of being accepted to Brown, while a female's chances were 1 in 25.

As far back as 2006, Jennifer Delahunty, then the dean of admissions and financial aid at Kenyon College, apologized in The New York Times to worthy females who were denied admission to the top-50 liberal arts college. She explained, "The reality is that because young men are rarer, they're more valued applicants."

The majority in the Harvard case implicitly insists on the importance of academic achievement in making admissions decisions. The average high school grade point average of females is 3.1 and of males is 2.9.

Despite their lower overall high school GPA, do males in the top tier of academic performance outmatch their female classmates? Apparently not at Harvard. This spring, Sophia Freund Prizes were awarded to 40 Harvard seniors who graduated summa cum laude, the highest academic achievement. Twenty-four, or 60%, of the prizewinners were women. More generally, a college diploma hikes a woman's salary even more than a man's, according to a paper written for the Federal Reserve Bank of St. Louis.

These discrepancies did not go unnoticed during the oral arguments in the Harvard case. Justice Elena Kagan, former dean of Harvard Law School, pointed out the existence of "statistical evidence that suggests that colleges now, when they apply gender-neutral criteria, get many more women than men." She then asked, "Could a university put a thumb on the scales and say 'it's important that we ensure that men continue to receive college educations at not perfect equality but roughly in the same ballpark'?"

I never had Kagan as an instructor while at Harvard Law myself, but had she called on me in class to answer her question, my reply would have been straightforward and unequivocal. "Professor," I would have said, "the Civil Rights Act of 1964 outlaws such discrimination." If necessary, I would have read aloud Title IX of that act which states no one "shall on the basis of sex be excluded from participation in, be denied the benefits of, or be subjected to discrimination under any education program or activity receiving Federal financial assistance."

As Chief Justice John Roberts wrote in the Harvard case, "A benefit provided to some applicants but not to others necessarily advantages the former group at the expense of the latter." Favoring males for admission to college disadvantages females. It is against the law.

Academic and other achievements should count in college admissions. Gender should not.

Case closed.

History Repeats Itself — Almost

July 19, 2023

We all know history doesn't really repeat itself, but it sure does echo through the decades and centuries. As Nobel Prize-winning novelist William Faulkner wrote: "The past is never dead. It's not even past."

Here are a few examples of today's policy debates echoing those of days gone by.

— In the 1930s, Republicans attacked President Franklin D. Roosevelt's policy to use public works to combat the Great Depression as socialism. In the 2020 presidential campaign, Donald Trump accused Joe Biden of handing "control to the socialists and Marxists and left-wing extremists." In May of this year, Republican Rep. Marjorie Taylor Greene attacked President Biden's "Build Back Better" public works policy as socialism. (As a courtesy, someone might have reminded the representative that FDR won four presidential elections in a row.)

— Former Alabama Gov. George Wallace ran for president as an independent in 1968 and managed to garner almost 14% of the popular vote. To deal with urban unrest, he was ready to "call out 30,000 troops and equip them with two-foot-long bayonets and station them every few feet apart." In 2020, then-President Trump put forward his idea of how to deal with urban protests. He asked the secretary of defense about calling out the army to "just shoot" demonstrators. Echoes indeed.

— In the decade before the Civil War, Southern Democrats — who were anything but democratic — dominated American politics. South Carolina Sen. James Hammond expounded on the need for rule by a superior class "which leads progress, civilization, and refinement" as contrasted to those belonging to an "inferior" race with no right to vote. Arizona state Rep. John Kavanagh told his fellow legislators in 2021 that "everybody shouldn't be voting," and "we have to look at the quality of votes." This year, at least seven states have enacted laws that restrict voting — albeit not quite to the same extent as South Carolina did in the 1850s.

— The Declaration of Independence pronounced King George III of Great Britain to be "a Prince, whose character is marked by every act which may define a Tyrant." Former President of the United States Donald Trump declared in his first year in office, "I have the right to do whatever I want as president." A difference, of course, is that the crowned head of the colonies could not be voted out of office or indicted as could the elected head of the United States.

Maybe we *should* take more seriously what philosopher George Santayana said: "Those who cannot remember the past are condemned to repeat it." In 1967, 5.7% of college graduates majored in history. In 2019, the number was down by two-thirds to fewer than 1.2%. Maybe what we need is more people knowing more history.

Or maybe not. In 1938, British Prime Minister Neville Chamberlain said potential Nazi aggression involved "a quarrel in a faraway country, between people of whom we know nothing." Within a year, his country was at war against Germany. In 2023, Florida Gov. Ron DeSantis dismissed the Russian invasion of Ukraine as a mere "territorial dispute." One hopes the governor will come to learn that even disputes occurring far from his country's shores can prove significant. I just wonder why he didn't know it already — DeSantis, a member of the Yale class of 2001, majored in history.

Sigh.

Golden Ticket in the Game of Life Goes to the Wealthy

July 26, 2023

In the 2022 midterm elections, white voters without a college degree cast their ballots for Republican candidates by a margin of more than 2-1, an estimated 66%-32%.

Why would these voters, who earn on average half as much as college graduates, support candidates whose policies favor the wealthy? Why would they back GOP representatives who want to raise the age for full Social Security benefits? Why would they get behind a party who passed into law a 2017 tax cut that left the top 0.1% of U.S. households paying a lower tax rate than the bottom 50%?

A hint to the answer came to me as I read through a just-issued study from the National Bureau of Economic Research. It analyzed the admissions policies of 12 universities — Harvard, Yale, Princeton, Columbia, Brown, Pennsylvania, Dartmouth, Cornell, Stanford, MIT, Duke and Chicago. Fewer than 0.5% of all college students are enrolled in these "Ivy Plus" institutions. And yet their graduates are overrepresented by 20 times among Fortune 500 CEOs, 50 times among U.S. senators and 100 times among Rhodes Scholars.

Getting admitted to one of the Ivy Plus sure looks like a golden ticket in the Game of Life. White voters without a college degree by definition didn't win a ticket, and they know only too well their kids won't win either. In contrast, an applicant whose family income placed them in the top 0.1% were 2.5 times as likely to go to an Ivy Plus college as other applicants with the same test scores. The fix was in.

"What I conclude from (the NBER) study is the Ivy League doesn't have low-income students because it doesn't want low-income students," says professor Susan Dynarski of the Harvard Graduate School of Education.

It was Republican candidates and officeholders who gave voice to those who resented the fix. On the campaign trail in 2021, now-Senator J.D. Vance said, "I think if any of us want to do the things that we want to do for our country and for the people who live in it, we have to honestly and aggressively attack the universities in this country." In 2017 when the Republicans held the White House and both houses of Congress, they passed a law that taxes the endowments of the wealthiest universities. In his campaign to regain the White House, former President Donald Trump promised to "reclaim" campuses "dominated by Marxist Maniacs and lunatics."

The NBER study shows students who graduated from an Ivy Plus school get a major boost in their chances of joining the top 1% of earners. So, kids with rich parents have an increased chance of getting into an Ivy Plus school, after college the kids have an increased chance of becoming rich themselves and then their own kids will have an increased chance of getting in. Isn't it monarchies like the United Kingdom where privilege is supposed to be inherited, rather than democracies like the United States? Not anymore. The United States has sunk to 27th in social mobility behind the UK as well as other monarchies such as Japan and the Netherlands.

What can we do? A lot. Here's a start.

First, the United States can settle on policies that increase income for the less affluent. Progress is being made there. Since 2020, the wages of the lowest-paid tier of workers have been increasing more rapidly than other tiers. Biden administration initiatives are bringing back manufacturing jobs that don't require college degrees. Factory construction is booming.

Next, we can improve education in this country, especially for children of the less affluent. In the most recent results from the

Programme for International Student Assessment, the United States placed 22nd on average in reading, math and science scores among 78 nations. Nothing is more important in educating our youth than high-quality teachers, and yet teachers are paid 24% less than other college graduates. To attract and retain outstanding teachers, increase their salary. If the Ivy Plus grads are indeed representative of the best and the brightest, it's easy to see why they go to work in consulting and investment banking. They get paid three times more than grads going into K-12 teaching. Wouldn't it be better for them to pass on a great education to many in the next generation rather than an inside track to wealth for a few? Again, the answer is to raise the salary for teachers.

Those white Republican voters are frustrated with good reason. The NBER study implies there's a lock on the doorway leading to the American Dream. Time to pass out more keys — a lot more keys — to them and their children.

Trump Did Not Win the Judicial Lottery This Time

August 2, 2023

By the luck of the draw, U.S. District Court Judge Tanya Chutkan was assigned to preside over former President Donald Trump's trial for conspiring to overturn the 2020 election results. I doubt Judge Chutkan, who is Black and Jamaican-born, would have been Trump's first choice given his history of attacking powerful Black women.

What history? How about a few examples? Trump tweeted that Omarosa Manigault Newman, a Black woman who served as White House director of communications, was a "crazed, crying lowlife" and a "dog," and he maligned veteran Rep. Maxine Waters as a "low IQ individual." He told journalist Abby Phillips that she asks "a lot of stupid questions" and deemed White House correspondent April Ryan "a loser" who is "very nasty."

In 2019, Trump attacked liberal Reps. Alexandria Ocasio-Cortez, Rashida Tlaib, Ayanna Pressley and Ilhan Omar, suggesting that the four weren't born in America by asking, "Why don't they go back and help fix the totally broken and crime infested places from which they came." All four are women of color, with three Black and three American-born.

Professor Michael Eric Dyson, currently at Vanderbilt, has said Trump is playing a familiar racist card with such invective by "trying to keep in place Black women who have stepped outside of their bounds, and who have refused to concede the legitimacy of being a docile being in the face of white power."

Perhaps no one has been the recipient of more vicious attacks from Trump than Vice President Kamala Harris, whose father is a Stanford emeritus professor born in Jamaica. Trump called her a "monster" after the 2020 vice presidential debate and also untruthfully implied that, as the daughter of immigrants, Harris was ineligible to serve as vice president.

But wait, there's more bad news for Trump. Judge Chutkan, who sits in D.C., has also already handled a case where he was a party. In Trump v. Thompson, the ex-president sued to stop the National Archives from providing presidential records to the House committee investigating the Jan. 6 attack on the Capitol. Chutkan denied Trump's plea, writing in her opinion, "Presidents are not kings, and Plaintiff is not President." Her ruling was upheld by the circuit court and the Supreme Court. Moreover, in cases stemming from the events on Jan. 6, she has stood out from her colleagues on the bench for the tough sentences she's handed down to those found guilty of attacking the Capitol.

Trump must have celebrated his good fortune this past June when the Florida case where he is accused of mishandling national defense secrets and obstructing justice was assigned to Judge Aileen Cannon. Last year Judge Cannon took unprecedented steps to pause the ongoing criminal investigation of Trump's activities. (That ruling was overturned unanimously on appeal.) Now, given his record of attacking Black women including the most prominent woman in America with Jamaican roots, Trump cannot be too pleased to have the tough-minded Judge Chutkan assigned to the election denial case.

After reading the indictments in both the Florida and D.C. cases, I'd bet it will be difficult indeed for the two juries to find Trump not guilty of all 44 charges against him. In the end, however, who will preside over the cases matters less than the election results in November 2024. If Trump — or a close ally — should retake the White House, an attorney general who will dismiss charges or drop appeals in both cases is almost a certainty.

Chances are, then, the real jury in the federal cases against Trump will be the Americans casting their ballots in November 2024.

GOP Fiddles as America Burns

August 16, 2023

Republican politicians are taking their lead on energy policy from Emperor Nero who, according to legend, fiddled while Rome burned. No, wait, it's worse than that. While some GOP legislators and presidential candidates are just fiddling à la Nero, others are actually fanning the flames.

Science shows the emission of greenhouse gases as a byproduct of using coal, oil and natural gas for power and heating leads to global warming. A hotter planet leads to droughts which in turn leads to drier plants that catch fire more easily and burn more intensely. A hotter planet also leads to melting ice in the polar regions which in turn leads to rising oceans and flooding coastlines.

The past eight years have been the warmest on planet Earth since records have been kept. The hottest month in the last thousand centuries was last month. Phoenix sizzled this summer with the temperature reaching 110 degrees Fahrenheit for 31 consecutive days. The ocean temperature off the coast of Florida set new records while soaring over 100 F.

We've seen the effects of global warming in Hawaii, too, whose average temperature today is 2 degrees Fahrenheit warmer than in 1950. It's not a certainty that the recent fire on the Hawaiian island of Maui was directly caused by this climate change, but climate change is a likely suspect for triggering its fierceness. With over 100 deaths, the fire is the deadliest wildfire in the United States since 1918. A recent study found human-caused climate change nearly doubled the forest fire area between 1984 and 2015 in the western United States.

President Joe Biden, the clear leader for renomination by the Democratic Party, wants to cut U.S. greenhouse gas emissions in half by the end of the decade.

And what do the two leading contenders for the Republican nomination for president want to do about climate change and global warming? In 2017, then-President Donald Trump announced the United States was withdrawing from the 2015 Paris climate accord designed to cap the rise in global warming. (The Biden administration has rejoined the accord.) On the campaign trail this year, Trump claimed global sea levels are rising about an eighth of an inch every three centuries. According to the National Oceanic and Atmospheric Administration, global sea levels are rising that much *each year*.

Florida Gov. Ron DeSantis, the other leading contender for the GOP nomination, has rejected calls to do something about the warming planet, calling any such initiatives "left-wing stuff." Former Vice President Mike Pence, another contender, accused "radical environmentalists" of exaggerating the threat of global warming.

Rising seas are coming as a result of global warming as well. According to an article in Scientific American, "an estimated 4.3 million acres — an area nearly the size of Connecticut — will be underwater by 2050, including $35 billion worth of real estate." GOP Sen. Tommy Tuberville, whose state of Alabama borders the Gulf of Mexico, has co-sponsored legislation to prohibit any U.S. spending on the Paris climate accord, to promote oil and gas leases on federal land and to direct the government to ignore any environmental costs from use of carbon-based fuels.

Last year in West Virginia v. EPA, the six justices of the Supreme Court appointed by Republican presidents voted to cut off the Environmental Protection Agency's ability to regulate greenhouse gas emissions from power plants. In an angry dissent, Justice Elena Kagan wrote, "Whatever else this Court may know about, it does not have a clue about how to address climate change."

But it's not just Republicans on the national stage who are taking positions that fuel global warming. This year, for example, GOP lawmakers in Texas passed laws to spend billions to subsidize gas-fueled power plants on the one hand, while making nonpolluting wind and solar power in rural areas more expensive on the other.

On May 10, 2023, Republican Gov. Greg Gianforte signed a bill that barred Montana's agencies from considering greenhouse gas emissions or climate change in reviewing applications for energy projects. In response to a lawsuit by 16 young residents, a Montana court ruled this week that the state must consider climate change when deciding whether to approve or renew coal and gas projects. The judge found that "Montana's climate, environment, and natural resources are unconstitutionally degraded and depleted due to the current atmospheric concentration of (greenhouse gas emissions) and climate change." Republican Attorney General Austin Knudsen has vowed to appeal that ruling.

Speaking at a U.N. conference, renowned naturalist David Attenborough warned, "If we continue on our current path, we will face the collapse of everything that gives us our security" from food production, access to fresh water and habitable ambient temperature to ocean food chains. It's hard to say whether Republican politicians are influencing the voters or vice versa, but neither group seems to be listening to such warnings. A survey this month showed Republican voters by a 3-1 margin think that economic growth should be given priority over dealing with climate change. (Democrats rate climate change the higher priority by a 4-1 margin.)

In his song "Who by Fire," Leonard Cohen riffs on an ancient prayer and asks who will die "by fire" and who "by water." Here's hoping — despite today's politics — that the future holds a third and happier alternative for us humans.

It's Time for Law School Grads To Promise To Pursue Justice

August 23, 2023

It turns out the brains behind the plan to steal the 2020 presidential election using fake electors was a little-known lawyer named Kenneth Chesebro.

According to an email cited in the indictment of Donald Trump by a D.C. federal grand jury, Chesebro himself called the scheme he came up with "kind of wild/creative." The Trump campaign would submit "fake" electoral votes to be counted by Vice President Mike Pence so that supporters could "start arguing that the 'fake' votes should be counted." Despite devising and attempting to submit this plan "to submit fraudulent slates of presidential electors," Chesebro was not indicted along with Trump in the D.C. case. He was, though, indicted for seven counts in the Georgia state conspiracy case.

One thing on Chesebro's resume pops out. Like so many other engineers of recent attacks on democracy and the rule of law, he holds a Harvard or Yale law degree. (He was a member of the Harvard class of 1986.) Those two institutions are first and second in sending alumni to the Supreme Court, and eight of the nine current justices attended one or the other.

Chesebro, then, is just another addition to the rolls of graduates of those preeminent schools of legal learning who forgot or ignored anything they might have learned in the classroom about reverence for democracy and the Constitution. Here are a few prominent examples of others on that list:

— Stewart Rhodes (Yale Law, class of 2004), founder of the Oath Keepers, was convicted of seditious conspiracy for his role in leading the attempted coup of Jan. 6, 2021, that resulted in at least seven deaths.

— Texas Sen. Ted Cruz (Harvard Law, '95) played along with Chesebro's scheme — advertently or inadvertently — by pushing for an "emergency audit " of the presidential election results.

— Florida Gov. Ron DeSantis (Harvard Law, '05) signed into law the Stop WOKE Act which U.S. District Judge Mark E. Walker found violated the First Amendment to the Constitution. DeSantis signed another bill in 2021 criticized by the Brennan Center for Justice as "an omnibus voter suppression bill that will make it harder for Floridians to vote" and a third in 2023 deemed another instance of "voting rights in Florida ... under attack" by a chapter co-president of the League of Women Voters.

— Supreme Court Justice Clarence Thomas (Yale Law, '74) flouted judicial ethics when he participated in cases involving the validity of the 2020 election even while his spouse advocated overturning its results, and again when he accepted gifts from rich "friends" who have an interest in court decisions.

This is not a large sample, and it would not add much to its statistical significance to add Yale Law grad Sen. Josh Hawley (who raised his fist in support of the Jan. 6 insurrection) or Harvard Law grad Sen. Tom Cotton (who deemed slavery "a necessary evil"). Still, in one of my favorite quotations from the world of fiction, James Bond's deadly enemy Goldfinger remarked, "Once is happenstance. Twice is coincidence. Three times is enemy action." Including Chesebro, here we have seven.

Harvard and Yale Law School do a great job in making certain that their graduates do not starve after graduation. Four years out, their alumni rank in the top five of all law schools pulling down a median salary of over $200K per year. Do the alumni of the two schools, then, become addicted to the prospect of power and money? In treating an addict, the first step to solving the problem is admitting you have one. And, as seen, Harvard and Yale Law have a problem — with at least some of their alumni. They should do more, much more, to ensure their graduates are answerable to the higher cause of doing justice and supporting democracy.

For guidance, perhaps we can look to another profession whose practitioners also answer to a higher cause — medicine. For doctors, the health of patients should be paramount. Upon graduation, some medical schools have students subscribe to a modern version of the 2,500-year-old Hippocratic Oath. Penn State, for example, has med school grads recite: "By all that I hold highest, I promise my patients competence, integrity, candor, personal commitment to their best interest, compassion, and absolute discretion, and confidentiality within the law." There's nothing about power or money there.

Lawyers do take an oath when they are admitted to practice. For example, in order to join the D.C. bar, a lawyer swears to "demean myself uprightly and according to law" and to "support the Constitution of the United States of America." That's not much. What if, as a first step, Harvard and Yale took the lead among law schools in requiring their graduates to take an oath to do justice? For Americans, it might look something like this:

As an attorney, I commit to pursue justice, to treat people fairly, to defend democracy, to ensure guilt is found only on the basis of sufficient evidence, to provide zealous and responsible advocacy to clients and to protect and defend the Constitution of the United States.

As a graduate of Harvard Law myself, I sure as heck would support it.

The next step, a critical one, would be to adjust the teaching curricula at law schools to make certain they support such an oath.

As Abraham Lincoln (no, not a Harvard or Yale Law alum) said, "The philosophy of the school room in one generation will be the philosophy of government in the next."

Even if You Vote, You Probably Won't Be Picking the Next President

August 30, 2023

We speak of the national presidential election coming next year. That's the wrong way to look at it. In fact, there will be five concurrent state elections held on Nov. 5, 2024, to determine whether Joe Biden stays in the White House or whether the GOP candidate, most likely Donald Trump, evicts him.

As you probably remember from high school, each state gets assigned a number of electoral votes equal to the sum of its representatives on Capitol Hill — two senators plus the number of representatives in the House. (The District of Columbia is also allocated three electoral votes.) The total number of electoral votes is 538. A majority is required to win the presidency — that's 270.

In 2016, Republican nominee Trump won the presidency with 304 electoral votes over the Democrat, Hillary Clinton. In 2020, he lost it to Joe Biden, reaching a total of only 232 electoral votes. What changed? Arizona, Georgia, Michigan, Pennsylvania and Wisconsin moved from the GOP column to the Dems.

Not only does it look as though Trump and Biden will square off again, but it also looks as though the same five states will determine the winner of the presidency again. Despite the recent flood of indictments brought against the former president, national polls over the past three weeks show these two frontrunners essentially tied among American voters. But what matters is what's going on not across the country, but in those five most critical states.

The trend in those states is no friend to Trump or whoever else the GOP nominee might be. In 2016, four of the states had Republican governors. In 2020, three had Republicans in the statehouse. Going into 2024, only Georgia will.

Michigan in particular looks to be turning blue. In 2022, Gov. Gretchen Whitmer won re-election by over 10%, and the Dems won majorities in both houses of the state legislature for the first time in almost four decades. The authoritative Cook Political Report moved Michigan to leaning Democratic. Arizona, Georgia, Pennsylvania and Wisconsin are left as the only states rated "toss-ups."

That leaves a steep path for the GOP to regain control of the White House. No one would be surprised if they won Georgia and Arizona, but without Michigan, Republicans would have a political Mount Everest to climb. They would almost certainly have to win Pennsylvania. A summer poll in that state shows that 57% of Pennsylvanians approve of the job Democratic Gov. Josh Shapiro is doing, with only 23% disapproving.

I'd like to do away with the electoral college so the president is the candidate who wins the most votes from all Americans, not the one who can score in the five states teetering in the middle. Then GOP and Democratic nominees would be vying for my vote in California. Even though Trump lost the Golden State by 29% in 2020, he won more votes there than in any other state.

When asked why he robbed banks, notorious bank robber Willie Sutton replied, "Because that's where the money is." I would love to see presidential candidates campaigning where the popular votes are, not the electoral swing votes. That's probably a dream. At least I can take some consolation in missing the nonstop political ads that will inundate voters this fall in Phoenix, Atlanta, Pittsburgh, Detroit and Milwaukee.

A Superhero Defends What Makes America Great

September 6, 2023

It doesn't matter what astronomers say. The autumnal equinox may be a couple of weeks away, but Labor Day's passed and classes have started. Summer's done.

In thinking back over my last lazy, hazy crazy three months, two events stand out, both barbecues — one with a gaggle of family members and another with a gang of old high school classmates.

At the family function, I had a chance to catch up with my brother-in-law for the first time since he'd retired from a Bay Area police department. He'd just picked up a side hustle as a security guard. Not Jewish himself, his first gig will be to protect a local synagogue during this month's Jewish High Holy Days of Rosh Hashanah and Yom Kippur.

At the backyard picnic, a high school classmate told me of an incident in Palo Alto, California, where he and his wife had been accosted out of the blue in a pedestrian tunnel by thugs who blamed them for bringing COVID-19 to the United States. My classmate is Chinese American. His family has lived in the country for generations. The attack took place a few hundred yards from the Stanford campus, ranked No. 3 on the U.S. News list of best global universities.

What is going on? The Bay Area synagogue that is hiring my brother-in-law is only doing what is prudent. Just five years ago, a gunman murdered 11 people praying at Sabbath services at a Pittsburgh synagogue. In the last decade, the number of antisemitic incidents have increased almost five times in the United States. The attack on my classmate and his wife can be no surprise either. In 2021, anti-Asian hate crimes in San Francisco increased by 567%

from the previous year. It's a good day when there are no reports of race-based murders featured on the news. Aug. 26 was a bad day, where a masked white man shot to death three Black people in Jacksonville with a gun painted with a swastika.

My father fought in World War II and was there when the Dachau concentration camp was liberated. My classmate was in the army during the Vietnam War era. Is this the country they served? Are we not better than this?

The motto of the United States is "e pluribus unum" — out of many, one. To me, it means out of persons from all over the globe, we have forged one people — Americans. Today I am a resident scholar in the same dorm I lived in as an undergraduate decades ago. All four of my grandparents were born outside the United States. Every day, I see my own youth reflected back at me. I listen to students' stories and hear American stories — students whose parents or grandparents came to this country to seek opportunity. Every day, I see young adults of all races, all religions, all ancestries grappling with becoming adult Americans. It was my story, now it's their story, and it's still the American story.

Back in 1949, DC Comics released a poster of Superman talking to a diverse group of children. He explained that our country was "made up of Americans of many different races, religions and national origins." He told them, "If you hear anyone talk against a schoolmate or anyone else because of his religion, race, or national origin — don't wait: tell him that kind of talk is un-American."

Superman had it right. And we would do well to extend his advice from the schoolyard and campus to kitchen tables, places of worship, workplaces, neighborhoods, campaign rallies and legislatures around the country.

It's up to us to respond each time we hear un-American attacks. The answer is not to turn the other way or ban books. Politicians who open a Pandora's box of hate, racism and antisemitism to curry votes must be told that what they're doing is un-American.

Iron is a soft metal. It is only when mixed with other elements like carbon, manganese and molybdenum that it becomes hardened steel. Of course, the Man of Steel would understand that a blend of many elements leads to greater strength.

In College Sports, the Almighty Dollar Triumphs Over Education and Tradition

September 13, 2023

In 1958, Clark Kerr, president of the University of California, said, "The three major administrative problems on a campus are sex for the students, athletics for the alumni and parking for the faculty."

I am more than satisfied with my parking spot at the university where I work. Long married, I absolve my alma mater of responsibility for my sex life. What I want to talk about is college athletics. They're sure as heck not just for alumni anymore.

The traditional major college athletic conferences have broken into pieces and reassembled into Franken-leagues over the past few years. Consequently, traditional rivalries alumni cherish have disintegrated.

I grew up in Palo Alto, California. Stanford Stadium is across the street from my high school, and I went to just about every Stanford home football game between sixth and 12th grade. Stanford, a 25-mile drive from the Pacific coast, has committed to joining the Atlantic Coast Conference. Stanford's traditional rivalries with USC and UCLA will vanish after over a century. My friends and neighbors who are Stanford alums won't drive across the country to tailgate in Piscataway, New Jersey, for a football game with Rutgers like they would've headed to LA for a USC game. The reconfiguration of the leagues was not done for the benefit of alumni.

So, maybe it was done for the students? In addition to football, Stanford student-athletes who play basketball, soccer, baseball, softball, women's lacrosse, wrestling, women's gymnastics, cross country, golf, tennis, track, swimming and women's rowing will be flying across the country for games, matches, regattas and meets. It's hard to see how long plane rides and missed classes benefit students or their education.

Of course, Stanford is not the only school affected by rejiggering conference memberships. The University of Colorado hired the talented "Neon" Deion Sanders as head football coach last December and then jumped conferences from the Pac-12 to the Big 12. Sanders said he would try to push out current scholarship students to make way for new transfer students. He was successful. Out of a roster limit of 85, only 10 scholarship players from last year remain this year. Losing a scholarship or transferring schools due to new management doesn't serve the interests of affected students either.

So, if college athletics isn't run for the benefit of alumni or students, what the heck is going on? As in the Watergate scandal, it's best to "follow the money." Thanks to bloated football broadcasting rights, the Big Ten could offer USC and UCLA annual payments of approaching $80 million, more than twice what they could have expected from the Pac-12. After a century, they jumped ship to the so-called Big Ten, which will swell to 18 teams next fall.

College athletics have become big business. Division I athletics generated $15.8 billion in revenues in 2019, according to the National Collegiate Athletic Association. In 2021, the NCAA earned around a billion dollars for March Madness. With new TV contracts for football and basketball, the number should soar in coming years. None of the funds will be paid to students.

The highest-paid state employee in 40 of the 50 states is a college football or basketball coach. Highest-paid of all is Nick Saban, head football coach of the University of Alabama, who receives approximately $11.7 million from the state. (Alabama K-12 schools rank in the 40s in math and reading scores, student to teacher ratio, percentage of licensed or certified public K-12 teachers and median ACT scores.) Forty-eight of 50 employees on the list are men. The only women are Nos. 49 and 50 — vice chancellor of the

University of Maine and New Hampshire's chief medical examiner. The latter makes $261,538 per year, about 2% as much as Saban.

In 2021, the University of West Virginia finished a $55 million upgrade to its football locker room, training facilities, player lounges and more. This year, the university recommended eliminating 32 majors and cutting $7 million in staffing including 38 faculty members.

In his seminal "General Education in a Free Society," published in 1945, another university president, Harvard's James B. Conant, wrote that the first priority for college education is preparing students for "life as a responsible human being and citizen." A second priority is a "student's competence in some occupation." Conant believed participation in sports can further these goals by helping students acquire "initiative and resourcefulness." He says nothing about athletics as a dollar generator. And then again, neither did Clark Kerr.

Update: In last week's column, I expressed sorrow at the need for protection of synagogues against violence. Two days after the column posted, my own synagogue was subject to a bomb threat during Friday night services. Congresswoman and longtime friend Anna Eshoo was in attendance, scheduled to speak after prayers. Via email, I asked her for her reaction. She wrote, "It was heartbreaking for me to witness the evacuation of the Temple on Friday evening at the conclusion of the prayer service. Families and children threatened with great harm, generated by hate. We all need to renew our commitment to stand against antisemitism. Their faith has deepened mine."

Romney and Others Speak Out, but Too Little, Too Late To Be Forgiven

September 20, 2023

At least a few Republican politicians and officeholders have fessed up to the role of their party and its leader in undermining American democracy. I doubt very much whether they give a hoot if I forgive them or not for their role in creating the problem in the first place. Still, I've been thinking about whether I should.

My reflections were prompted by Republican Sen. Mitt Romney who has been reaping praise recently for pointing out the obvious: "A very large portion of my party really doesn't believe in the Constitution." The 2012 GOP nominee is often lauded as a man of principle, especially for his votes to convict former President Donald Trump in two impeachment trials. For years, though, Romney was more than willing to accept the support of extremists in his party to further policy goals. As Nobel laureate Paul Krugman says, "It's good to see Romney speaking up now, but the party he's criticizing is in large part a monster that people like him helped create." Moreover, I suspect Romney's statement would have carried more weight if he had made it before he decided not to run for reelection and if it weren't being used to publicize his biography coming out next month.

Romney is not the only prominent Republican whose support for democracy and the rule of law came too little, too late. Trump national security adviser John Bolton wrote that former President Trump had indeed committed the high crimes and misdemeanors necessary for impeachment. Among them was the threat to withhold military aid to Ukraine if that nation did not launch an investigation into Joe Biden. Bolton refused to speak out when conviction of Trump in the Senate was possible. He only made the accusation in a book published in time to become a bestseller but too late to have much effect on Trump's standing.

Here's another example. In the days just after the 2020 presidential election, Trump Attorney General William Barr seemed to support his boss's accusations of election irregularities when he tasked prosecutors with looking into the empty claims. The head of the Election Crimes Branch of the Justice Department resigned in protest. Two years later in testimony before the House of Representatives Jan. 6 committee, Barr said the claims made by Trump were "bogus" and "bull——."

Admittedly, obtaining my forgiveness isn't worth much to Romney, Bolton or Barr, but what would it take for them to earn it?

When the Holy Roman Emperor Henry IV sought absolution from the pope in 1077, he put on a hair shirt and waited outside the papal residence at Canossa for three days in a snowstorm. Tempting though it may be to set the bar there, I'm not requiring frostbite and itchy clothes to concede forgiveness for GOP bigwigs. But I still would like to find a workable standard.

The Middle Ages do offer another possibility. Maimonides, the great philosopher and physician to Saladin, the sultan of Egypt, lived a century after Henry IV. What Maimonides wanted to see for forgiveness was stopping wrongdoing, confessing the improper action, regretting the action and determining not to repeat it.

Wouldn't it be great if Romney, Bolton and Barr had followed Maimonides' advice? But they expressed little sorrow and certainly no apology for failing to take action to protect democracy and the Constitution sooner or more strongly.

Let's go back into history again, but not quite as far back as the Middle Ages. One of Trump's predecessors in the White House, Richard Nixon, said this about the Watergate break-in: "Well, when the president does it, that means that it is not illegal." No acknowledgment of improper action there. His counsel Charles Colson took another path. Pleading guilty for conspiring to cover up the break-in, Colson told a federal judge he'd been "an arrogant self-assured man in the ruthless exercise of power." He later reminisced, "My biggest regret is that I saw things going on that I should've known were wrong or I knew were wrong but then I rationalized them away. I didn't say anything. I should've spoken up a number of times and ... didn't." Colson spent seven months in federal prison and went on to found the Prison Fellowship, a nonprofit organization to support, teach and advocate for prisoners, former prisoners and their families.

Maimonides would assuredly say Colson deserves forgiveness. But what about GOP stalwarts such as Romney, Bolton and Barr? No way. By the time they spoke out, it was too little, too late.

Potomac Fever Still Infects the Senate

October 4, 2023

The past week or two, I've been thinking about two senators in particular — the late Sen. Dianne Feinstein from California and current senator from New Jersey Robert Menendez. She needed to resign and wouldn't. He needs to resign and won't.

Don't get me wrong. Sen. Feinstein, who died on Sept. 29 at age 90, is a hero of mine. She spearheaded a ban on assault weapons — unfortunately now expired — that saved hundreds if not thousands of American lives. As head of the Senate Intelligence Committee, she took on the CIA and revealed the interrogation techniques it used against suspected terrorists were both brutal and ineffective. (Annette Bening even starred as Feinstein in a movie about the episode called "The Report.")

But she wouldn't leave when it was time to go. Questioning Twitter's then-CEO Jack Dorsey in November 2020, she repeated a question with no memory of already having asked it moments before. This past spring, her absence from meetings of the Senate Judiciary Committee due to illness prevented the confirmation of federal judges.

Feinstein said, "I understand that my absence could delay the important work of the Judiciary Committee." Ill and feeble she might be, but she still refused to give up her seat. Why? If she had resigned, her replacement would have been chosen by California Gov. Gavin Newsom, a fellow Democrat. Her successor was bound to vote much as she would. Given her physical and mental condition, the chances of Feinstein adding to her illustrious list of accomplishments were nil. She wasn't staying because she could serve her constituents or the country better than a replacement. She was holding on for herself.

Almost seven decades ago, John F. Kennedy, who served eight years as a senator from Massachusetts, noted in his Pulitzer Prize-winning "Profiles in Courage," "The virus of Potomac Fever, which rages everywhere in Washington, breeds nowhere in more virulent form than on the Senate Floor." And what is that fever? Urban Dictionary defines it as, "A disease peculiar to the greater Washington, DC, metropolitan area that presents chiefly as an intense desire in the infected to be associated with the power and prestige of the United States Federal Government." Apparently, Feinstein suffered from an acute case of Potomac Fever which was virulent enough to override a lifetime of service to her constituents and the country. What a shame.

On the other hand, Sen. Robert Menendez of New Jersey is alive and breathing even if his political career is in mortal danger. He has been indicted for taking bribes to bolster aid to Egypt and to disrupt both state and federal criminal cases. FBI agents executed a search warrant of his home where they found over half a million dollars in currency, some of which bore the fingerprints of the persons who allegedly bribed him. In addition, agents found over $100,000 in gold bars and a Mercedes-Benz which also allegedly represented payoffs.

And yet, Menendez refuses to resign. If there were only the counterpart of the COVID-19 home test for Potomac Fever, I'd bet Menendez's test would be positive. He says that after any trial, "Not only will I be exonerated, but I will still be New Jersey's senior senator."

That's fine for him, but does the prolonged period between indictment and verdict benefit his New Jersey constituents and the people of the United States? How effective a senator can he be with this sword hanging over his head? He doesn't need a seat in the Senate to fight the charges.

Menendez called the indictments the product of an "active smear campaign." This feeds into Republican accusations that the

Justice Department has been weaponized against the Biden administration's enemies — especially former President Donald Trump. Republican Sen. Tom Cotton has said Menendez should not be forced from office "by Democratic politicians who now view him as inconvenient to their hold on power." Tell me why Democrats would want to chase Menendez from office if he were innocent. He has voted 100% of the time with President Joe Biden in this congressional session.

It must be tempting, too, for Republicans to want Menendez in office where he would be vulnerable in his 2024 reelection bid. Again, if he did resign, a Democratic governor would appoint his replacement who inevitably would vote much the same as he did. Sorry, Senator, you are not the indispensable man. You are preoccupied with your plight and at the same time. suffering from Potomac Fever. Staying in office is not what's best for your constituents or the country.

In "Profiles in Courage," Kennedy also asks, "Where else, but in the political profession is the individual expected to sacrifice all — including his own career — for the national good?" Yet isn't that what we should expect of those we elect to high office? It may be only a naive dream, but the goal of all hundred senators ought not be reelection but doing what's right for their constituents and country.

Why Did Hamas Attack Now? What's Next?

October 11, 2023

Why did the murderous Hamas attack on Israel happen now? What comes next?

First, why now?

Just last month, U.S. Secretary of State Anthony Blinken said, "If you have the leading Islamic country in the world making peace with Israel, I think that truly is transformative." All year, the Biden administration has been boasting of its work to bring Saudi Arabia and Israel together to bring peace to the Middle East.

Such a deal would indeed be transformative, but in a way that challenges the Hamas Covenant's call to "obliterate" Israel. The deal would almost certainly have included concessions to Palestinian Arabs intended to bring regional peace closer. So, Hamas took to terrorism to undo the deal. Those despicable videos of ruthless murders of innocent Israeli citizens were posted and publicized as a warning to potential peacemakers. Hamas is threatening next to "regrettably" execute Israeli civilian hostages.

A peace agreement among three of its sworn enemies would also be a devastating blow to Iran's strategic position in the Middle East. Iran supplied Hamas with the funds and arms that made the terrorist raids possible. Iran must have urged, ordered or consented to the attacks.

Political crises in both Israel and the U.S. also made it a favorable time to launch the attacks. Israeli Prime Minister Benjamin Netanyahu's intention to limit judicial power led to mass street protests last spring. Israeli air force pilots threatened not to report for duty. The Ministry of National Security, which oversees the border police, is headed by Itamar Ben-Gvir, who was appointed for the right-wing votes he could bring to the Netanyahu coalition and not for any expertise or administrative ability.

And what about the United States? On the day of the attack, there was no speaker of the House of Representatives. How long might this political stalemate delay any emergency funds for Israel? The Republicans, who hold a majority in the House, seem ready to step away from support for Ukraine against Russian aggression and terrorism. Could Iran and Hamas have drawn a lesson there? On the other side of Capitol Hill, Sen. Tommy Tuberville is single-handedly corroding U.S. military readiness by blocking the promotions of senior officers.

The ramifications of the Hamas terrorist attacks will spin out over years if not decades. But there are short-term consequences I'd put money on.

Netanyahu positioned himself as the indispensable protector of his country's security. He failed. Only two weeks before the surprise Hamas attack, he told the United Nations General Assembly that Israel was "at the cusp" of that peace agreement which "will go a long way to ending the Arab-Israeli conflict." A predecessor as prime minister, Golda Meir, was pushed out of office within a year for allowing Israel to be surprised by an attack a half-century ago. Netanyahu's fate will be the same.

The Saudis couldn't let Iran be seen as the protector of Palestinian Arabs while they themselves aligned with the Jewish state. As a result, the Saudi Arabian foreign ministry did not condemn the Hamas attacks, but instead pointed to Israel's "occupation, the deprivation of the Palestinian people of their legitimate rights, and the repetition of systematic provocations" as responsible. The march toward a Saudi peace agreement with Israel is now frozen in place if not in full retreat.

Over two decades, Israel hunted down the terrorists who murdered Israeli athletes at the 1972 Munich Olympics. The country will be just as single-minded with the Hamas leaders and terrorists responsible for the deaths of over a thousand citizens in recent days. (As a percentage of its population, 1,000 Israeli deaths is equivalent to 12 times the number of Americans who died in the crash of the Twin Towers on 9/11.) Remember, there are videos of the perpetrators. Like its nemesis Netanyahu, Hamas is bound to lose its power over the Gaza Strip.

Only in the longer term do things begin to look more hopeful. The United Arab Emirates was "appalled" by the actions of Hamas. Saudi Arabia should also come to see killing babies and taking hostages is not a basis for sympathy. Any resuscitation of the peace agreement between Israel and Saudi Arabia will have to include consultations with the Palestinian Arabs on the benefits an agreement will bring to them.

Lord Palmerston, the 19th century British prime minister, said that Britain had no eternal allies or enemies, only eternal interests. Even in the wake of the heinous terrorist attacks, it is in the interests of both Israel and Saudi Arabia to stand for peace and stability and to oppose Iranian-fostered terrorism. I look forward to a future where Hamas will be crippled or gone; a new prime minister will hold office in Israel; Saudi Arabia will make peace with Israel; and Palestinian Arabs have set forth on the road to justice and democracy.

For Better or Worse, Jackass CEOs Are the Ones Who Change the World

October 18, 2023

According to Forbes Magazine, Elon Musk, CEO of the electric car manufacturer Tesla, is the world's richest man with a net worth of over $250 billion. Tesla itself is the world's eighth-most valuable company.

A recent 688-page biography of Musk by Walter Isaacson hit No. 1 on the New York Times bestseller list. In her review of the book, Harvard historian Jill Lepore writes, "The book upholds a core conviction of many executives: sometimes to get s— done you have to be a (jerk)." She goes on to call out Musk's "pettiness, arrogance, and swaggering viciousness."

There's little doubt about Musk being a jerk. In the book, Isaacson reports, "(Musk) didn't have the emotional receptors that produce everyday kindness and warmth and a desire to be liked." There's a joke that went around Silicon Valley comparing Musk to the sun: The closer you get, the more you get burnt. His subordinates have fallen like redwoods in a clear-cutting operation. In a nine-month period, 44% of his direct reports left compared to a 9% average at peer companies. He called a British diver who helped in the 2018 rescue of Thai schoolboys from a cave a "pedo" — slang for a pedophile. I don't know him, but he sure doesn't sound like a nice fellow.

In my time in Silicon Valley, I did cross paths with Apple co-founder Steve Jobs, the subject of another hefty biography by Isaacson. How did Jobs treat his employees? Isaacson notes, "He could stun an unsuspecting victim with an emotional towel-snap, perfectly aimed." Silicon Valley historian Leslie Berlin wrote, "His management style was dismissive." No wonder, given his tendency to divide his subordinates into two categories: "insanely great people" and "crappy people." He also allegedly orchestrated an illegal conspiracy among tech companies to keep salaries down. He didn't think rules applied to him.

Apple is the world's most valuable country with a market cap approaching $3 trillion. No. 2 is Microsoft. Back in 2001, a federal court found that Microsoft, under the leadership of Microsoft founder Bill Gates, had violated U.S. antitrust laws.

Facebook, founded by Mark Zuckerberg, allowed its platform to be used by Russians in an attempt to influence the 2016 U.S. presidential election despite warnings. Earlier this year, he laid off over 10,000 employees from the company, now known as Meta Platforms and No. 7 on the list of the world's most valuable companies. Heidi K. Gardner, distinguished fellow at Harvard Law School, said using email to sack the employees with little or no warning implied Zuckerberg treated employees as "chess pieces that can be moved about and discarded at will."

Are Musk, Jobs, Gates and Zuckerberg, then, the heirs to the robber barons of the late 19th and early 20th centuries? John D. Rockefeller was America's first billionaire. His Standard Oil crushed competitors and was broken up by the trustbusting President Teddy Roosevelt. Henry Ford owned the notoriously antisemitic The Dearborn Independent, disseminated at every Ford franchise in the country. The paper published front-page articles blaming the world's problems on "The International Jew." Andrew Carnegie founded Carnegie Steel, the pioneer in efficient steel production. In July 1892, the company hired Pinkerton detectives armed with rifles to break a union-led strike at a plant in Homestead, Pennsylvania. Twelve died in the confrontation.

The seven men (and they *are* all men) mentioned above were CEOs of start-up companies that exploded in size and changed the world — by developing the oil, steel, auto, personal computer, handheld, social networking and electric vehicle industries. All seven started or joined their companies when they were young, ranging in age from 19 for Zuckerberg's founding of Facebook to age 39 for Ford starting his car company.

All were obsessed with oversized goals. For example, Musk's goal for Tesla is "to accelerate the world's transition to sustainable energy." In recruiting Pepsi president John Sculley to Apple, Jobs asked him, "Do you want to sell sugar water for the rest of your life or come with me and change the world?" Henry Ford's aim was "a car in every garage." In 2017, Facebook said its mission was "to give people the power to build community and bring the world closer together."

Jessica Grose recently wrote an opinion piece for the New York Times entitled "C.E.O.s Don't Need to Be Monsters." She's right, of course — in general. However, she appears to be wrong for those few CEOs who can drive a startup into the top 10 in market cap while changing the world.

Lying Proves a Winning Strategy in Both Middle East and United States

October 25, 2023

Mark Twain supposedly said, "A lie can travel around the world and back again while the truth is lacing up its boots." Whether he did actually make that remark or not, its underlying truth has been made crystal clear in recent days.

On Oct. 17, the Gaza Health Ministry accused Israel of bombing Al-Ahli al-Arabi Hospital in Gaza City and killing 500 people. Based on intelligence reports and intercepts, President Joe Biden said the next day that Israel was not responsible but rather "the other team." The U.S. intelligence community determined with "high confidence" that the missile was not shot by Israel. Britain, Canada and France agree. A video analysis by The Wall Street Journal showed how a failed rocket shot from inside Gaza caused the explosion. Hamas, the organization which controls Gaza, has put forward no evidence to the contrary.

And yet, Hamas, designated a terrorist organization by the U.S. and the European Union, turned a tragedy into a victory. By getting its story of Israeli responsibility out first, it triggered protests in Lebanon, Iraq, Jordan, Kuwait, Egypt, Tunisia and the West Bank. Hamas was able to stop moves toward peace between its enemy Israel and nearby countries. Jordan's King Abdullah canceled the summit meeting with President Biden and Egyptian president El-Sisi. Saudi Arabia, which had been moving closer to recognizing Israel's right to exist, now condemned the country.

In the United States, Rep. Rashida Tlaib of Michigan refused to accept evidence that Israel did not bomb the hospital. A longstanding opponent of Israel, she accused Israel of "oppressive & racist policies" in 2019. On Oct. 17 of this year, she posted on social media, "Israel just bombed the ... Hospital killing 500 Palestinians (doctors, children, patients) just like that." She threatened Biden, "We will remember where you stood." She refused to apologize even after the evidence emerged that the deaths at the hospital were not caused by Israel, saying, "Both the Israeli and United States governments have long, documented histories of misleading the public about wars and war crimes." The idea the bomb originated within the Gaza Strip simply did not fit her worldview.

We Americans can look closer to home than the Middle East to find another compelling example of how lies spread early can win a propaganda war.

Hours after the polls closed in the November 2020 presidential election, ballots were still being counted. The networks had not yet picked a winner. Nevertheless, then-President Donald Trump lied in claiming victory: "Frankly, we did win this election." A week later he tweeted, "RIGGED ELECTION. WE WILL WIN." He continued to support the lie on Jan. 6, 2021: "We had an election that was stolen from us." It didn't matter that his legal efforts to have the supreme courts in the swing states Arizona, Nevada, Pennsylvania and Michigan support this belief all failed. It didn't even matter when the official count of electoral votes showed Biden had won.

The lie that Trump triumphed was made early and lives on. In fact, it is gaining strength. According to a July poll by CNN, 69% of Republicans and Republican-leaners believe President Biden did not legitimately win the presidency despite the evidence. That's up from 63% earlier this year. The more evidence showing that Trump is lying, the more his believers cling to the lie.

This is what psychologists call the "backfire effect," when evidence to the contrary leads to people embracing their belief even more strongly. Academics have shown that backfire effects tend to occur when the issue is an integral part of an individual's political identity. Thus, the more evidence put forward that Israel did not bomb the hospital and that President Biden won the election, the more some people will believe the opposite.

Two thousand years ago, the Roman philosopher Seneca the Younger wrote, "Truth hates delay." Delay was necessary to come up with the truth about the hospital bombing as the United States, France, Canada and the U.K. evaluated intelligence reports. Moreover, Seneca did not live in the age of the internet. Even respected sources of news such as The New York Times raced to put up Hamas' lies. It was only six days after the explosion that the Times acknowledged its "early versions of the coverage — and the prominence it received in a headline, news alert and social media channels — relied too heavily on claims by Hamas, and did not make clear that those claims could not immediately be verified."

As for the 2020 presidential election, states required days to count all the ballots. To falsely declare he won took Trump only a few hours after the polls closed.

How easy it is to make some people believe a lie that fits their beliefs, and how hard it is to undo that work.

Mr. Speaker, No Time To Abandon Policy That Made America Great

November 1, 2023

I was gratified to learn that Mike Johnson, the newly elected Republican speaker of the House of Representative, believes immigration is the most serious threat to the country. I'm not sure it's the most serious threat, but it's in my top half-dozen.

Then I discovered that Johnson wanted to keep immigrants *out*. I want to let them *in*, just as Ronald Reagan did. In his last speech as president, he declared, "Thanks to each wave of new arrivals to this land of opportunity, we're a nation forever young, forever bursting with energy and new ideas." Without new Americans, Reagan believed, "Our leadership in the world would soon be lost."

What would this country be like today without immigrants or their children or grandchildren? I spent much of my working life toiling in California's Silicon Valley, the hub of world technology. What would the Valley have been like without Apple co-founder Steve Jobs, the son of a Syrian immigrant? And what about other companies such as search giant Google (co-founder born in the Soviet Union), electrical vehicle company Tesla (CEO born in South Africa), next-generation chip leader Nvidia (founder born in Taiwan), and so many more?

Nowadays I write novels. To learn from the masters, I read their works. In the last 50 years, seven Americans have won the Nobel Prize in Literature. Four of them, including Saul Bellow and Isaac Bashevis Singer, were themselves born outside the U.S., and Bob Dylan and Louise Glück were the grandchildren of immigrants from Eastern Europe. Just as with technology, American literature (and music) would be much the lesser without them. This is true in virtually any field of endeavor from architecture to sports to medicine. As a matter of fact, millions of people around the world are alive thanks to this year's Nobel Prize winner in medicine: Hungarian-born Katalin Karikó, a researcher at the University of Pennsylvania, laid the groundwork for development of the COVID-19 vaccine.

The children of immigrants play leading roles on the national political stage, too. President Barack Obama's father was born in Kenya. The mother of his successor as president, Donald Trump, was born in Scotland. How different would 21st century American politics be without those two game changers? And what about other aspirants to the presidency past and present, including Vice President Kamala Harris (parents born in India and Jamaica), Sen. Ted Cruz (father born in Cuba) and current candidate Vivek Ramaswamy (parents born in India)?

Currently a resident scholar at Harvard, I live among students who themselves, or whose parents, come from countries from Albania to Zimbabwe. Talking to them reminds me of my own background. I, too, am the progeny of immigrants, who came to this country to escape persecution and to take advantage of the opportunities it offered. Current law has us sending international students home after graduation even if they buy into the American dream and want to stay. The late Bob Noyce, inventor of the microprocessor and co-founder of Intel, once joked to me that foreign students who earn a Ph.D. in engineering at an American university ought not be sent home — they should be *required* to stay in the U.S.

Now, don't get me wrong. I am not suggesting the U.S. should swing open its gates and let all enter no matter what the law says. What I do mean to suggest is, first, that rhetoric attacking immigrants should cease. Trump should apologize for calling Mexican immigrants rapists. The new speaker of the House, a Trump supporter, should stop dissing immigrants by saying Democrats want to "turn all these illegals into voters for their side." If Johnson, a self-described "Bible-believing Christian," doesn't want to study Reagan's speeches, he can turn to the Book of Leviticus, which could not be clearer: "The foreigner residing among you must be treated as your native-born. Love them as yourself, for you were foreigners in Egypt."

Instead of spouting partisan rhetoric, Speaker Mike Johnson should be working, on the one hand to protect American borders, and on the other to ensure America remains a beacon of freedom and opportunity. He should support the administration's request for funding that would expedite processing refugees at our southern border and deportment of those who have no right to stay. It's time to pass laws to update our immigration laws to ensure this country continues to benefit from the work ethic and brilliance of new Americans and continues to be a haven for the oppressed.

In 1963, President John F. Kennedy said welcoming immigrants is "what this country has stood for for 200 years." In 1989, Reagan said immigrants "give more than they receive. They labor and succeed. ... They renew our pride and gratitude in the United States of America, the greatest, freest nation in the world."

Time to heed those words. And to act on them.

A Careful Look in the Mirror Shows It's Hamas, Not Israel, That Supports Genocide

November 8, 2023

Mirror politics is accusing your opponents of doing the very thing you yourself are doing or wish to do. That's what's going on in the Middle East right now when anti-Israel politicians, writers and academics accuse Israel of genocide.

The term genocide is thrown around a lot these days, but it's carefully defined by the United Nations 1948 Genocide Convention as "acts committed with intent to destroy, in whole or in part, a national, ethnical, racial or religious group."

In 1948, Israel's population was 82% Jewish and 18% non-Jewish citizens, overwhelmingly Arab. Today, it's 73% Jewish and 27% non-Jewish. Moreover, Arabs (including the ethnically Arab Druze minority) make up almost half of new doctors in Israel. The numbers of Arabs generally and Arab doctors particularly would hardly increase during a campaign of genocide by Israel.

The Gaza Strip was occupied by Israeli troops during the 1967 Arab-Israeli War. According to the U.S. Census Bureau, Gaza's population in 1970 was 345,000 people. Israeli troops withdrew in 2005. According to the CIA, its population is now 2.1 million. Despite this huge population growth, Israel is accused of genocide by politicians, journalists, governments and professors who should know better.

Gaza civilians and Hamas both understand Israel would prefer not to harm the innocent. That's why Gaza civilians knew they were safe as they moved through a humanitarian corridor protected by an Israeli army tank. That's why Hamas fires rockets from or near schools, hospitals and mosques. As a 2019 NATO report noted, any Israeli retaliation allows Hamas "to accuse (Israel) of committing war crimes."

Rep. Rashida Tlaib of Michigan says President Joe Biden is supporting Israeli genocide. A writer for the New York Times signed an open letter accusing Israel of trying to "conduct genocide against the Palestinian people." A Yale professor deemed Israel a "murderous, genocidal settler state." Along with more than half a dozen other countries, South Africa has withdrawn its ambassador to Israel, calling its conduct "genocide."

This is all mirror politics. Israel withdrew from Gaza in 2005 to allow its population self-determination. Last month, the Hamas rulers of Gaza sent terrorists into Israel where they brutally murdered 1,200 people and took another 240 hostage. Israel said first that it would delay sending troops into Gaza and then that it would support a ceasefire if the hostages were released. On Oct. 27, the New York Times ran a story headlined, "As Gazans Scrounge for Food and Water, Hamas Sits on a Rich Trove of Supplies." Hamas would rather let Arabs in Gaza die than move toward peace. Why? Because Hamas' paramount aim is genocide.

The Hamas Covenant calls for Islam to "obliterate" Israel and to "vanquish" all Jews. As Biden said of Hamas, "Its stated purpose is the annihilation of the State of Israel and the murder of Jewish people." Hamas does not deny it. When an interviewer on Lebanese TV asked senior Hamas official Ghazi Hamad whether Hamas's war aims include the "annihilation of Israel," Hamad responded, "Yes, of course."

The Israeli war aim is to free the hostages and destroy Hamas. It is not to kill peaceful residents of Gaza for no reason.

Gaza is surrounded by Israel and Egypt. The latter's actions show it, too, supports the elimination of Hamas. The Economist, a British magazine with an international reputation for trustworthiness, recently wrote, "The only way out of the cycle of violence is to destroy Hamas's rule." As the legendary prime minister of Israel Golda Meir told American President Gerald Ford, "We can't negotiate with terrorists who just want us out."

When anti-Israel protestors shout, "From the river to the sea, Palestine must be free," they are chanting code words calling for genocide of 7 million Jewish citizens of a country established and recognized by the U.N. As a recently passed bipartisan resolution of the House of Representatives put it, the slogan is "widely recognized as a genocidal call to violence to destroy the state of Israel and its people." And what about the 2.6 million *non-Jewish* citizens of Israel? Polling shows 74% of them identify as Israeli or Arab-Israeli versus 7% who identify as Palestinian. What happens to them?

During the Cold War, those in the West who supported nuclear disarmament to bring about world peace were called "useful idiots" by the Soviet Union's KGB. Too many protestors who think they are supporting peace in the Middle East are the useful idiots of Hamas genocide.

It's possible to support a solution of two states, one majority Arab and one majority Jewish, without accusing Israel of genocide. It's possible to envision Palestinian Arabs setting forth on the road to justice and democracy without genocide. But a peaceful future is only possible if Hamas is defeated. Ongoing warfare, more deaths and potential genocide are the inevitable consequences of continued Hamas rule of Gaza.

For those who see Israel as the entity embracing genocide in the conflict, I suggest you look around. You may be walking down a hall of mirrors.

Beware of Dictatorships Bearing Gifts (Even if They're Cute and Cuddly)

November 15, 2023

Earlier this month, three giant pandas on loan at the National Zoo in Washington, D.C. were crated up and loaded on a FedEx jet for a trans-Pacific flight. China had requested their return. Frequent visitors to the zoo were left weeping at their departure.

Me? I say good riddance.

Now, I have nothing against pandas. I had a toy panda as an infant and remember it fondly still. But almost all *living* pandas come from Tibet, which was invaded and conquered by China in 1950 and annexed in 1959. The head of the Tibetan government, the Dalai Lama, fled to India and remains head of the Tibetan government-in-exile.

According to the Latin poet Virgil, the priest Laocoon warned, "Don't trust the horse, Trojans. Whatever it is, I fear the Greeks, even those bearing gifts." And Americans shouldn't trust pandas from the Chinese government. Those black and white cuties ostensibly stood for peace and goodwill but underneath served as a cover-up of aggression and authoritarianism.

Upon the departure of the pandas, Chinese diplomat Xu Xueyuan said they had "contributed strongly to the mutual understanding and friendship between the Chinese and American peoples." She might have overstated the case, but Panda Diplomacy did contribute, at least a little, to the success of China's aim to maintain its hold on Tibet and integrate it into the rest of the nation. In 2014, President Barack Obama said that the U.S. recognized Tibet as part of China.

Obama went on to "encourage Chinese authorities to take steps to preserve the unique cultural, religious and linguistic identity of the Tibetan people." But American encouragement had little effect on Chinese policy. A U.S. Department of State report issued in 2022 found "significant human rights issues" in Tibet including "torture," "extrajudicial killings by the government," "severe restrictions on freedom of religion," "coerced abortion" and "violence or threats of violence targeting Indigenous persons."

Schools are eliminating the teaching of Tibetan culture and history. Reports indicate over three-quarters of Tibetan children have been shifted to state-run boarding schools. The Chinese government has incentivized members of the Han ethnic group, the overwhelming majority in China, to move to the Tibet Autonomous Region, about half of historic Tibet. According to Chinese censuses, the Han percentage of the population in the TAR increased from 8% to 12% from 2010 to 2020. (My guess is that the number is higher.) Tibet is being exploited by "major development projects" that, again according to the State Department, "disproportionately benefited non-Tibetans and contributed to the considerable influx of Han Chinese into the TAR."

Oxford Languages defines colonialism as "the policy or practice of acquiring full or partial political control over another country, occupying it with settlers, and exploiting it economically." It sure looks as though that's what's going on in Tibet. The Chinese government is following the playbook in Tibet that it uses in dealing with other ethnic minorities. However, it has not advanced as far in the TAR as it has in Xinjiang province where over a million ethnically Uyghur residents were put in concentration camps.

President Joe Biden met with Chinese President Xi on Nov. 15. Did he even mention Tibet? Almost certainly not. Our relations with China — the U.S.'s biggest trading partner and biggest military rival, and by two times the world's biggest carbon emitter — have higher priorities. Issues of war and peace aside, the American government knows only too well that 22% of all U.S. imports come from China. In 2019, 70% of shoes purchased in the U.S. were made in China. More than 95% of Apple's iPhones, AirPods, Macs and iPads are made in China. Going without pandas might generate tears, but Americans are not about to go around barefoot and disconnected.

What about nongovernmental left-wing protests over Chinese policy in Tibet? Anti-Israel activists justify attacks on that country because of its alleged colonialism. (The claims are false, but we'll address that another day.) Why no protests against actual Chinese colonialism in Tibet? The far left wouldn't be swayed because Chinese imports to the U.S. are 200 times Israel's. It cannot be a matter of Muslim solidarity — while the Tibetans are Buddhist, Uyghurs are Muslim, and there's not much protesting going on about them either. Is it simply a matter that Jews form the majority in Israel, but not China?

Alas, pandas are soft and fuzzy, but international affairs are not.

"Giant pandas belong to China," Chinese diplomat Xu Xueyuan said.

No, they don't, say I — while typing the words of this column on a Chinese-manufactured laptop.

A Big Thanks to America's Women Voters

November 22, 2023

I admit I am not thankful for the climate change deniers, assault weapons supporters and election rejecters so prevalent on the American political scene. What I am thankful for this holiday season is that stalwart bloc of voters in favor of doing something about climate change, mass murders and attacks on democracy.

Who are they? American women.

The press tends to look at the November 2024 presidential election in terms of red versus blue states, college-educated versus non-college-educated voters, and white voters versus voters of color. Fair enough, but in my view even more important is the contest between women and men voters.

Then-President Donald Trump encouraged a takeover of the U.S. Capitol on Jan. 6, 2021, in support of his claim to have won the 2020 presidential election. This fall, he's used neo-Nazi language by calling his political opponents "vermin" and saying immigrants are "poisoning the blood of our country." In a second term, he has said he would appoint a special prosecutor to "go after" President Joe Biden and use the Justice Department to investigate and indict political enemies and critics. Former federal appellate Judge J. Michael Luttig and other prominent conservative lawyers have written that Trump and his allies are "explicitly threatening to upend fundamental tenets of the American constitutional system if returned to power."

And what's the overall reaction of American voters to the dangers another Trump term poses? In a recent NBC poll, the former president leads Biden by two percentage points. If not for the 19th Amendment that extended the right to vote to women, the margin would be far greater. That's because male voters are ready to return

Trump to the White House by a 55% to 35% tally. Women, on the other hand, reject Trump and what he stands for by 13 points, 52% to 39%.

Still, women do have a lot of work to do to deter a Trump-led turn away from democracy. In 2016, Trump lost the popular vote to Hillary Clinton by over 2%. The eccentricities of the Electoral College delivered the White House to him nonetheless.

American women show good sense not only on who should sit in the White House but also on other critical issues. Let's look at two of them: mass shootings and climate change.

In each of the eight deadliest mass shootings in America between 2012 and 2022 — including those in Sandy Hook, Las Vegas and Uvalde — the murderer used an assault weapon. It's no surprise, then, that 70% of American women want to see a ban on such weapons. It is unfortunate, though, that such a ban is supported by only a minority of men.

The United Nations has called climate change "the single biggest health threat facing humanity." How so? By its effect on "air pollution, disease, extreme weather events, forced displacement, pressures on mental health, and increased hunger and poor nutrition." Fifty-nine percent of women in a recent survey believe climate change is indeed causing such serious effects, 10% more than among men.

So, what's going on with these broad discrepancies between the viewpoints of men and women? Why would women take a stand against authoritarianism, mass murders and climate change more often than men? I don't know, but in any case, I am thankful to those tens of millions of women (and the smaller number of men) for doing what they can to steer the country in the right direction.

This Thanksgiving season, then, I am hoping not for a blue wave or a red wave in next year's elections but for a tsunami of women at the polling booths.

'Settler Colonialism' Applies to This Country, Not That One

November 29, 2023

There is a nation prominent on today's world stage whose origins are rooted in settler colonialism and white supremacy. No, it's not Israel. Though a proud American, I must confess with shame that it's the United States.

First let's discuss Israel. American partisans of Palestinian Arabs accuse Israel of settler colonialism — that the country has been populated by white Europeans who displaced indigenous people of color.

There have been Jews in the Holy Land for over 3,000 years. A 1993 archeological find confirmed the existence of a King David and successors. Jews, then, are indigenous peoples themselves.

Of course, Arabs have lived for millennia in what's now the state of Israel, too. In fact, a recent study by geneticist Michael Hammer of the University of Arizona shows that 70% of Jewish men and half of Arab men are descended from the same paternal ancestors going back to prehistoric times. (Claims that Jews are descended from the Turkish tribe known as Khazars are pseudoscience invoked by Israel's enemies and antisemites.) The Israeli Law of Return allowing Jews to move back to Israel is aptly named.

During and after Israel's 1948-49 War of Independence, around 700,000 Arabs left or were expelled from what is now Israel. Over the next 50 years, almost 900,000 Jews were pushed out of Arab lands — about two-thirds of them were resettled in Israel. Sadly, this was, in essence, a population swap or ethnic cleansing. Around the same time, a population swap following the independence of India and Pakistan in 1947 saw between 14 million and 18 million people move from one country to the other.

In 1948, Israel's population was 82% Jewish and 18% non-Jewish citizens who were overwhelmingly Arab. Today, the numbers are 73% Jewish and 27% non-Jewish. So over the last 75 years, Israeli Arabs grew as a percentage of Israel's population; they were not displaced. Moreover, calling the Jews white Europeans is misguided; almost half of Israel's Jews trace their recent ancestry to the Arab and Muslim world and another 3% from Ethiopia.

What about the United States? Of course, there were no national censuses conducted before Columbus arrived in the New World. Estimates made by experts in the last 20 years for the indigenous population in North America in 1491 range from 3.5 million to 7 million. The U.S. census in 1900 showed 237,196 Native Americans out of an overall population of 76 million, or 0.3%. Massacres, starvation and disease had decimated the Native Americans.

Motivated by a sense of "manifest destiny," white Americans believed they had a divine mandate to conquer and settle the continent from sea to sea. The displacements, suffering and deaths of Native Americans were not overlooked. They were part of the plan. In 1830, Congress passed the Indian Removal Act. Treaties with Indian tribes were disregarded. In 1851, California's first governor, Peter Burnett, told the state legislature to expect war "until the Indian race becomes extinct."

Americans have long gloried in their colonial settler past. Colonial houses and colonial art are still sought after. After dying at Little Big Horn, Col. George Custer was made a martyr. His troops were there to force members of the Sioux tribe onto a reservation. Recently, former House Speaker Kevin McCarthy said, "In every single war that America has fought, we have never asked for land afterwards." He should bone up on his history. Even setting aside the Mexican-American War, Wikipedia lists over five dozen American-

Indian Wars between 1776 and 1918. According to one estimate, the United States has taken over some 60% of its territory from native peoples since the Declaration of Independence.

Are Americans ready to give up the land on which they live, commute, study, work and vacation to the descendants of indigenous peoples who were displaced? In his bestselling book "Palo Alto: A History of California, Capitalism, and the World," author Malcolm Harris suggests that Stanford University kick off the process by returning its land to members of tribes who lived there centuries ago. How likely is Stanford to give up its 8,180 acre campus in the midst of Silicon Valley? How many Americans would be willing to give up their homes to compensate for the sins of their forebears? What about recent immigrants whose ancestors did not even live in the United States?

Supreme Court Justice Neil Gorsuch has attacked those who "just cast a blind eye" at the "sadly familiar pattern" involving Native Americans where "promises were made, but the price of keeping them has become too great." Well said, Mr. Justice, but can you imagine any future where most of the land of the United States is turned over to the descendants of displaced tribes?

In this year's National Book Award winner "The Rediscovery of America," Ned Blackhawk asks, "How can a nation founded on the homelands of dispossessed Indigenous peoples be the world's most exemplary democracy?"

That's the irony of Americans protesting against Israel. They're accusing Israel of what their own country is guilty of. The protesters cry out that a state of Palestine should displace Israel "from the river to the sea." That's misguided and wrong. Logic and history dictate they should instead be shouting, "From sea to shining sea, give Native Americans back their territory."

Here's a message for those Americans who condemn Israel for settler colonialism: It's a lot easier to peer through a distorted telescope at a faraway country than to look into a mirror for a clear view of yourselves.

Got COVID for Thanksgiving and I'm Grateful

December 6, 2023

For almost four years, I eluded the COVID-19 virus that was stalking me, family and friends, fellow Americans and all humankind. I figured I was safe when I sat down for a family Thanksgiving dinner, but it turned out I was a sitting duck (turkey?) for my pathological pursuer. And how do I feel about all this? Thankful.

By avoiding the virus for so long, I missed the most dangerous variants and could get the latest version of the vaccination. So, I ended up not with a life-threatening disease, but what feels like a mild cold. I'm going to miss a holiday party I sorely wanted to attend. As my mom used to say to my toddler self after I scraped a knee, "You'll live."

And I will indeed live on, grateful to Nobel Prize winners Katalin Kariko and Drew Weissman for their discoveries that enabled speedy development of COVID-19 vaccines. It hurts me to say it, but I am even thankful to former President Donald Trump for backing Operation Warp Speed, which used the discoveries of the Nobel laureates to develop an effective COVID-19 vaccine in less than a year.

I'm used to resenting Big Pharma, but not this time. I am grateful for the role Moderna and Pfizer played in getting that vaccine out. Millions more would have died around the world if the COVID-19 vaccine had taken as long from discovery to deployment as the previous recordholder, the mumps vaccine, which took four years.

So, it's all worked out pretty well for me. But despite the miraculously speedy development of vaccines, it could've worked out better for others over the past four years. And it could work out better for others going forward.

Around 1.2 million Americans have died of COVID-19 since the pandemic began. The mortality rate for those who were unvaccinated was 250% higher than those who were. That means hundreds of thousands of Americans died unnecessarily.

And even with this lesson in front of them, over 80% of U.S. adults have failed to get the updated COVID-19 vaccine since it became available in late September. The life expectancy of Americans has doubled since 1900, and vaccinations are a major reason. Do tens of millions of Americans want to go back to the days of smallpox and polio epidemics?

Among a certain part of the population, the answer at least appears to be yes. The death rate from COVID-19 has been greater in Republican-leaning counties. Florida's Republican Gov. Ron DeSantis has accused the federal government of mishandling vaccine rollout even while it appears his administration is doing the mishandling. A New York Times analysis found that "unlike the nation as a whole, Florida lost more lives to Covid after vaccines became available to all adults, not before."

Despite a lack of any evidence whatsoever, presidential candidates DeSantis and Nikki Haley have implied getting vaccinated can interfere with a woman's fertility.

Robert Kennedy Jr. became prominent on the national scene as an anti-vaxxer. He hasn't noticeably changed his views as he runs for the presidency as an independent. He said in a July interview, "There's no vaccine that is safe and effective."

That's just not true. Do not listen to what DeSantis, Haley or Kennedy Jr. are saying about COVID-19 vaccinations. According to the Department of Health for the state of Washington, "From October 06 to November 02, 2023, unvaccinated individuals were between 2 and 4.5 times more likely to be hospitalized with COVID-19 compared to those who received at least one booster dose."

Most of the deaths from COVID-19 befall those Americans over age 65. That cohort constitutes 16% of the U.S. population but has accounted for an estimated 75% of the COVID-19 deaths. But only a third of those senior citizens have received the latest COVID-19 vaccine. Over half of Americans have no intention of getting it.

For Americans over 65, just go get the latest shot. It's protection against hospitalization and death. For those under 65, even if your chances of hospitalization and death are low, you probably will, like me, get a milder case should you catch it and at the same time decrease the chances of infecting someone over 65.

I live on a college campus amid hundreds of students. They should be getting vaccines before they go home — if not for themselves, then for the older generation. No one wants to give a COVID-19 infection to a grandparent as a holiday gift.

President Joe Biden has declared the COVID-19 pandemic to be over. Maybe so, but as a friend wrote to me upon hearing I was infected, "We might be done with Covid, but Covid is not done with us."

The newest variant appears more contagious than previous ones. COVID-19 rates are rising. Hospitalizations due to COVID-19 were up 10% Thanksgiving week (when I was infected!), the most recent week where data are available.

Come on, fellow Americans. Get vaccinated. It's easy and safe. You don't want to die. I believe in your good hearts. You don't want a loved one to die whether infected by you or a stranger. Neither does anyone else.

When It Comes To Current Events, Best To Learn Before Shouting

December 13, 2023

H.G. Wells, the novelist who wrote "The Time Machine" and "The War of the Worlds" at the end of the 19th century, figured human history was "a race between education and catastrophe." I fear catastrophe is winning.

When it comes to dealing with the future of the American republic, with antisemitism and with the war in the Middle East, too many Americans find it's easier to spout a slogan than to learn the facts.

When Donald Trump ran for the presidency in 2016, he crowed, "America First." But those words have an ominous meaning in American history. Before World War II, the aviator Charles Lindbergh spearheaded the America First Committee which expressed admiration for Nazi Germany and warned against the danger posed to the United States by Jewish "ownership and influence in our motion pictures, our press, our radio, and our government." Stephen Jacobs, a Holocaust survivor, said in a 2018 interview that Trump's America "feels like 1929 or 1930 Berlin."

In recent weeks, Trump has resorted to even more Nazi rhetoric. He's accused immigrants of "poisoning the blood of our country." In 1935, Hitler promulgated "the Nuremberg Law for the Protection of German Blood and German Honor." An adage often attributed to Mark Twain says, "History doesn't repeat itself, but it often rhymes." Too bad it's rhyming with Nazi racism.

In recent weeks, too, Ivy League universities stand accused of tolerating antisemitism on their campuses. For anyone who follows the history of American higher education, these allegations echo through the years. Columbia was the first of the Ivies to have large numbers of Jewish students. According to professor Jerome Karabell's book "The Chosen: The Hidden History of Admission and Exclusion at Harvard, Yale, and Princeton," a ditty popular a century ago went like this: "Oh, Harvard's run by millionaires/ And Yale is run by booze/ Cornell is run by farmers' sons/ Columbia's run by Jews."

Columbia responded to this kind of slur on its reputation by putting a quota on the number of Jews it accepted. Yale capped Jewish admissions at 10-12% up to the 1960s. In the 1920s, a Jewish assistant professor at Harvard said students had taken to "Jew-baiting" as a "new kind of college sport." No wonder Jews are sensitive about antisemitism on the university campuses today.

It's popular among those who oppose the existence of the state of Israel to attack its supposed support of white European settler colonialism. That's a strange thing to be claiming during the Jewish holiday of Hanukkah, which celebrates the establishment of a Jewish kingdom in the land of Israel over two thousand years ago. Over the last two millennia, it's been the Romans, the Ottomans and the British who were the colonials. The Jews are the indigenous people. White European? Over half of Israeli Jews come from Arab and Muslim lands in North Africa and the Middle East. Twenty-one percent of the country are Arabs.

A slogan often chanted on campus and at anti-Israel demonstrations is "from the river to the sea, Palestine shall be free." In a poll of 250 college students sponsored by UC Berkeley professor Ron Hassner, almost half of the supporters of the slogan were unable to identify which river and sea were being referred to. When asked about the Oslo Accords signed between Israel and the Palestine Liberation Organization in the 1990s, over a quarter of the chant's supporters claimed no such peace agreements had ever been signed at all. After learning some basic facts about the Middle East, over two-thirds of the students went from supporting "from the river to sea" to opposing it.

A free Palestine? The last election in the Palestinian Arab West Bank and Gaza were held in 2006. I'm no fan of the current government of Israel, but there have been five parliamentary elections there in the past five years. Israeli Arabs, who as noted are over a fifth of the country's population, were among the voters each time.

Rabbi David Wolpe, currently a visiting scholar at the Harvard Divinity School, wrote that "Part of the problem is a simple herd mentality — people screaming slogans whose meaning and implication they know nothing of."

Aldous Huxley, the author of "Brave New World," lamented, "That men do not learn very much from the lessons of history is the most important of all the lessons of history." Maybe it's time to change that so we can better understand what's going on around us.

Biden Being Trumped in the Polls and in Storytelling

December 20, 2023

A sign in Bill Clinton's election headquarters back in 1992 reminded his campaign team that the key issue was "the economy, stupid."

The words captured a cliche — that Americans vote their pocketbooks. If only it were still true, Joe Biden would win reelection in a romp.

This month, the Dow Jones Industrial Average broke through the 37,000 level for the first time. Inflation has plummeted from 9.1% in January 2022 to 3.1% last month. Consumer spending is strong. The economy grew at a sizzling 4.9% last quarter. Unemployment remains below 4% with over 14 million new jobs added since Biden took office.

And yet. And yet.

In a poll this month, registered voters believe by a 3-1 margin that the economy has gotten worse in the past two years. According to an October survey, 59% of Americans think we are in a recession. A survey from the previous month showed Americans prefer to have Republicans handling the economy by 14%, the largest margin in over three decades.

It's no surprise, then, that Biden is trailing Trump in the polls. "It's the economy, stupid" might have worked in 1992, but it ain't working in 2023. Why not?

Because the almost-certain Republican nominee Trump is telling a better story.

For those Democrats and disgruntled Republicans who look at Trump and see only bullying, greed and racism, they are missing the point. Trump has a story that resonates with tens of millions of voters. He says he wants to make America great again. He harks back to times when American factory workers were unchallenged by China and when women had no dominion over their own bodies. He feeds off resentment from those who think they are getting a raw deal, who believe government aid is going to the undeserving and who disdain spoiled graduates of Ivy League universities their children have no chance of attending. He tells voters they are getting overrun by immigrants: non-Hispanic whites were 89.5% of the population in 1950 but will be a minority by 2050.

So, what's Biden's story? Saying he is the greatest job-producing president in history just does not resonate. His attempt to take a page from Clinton's 1992 playbook does not work in 2023. Neither does a friendly Uncle Joe lost in the distant past. Nor does a role as comforter-in-chief.

So can Biden overcome what Yale professor Jeffrey Sonnenfeld calls the "ageism and cynicism" of the American public?

Biden could learn something from the three presidents in the last hundred years who told Americans a story that was believable and inspiring. Franklin D. Roosevelt promised the government would offer a New Deal amid the Great Depression. John F. Kennedy stirred a new generation "tempered by war" to defend "freedom in its hour of maximum danger." Ronald Reagan told Americans they were building "a shining City on a Hill" according to "some divine plan ... to be sought out by those who were possessed of an abiding love of freedom and a special kind of courage." Americans bought into their stories of a New Deal, a defender of freedom and a country blessed by the Almighty.

Why? Because all three focused on the future while finding inspiration in the past. Each reached out to Americans, not as a spokesperson for any one group, but to all who believed in what's to come. Reagan captured this concept by saying, "as long as we remember our first principles and believe in ourselves, the future will always be ours ..."

Now, President Biden stands for a better future for Americans, one where good jobs are available, where laws are enforced without fear or favor, where personal freedoms are freely exercised, where there's compassion for those who suffer, where democracies stand together against aggression, and where educational opportunity is open to one's children and grandchildren. His problem? He holds the strands of a compelling story but has not woven them together into something believable. Even if he did, he couldn't tell it with the soaring rhetoric of a Roosevelt, Kennedy or Reagan. But he could weave it together and convey it with sincerity, earnestness and proof of a job well done.

He could add to his accomplishments with programs to make higher education more accessible, to support child care and to enforce current immigration laws, while continuing to build infrastructure, restore manufacturing, defend democracy, protect individual freedoms and sponsor immigration reform.

Trump seems to look backward to the olden days. A winning story for Biden, even at age 81, would be forward-looking, providing a vision, telling us what tomorrow promises. However, if Biden cannot tell a better story than the one he is telling, he will lose.

As Bobby Kennedy said in his campaign for the presidency over a half century ago, "There is a contest on, not only for the rule of America, but for the heart of America." And the question for next November is whether it will be Trump or Biden's story that will win America's heart.

No Wiggle Room in Determining Trump's Eligibility for Presidency

December 27, 2023

Over the years millions of American parents must have told their children, "In America, anyone can become president."

Of course, that's not quite true. To become president, a person needs to be a citizen born in the United States who has reached 35 years of age and resided there for 14 years. They must also have taken the oath of office and not already served as president for more than six years.

Limits on who can become president are inherently anti-democratic. They don't allow votes to be cast for those not qualified. Maybe you think the late Henry Kissinger was such a foreign policy wizard he should've been elected president back in the 1980s. Tough. He was born in Germany and ineligible. Or maybe you would prefer Taylor Swift to have beaten both Donald Trump and Joe Biden for the presidency in 2020. Sorry, Time Magazine's Person of the Year was only 31 back then.

Oh yeah, there's one more restriction of special concern to Trump, running again in the 2024 presidential race. According to the Constitution's 14th Amendment, a candidate cannot have "taken an oath ... as an officer of the United States ... to support the Constitution of the United States (and) have engaged in insurrection or rebellion against the same, or given aid or comfort to the enemies thereof."

Trump entered politics by falsely claiming Barack Obama was born in Kenya, not the United States, and therefore ineligible to be president. In one of history's most malicious or delicious — depending on your politics — twists of fate, he may now be ineligible himself as someone who engaged in an insurrection against the U.S. or as someone who gave aid or comfort to its enemies.

In November, a trial court in Colorado found Trump's activities on and around Jan. 6, 2021, "easily satisfy" engagement in an insurrection "through instigation or incitement." But then it went on to hold, as president, Trump did not hold an office of the United States and thus ought not be removed from the ballot. How can that be when the Constitution prescribes the oath a prospective president must take before entering the "Office"? Someone can take an oath of office and not be an officer? Come on, Your Honor, be serious.

Upon appeal, the Colorado Supreme Court confirmed the district court's holding that Trump had engaged in an insurrection. It overruled as a matter of law the trial court's contrived interpretation that someone who took an oath of office is not an officer.

Dissenting from the majority, Justice Carlos Samour wrote that being excluded from the ballot deprived Trump of running without "due process" including a "fair trial." No. As Harvard Law professor Lawrence Tribe noted, the process was "elaborate" and "fair." He continued, "The Constitution itself contemplates that this is not like a criminal trial. ... It simply says, that for the privilege of wielding power over others, you must be someone who has not tried to overturn the Constitution after swearing to uphold it."

Samour's dissent also warned against "risking chaos in our country." It's a fair point. Trump himself has already called for "termination" of those parts of the Constitution that kept him from retaining the White House. And chances are good he would do the same again if he should lose the nomination or general election in 2024. The majority of the Colorado court said it understood the risk but affirmed their "solemn duty to apply the law, without fear or favor, and without being swayed by public reaction to the decisions that the law mandates we reach."

The majority of the Colorado Supreme Court read the Constitution as written. You can be elected president if a convicted felon. You can win even if running from a prison cell. You can be a racist who calls fellow citizens vermin. But you must be over 35 and not have engaged in an insurrection. As Justice Neil Gorsuch of the U.S. Supreme Court wrote in 2020, "When the express terms of a statute give us one answer and extratextual considerations suggest another, it's no contest. Only the written word is the law."

The Colorado Supreme Court's holding that Trump is ineligible will inevitably be reviewed by Justice Gorsuch and his eight colleagues on the U.S. Supreme Court, especially since only a week after the Colorado decision, Michigan's highest court held that Trump *should* remain on the primary ballot in that state.

Pundits, columnists, politicians and editorial boards have decried the possibility of Trump being anti-democratically excluded from another term. I understand and sympathize. There's just one problem — those pesky words of the Constitution. We don't get to pick and choose which parts we accept as the law of the land and which parts we ignore.

The U.S. State Department has condemned a new "sovereignty and protection" law in Hungary that might be used to "intimidate and punish" Hungarians critical of the government — notwithstanding the country's constitutional protection of freedom of expression. According to newspaper reports, if he takes back the presidency, Trump is already contemplating disregarding American constitutional considerations and having the Justice Department investigate his critics and "go after" Biden.

So, what it comes down to is this: Will the Supreme Court read the 14th Amendment as written or not? I anxiously await its verdict.

Who I Am Determines What I Write

January 10, 2024

What I've been thinking about this first month of 2024 is how much *who* I am determines *what* I write each week in this column.

So, for better or worse, here are a dozen elements that have helped make me the person I am.

1. I'm a supporter of the American democratic experiment. I worked as counsel to a U.S. Senate committee. The Constitution was ratified in 1789 to "establish Justice, insure domestic Tranquility, provide for the common defense, promote the general Welfare, and secure the Blessings of Liberty to ourselves and our Posterity." This country has come a long way from its beginnings and yet there is still much to do to form a "more perfect Union."

2. I'm a novelist. I write stories. I read them, too. The Nobel Prize winner for literature Gao Xingjian wrote, "It's in literature that true life can be found. It's under the mask of fiction that you can tell the truth." Schools should impart to students a love for reading, storytelling and learning. Something needs to be done as well to support those who write the stories that we love and learn from. (A recent survey of just under 6,000 published authors shows their 2022 median income was around $5,000.)

3. I'm an entrepreneur. I worked for three decades in Silicon Valley. I believe in American ingenuity and capitalism. Certainly, the government needs to set rules (such as ones against illegal monopolies) and standards (such as how genetic engineering should be used) for business, but it should do so without creating needless barriers to innovation and progress.

4. I'm a resident of a college dorm. Of course, my undergraduate neighbors will need to support themselves after graduation. But as then-presidential candidate Robert Kennedy

lamented over 50 years ago, we have "surrendered personal excellence and community values in the mere accumulation of material things." In addition to providing the skills needed to make a living, we must provide our progeny the tools to lead a good life.

5. I'm a believer in religion. I believe we should work to leave the world a better place than we found it. The way religion works for me is personal. I am committed to letting others observe their personal beliefs, too, so long as those beliefs lead to respect for the beliefs of others.

6. I'm a family man. Nothing is more important to me than my spouse and children. I believe in the centrality of family to our lives. Does that belief make me a conservative? Sure. Families have been around for thousands of generations. But I don't care how the family is constituted, whether it includes multiple races, different religions, widely varied DNA, diverse political leanings or LGBT members as my own extended family does. I don't think the government or other people should care either. Does that belief make me a liberal? Sure to that, too.

7. I'm a father. I want a better world for my four children. I want my three adult daughters to have the freedom to deal with their own bodies as they wish without undue government interference.

8. I'm a son. My father fought against Nazism to preserve democracy and was there at the liberation of Dachau, the concentration camp. His legacy makes me a strong supporter of democracy, a stubborn enemy of authoritarianism and a determined opponent of racism and antisemitism.

9. I'm a grandson. None of my grandparents were born in this country. As Ronald Reagan declared in his last address as president, "Thanks to each wave of new arrivals to this land of opportunity, we're a nation forever young, forever bursting with energy and new ideas." I'm a sucker for that American dream.

10. I'm a grandfather. To allow parents to make ends meet, the federal government should be doing more to support child care.

The governments of other rich countries contributed an average of $14,000 per year for a preschooler's care in 2021. The United States? $500. Helping with child care is an investment that enables families to better support themselves and live more enriching lives. It also causes the overall economy to grow.

11. I'm a voter. It does no good to complain about the direction taken by our school district, city, county, state or federal government if we don't vote.

12. I'm an American. I feel so fortunate to have grown up in this country of opportunity and freedom. While my column may at times come across as critical of the American people and their government, I write because I care.

So, for better or worse, now you know a little more about where I'm coming from. As Bill Murray called out in the classic comedy "Stripes," "That's the fact, Jack."

I wish you all a year of joy, commitment, learning, fulfillment and good health.

'A Rendezvous With Destiny' Awaits Us in 2024

January 17, 2024

I was 8 when my dad took a job with Ampex Corporation, the video recording pioneer. He used to joke that company sales only did well every fourth year when the networks upgraded their equipment for the summer Olympics and U.S. presidential election.

Well, this is one of those Olympic and election years, and I'm wishing and hoping it's a good one. At the same time, nightmares of what could go wrong in 2024 for us Americans haunt my sleep. Like what? Well, here are the five that keep me up in the night's darkest hours.

— Former President Donald Trump winning back the White House. Could he really win despite 91 charges in four criminal trials, despite a New York court holding him liable for sexual abuse, despite the violent attempt to overturn the results of the 2020 election? The polls say yes. And Trump says he'd be a dictator on his first day in office and that election fraud would enable him to terminate "all rules, regulations, and articles, even those found in the Constitution." Forty percent of his Republican supporters believe "true American patriots may have to resort to violence in order to save our country." I doubt American democracy could survive four years of lawlessness and chaos brought about by Trump's election.

— Appeasement of Russia. The lesson of World War II is that appeasement does not deter aggression. When British Prime Minister Neville Chamberlain struck a deal to give a hunk of Czechoslovakia to Nazi Germany in 1938, he declared it was "peace for our time." Less than a year later World War II began. Vladimir Putin's Russia invaded its neighbor Ukraine in 2014 and seized Crimea. A namby-pamby response from the United States and its

NATO allies whetted the appetite of Russia's dictator, and he came back for seconds in 2022. If we abandon Ukraine now, Putin will help himself to a third course.

— War or peace in the Middle East. No country can tolerate a neighbor who sends terrorists across the border to murder, rape and massacre, and Israel is no different. The Israeli Defense Forces have rules to avoid killing civilians. Still, they can and should do better even if the Hamas terrorists hide among noncombatants in hospitals and schools. Iran is stirring the pot in Iraq, Lebanon and Yemen: The chance of a wider war looms. Israel has a right to live in peace, and so do the Palestinian Arabs of the Gaza Strip and the West Bank.

— The crisis in American universities. During the academic year, I live and eat with undergraduates. One thing I see for sure is that the diversity of the student body makes a college exciting and intellectually stimulating. Racism, antisemitism and prejudice have no place there. At the same time, free expression is fundamental to a university's mission. According to the (London) Times Education Supplement, seven of the top 10 universities in the world are American. The legacy of our world-leading institutions of higher learning would be imperiled if the right balance is not struck among the core principles of diversity, lack of prejudice, and free expression. Danger lurks, too, if the federal government becomes too involved in deciding who should be admitted to our universities and what opinions are acceptable in their classrooms, textbooks, archives and labs.

— Antisemitism in the United States. Last month's Harvard CAPS-Harris Poll found one-third of 18-24 year-olds view Jews as oppressors. The Anti-Defamation League reports that antisemitic incidents in the U.S. including attacks on Jewish owned-businesses and synagogues increased by 337% in the two months following the Oct. 7 terrorist attack on Israel. Jews constitute only 2% of the American population. When the whites of a person's eyes turn yellow, it can mean liver cancer is eating away their insides. The turn upwards in antisemitic incidents in America means something is rotten in this country's soul. Prejudice and racism will spread beyond Jews if the sickness is not treated.

My list doesn't include the hazards of a Chinese invasion of Taiwan, a deadly hurricane or flood caused by climate change, a recession, artificial intelligence run amok or another pandemic. Why not? Because they only trouble me in the daytime.

Looking back over 2 1/2 centuries, we can spot a few years that were turning points in American history. Examples include 1776 when the American colonies declared their independence, 1861 when a war between the states over slavery broke out, 1941 when Pearl Harbor was attacked and 1968 when Martin Luther King Jr. and Robert F. Kennedy were murdered. This year looks to me like just such a turning point.

President Franklin D. Roosevelt told Americans they had a rendezvous with destiny in 1938. So do we in 2024. For better or worse.

Lincoln and Reagan Wouldn't Recognize Today's Republican Party

January 24, 2024

Are the candidates running for office as Republicans really impostors?

The Republican Party was formed in 1854 to stand against the expansion of slavery. Now, Nikki Haley, one of the two leading candidates for the Republican nomination, says "the United States has never been a racist country." The Supreme Court ruled in 1857 that enslaved African Americans were not citizens of the United States. So, slavery wasn't racist, Gov. Haley?

Republican President Theodore Roosevelt signed the bill establishing the U.S. Forest Service, and Republican President Richard Nixon signed the bill establishing the Environmental Protection Agency. The administration of former President Donald Trump, who is running again for the White House, slashed over 100 environmental rules and policies relating to water pollution, emissions, toxic waste, wildlife and oil drilling.

For most of the last century, the Republican Party was known as pro-business. The cover of the current issue of the British periodical The Economist warns, "He's winning: Business Beware." The reference is to Trump and the way his "most chaotic tendencies could threaten America, including its companies." The Republican Party used to stand for balanced budgets and free markets, but in its lead story, the magazine warns of tax cuts leading to greater deficits and inflation as well as higher tariffs inhibiting international trade and raising consumer prices.

The interstates in this country are officially known as the Dwight D. Eisenhower National System of Interstate and Defense Highways. Why? Because that Republican president pushed through passage of the Federal-Aid Highway Act of 1956. Former President Trump's pronouncements of "Infrastructure Week" became a long-running joke during his administration. It was left to his successor, the Democrat Joe Biden, to get the $1 trillion Infrastructure Investment and Jobs Act and the $1.85 trillion Build Back Better Act passed to rebuild roads and bridges and invest in airports, public transportation, electric delivery systems, high-speed internet and clean water.

In his final speech as president, Republican icon Ronald Reagan said, "We lead the world because, unique among nations, we draw our people — our strength — from every country and every corner of the world." In announcing his run for the presidency, Trump called immigrants from Mexico "rapists." Mike Johnson, the Republican speaker of the House of Representatives, has named immigration as "the true existential threat to the country."

For most of President Eisenhower's administration, the individual income tax rate for the richest Americans was 91%, while for those at the lowest level it stood at 22%. After Trump pushed through the Tax Cuts and Jobs Act in 2017, the effective tax rate on the bottom half of earners was higher than for billionaires. That doesn't seem fair, does it? Despite the high tax rate, economic growth was stronger under Eisenhower than under Trump.

The postwar Republican party stood for defense of democracy abroad. As the first military commander of NATO, future President Eisenhower reminded Congress what could be achieved when the United States bound up its "heart and soul in material ways with our friends overseas." As president, Trump threatened to pull the United States out of NATO. The Republican majority in the House of Representatives, encouraged by Trump, is stonewalling support of Ukraine against Russian aggression.

A 1977 poll found more Republicans supported abortion rights than Democrats. In 2022, the Republican-appointed judges on the U.S. Supreme Court took away the right to abortion they had extended to women in Roe v. Wade. Since then, Republican legislatures in 14 states have completely banned abortions. And the potential for more governmental intrusion looms. Justice Clarence Thomas has suggested the Supreme Court "should reconsider" a case that protected use of contraceptives by married couples.

In his 1960 State of the Union address, President Eisenhower declared the federal government's first duty was to protect the right to vote "against all encroachment." According to the Brennan Center for Justice, at least 14 states passed laws in 2023 making it harder to vote. The state legislatures of all but one of those states had Republican majorities.

And perhaps most important of all, the Republican Party once stood for support of the Constitution. Abraham Lincoln said, "We the people are the rightful masters of both Congress and the courts, not to overthrow the Constitution but to overthrow the men who pervert the Constitution." In contrast, Donald Trump said to regain office, he might have to support "termination of all rules, regulations, and articles, even those found in the Constitution." According to a poll taken last summer, a third of Republicans believe "true American patriots may have to resort to violence in order to save our country."

The Republican party of Lincoln, Roosevelt, Eisenhower and Reagan indeed has a glorious past marked by stalwart support of legal immigration, the right to vote, free enterprise, anti-racism, limited government, democracy abroad, environmental protection and infrastructure.

But that grand old party is no more, alas.

A Three-State, Not Two-State, Solution Best Bet for the Middle East

January 31, 2024

When it comes to developing long-term solutions to end the Israel-Hamas war, policymakers are spitting in the wind.

On Oct. 8, the day after the murderous Hamas assault on Israel, Secretary of State Anthony Blinken said the "best way" to resolve differences between Israel and Palestinian Arabs "remains a two-state solution." This month, U.N. Secretary General Antonio Guterres said, "Any refusal to accept the two-State solution by any party must be firmly rejected."

I do support both Palestinian Arabs and the citizens of Israel living in peace in their own separate democratic countries. But a "two-state solution" envisions Israel being joined on the world stage by a single independent Palestinian Arab nation. The fatal flaw with any such plan is that the latter would exist in two separate pieces — the West Bank where the Palestinian Authority now holds sway and the Gaza Strip where the terrorist organization Hamas wields power. The two parts would be divided by Israel itself.

The dismal history of nations split in two should provide a lesson to Blinken, Guterres and any other diplomats seeking peace in the Middle East.

— The most glaring example is Pakistan. Faced with communal violence between Hindus and Muslims in 1947, the British partitioned their colony of India into two countries, but three pieces. The largest piece kept the name of India. The Islamic Republic of Pakistan was separated by Indian territory into West Pakistan and East Pakistan. A common religion did not provide a strong enough glue to hold Pakistan together. After war and violence with deaths estimated at 3 million, East Pakistan broke away and declared independence as Bangladesh in 1971.

— The Treaty of Versailles after World War I divided Germany into two segments. East Prussia was separated from the bulk of the country by Polish territory. According to the journalist and historian William Shirer, Germans believed "the most heinous crime of the Versailles peacemakers had been to separate East Prussia from the Reich by the Polish Corridor." The German solution to rectifying the grievance was to invade and conquer Poland at the outset of World War II.

— In the Arab world itself, Egypt and Syria merged into the United Arab Republic in 1958. The two parts of the UAR were separated by the territories of Israel, Lebanon and Jordan. In 1961, Syria rebelled against Egyptian domination. Even though Gamal Abdul Nasser, the Egyptian leader, reacted by confirming his commitment to Pan-Arabism, he decided not to send troops to the Syrian part of the UAR to maintain the union.

— A 1994 agreement between the Palestine Liberation Organization and Israel created the Palestinian Authority to administer Gaza and the West Bank, two territories separated by the State of Israel. In 2005, Israelis troops withdrew from the Gaza Strip. The next year, Hamas seized control of the Gaza Strip while the Palestinian Authority continued to hold sway in the West Bank.

So, the unity between Gaza and West Bank has broken apart once before. Is a solution for a single democratic Palestinian Arab state more viable now? No. But there could be one for two democratic states. The United States and the United Nations should move toward, not a two-state solution, but a three-state one.

But would the West Bank and the Gaza Strip be viable as standalone countries?

Why not? The West Bank would be a small standalone country, roughly half the size of Jamaica. Like that Caribbean nation, it has an economy based on agriculture and tourism. The

West Bank's per capita gross domestic product is already higher than that of neighboring Jordan. The Gaza Strip is far smaller, but even so, its potential is promising. Singapore, Dubai and Hong Kong provide workable models for flourishing city-states with economies founded on trade, seaports, manufacturing and finance.

The best predictor of the future is the past. The history of divided countries indicates a two-state solution to the war now raging would be no permanent fix. What's happened already in this century to divide the West Bank and Gaza Strip makes the chances of a lasting remarriage between them a 100-1 long shot. It makes little sense to try it again at those odds. The stakes are too high.

On the other hand, models do exist for both potential Palestinian Arab states. In the early years of their independence, political and economic support could be provided by the United States, the European Union, Saudi Arabia and the United Arab Emirates.

Secretary Blinken and Secretary General Guterres, history tells us an attempt to reach a two-state solution to the Israel-Palestinian Arab conflict is bound to fail. A solution that includes three states has a chance, maybe even a good one, to lead to peace and prosperity.

Attacking Israel Crosses Line Into Antisemitism

February 14, 2024

For years, I have listened to friends and colleagues attack the policies of Israel and even question its right to exist. They always follow up their statements by saying that being anti-Zionist is not the same thing as being antisemitic. Events following Hamas' murderous attack on Israel last October have shown me this may be in true in theory, but it definitely is no longer true in practice.

First, let's get some definitions out of the way. Antisemitism is hatred, prejudice and discrimination directed against Jews because they are Jews. Anti-Zionism is attacking Israel's right to exist, often by holding it to different standards than other nations.

Anti-Zionism becomes antisemitism when American citizens who are Jewish are blamed for the actions of the State of Israel, a foreign country over 6,000 miles away. According to the Anti-Defamation League, the number of antisemitic incidents in the U.S. rose 361% from the previous year in the three months following the Oct. 7 Hamas attack on Israel. These included a "dramatic increase in bomb threats" directed at synagogues. A personal note here: A swastika spray-painted on the sidewalk near a neighborhood park in my hometown outrages me at what is happening in this country.

It's antisemitism as well when Israel, the only majority Jewish nation in the world, is judged differently than other countries or other parties to the Middle East conflict. Samuel J. Dubbin, a former special assistant to the U.S. attorney general, notes "the drumbeat that Israel should accept threats to its security which would never be suggested for any other nation."

Hamas launched a murderous assault on Oct. 7 that killed over 1,200 people living in Israel. As a percentage of Israel's population, that attack was more than 12 times deadlier than the 9/11 terrorist attack on the United States. While exercising its right as a sovereign nation to defend itself, Israel was condemned for civilian deaths, rightfully so in some cases. However, Hamas' tactic of hiding its armed personnel among civilians and using hospitals to shelter troops is either denied or brushed aside by anti-Israel protesters and Hamas apologists.

At demonstrations against Israel I've witnessed this winter, protesters have demanded an immediate ceasefire which would leave the terrorist organization Hamas in control in Gaza. The responsibility for a ceasefire falls completely on Israel. There's no mention that Hamas itself violated a 2021 ceasefire when it launched its attack on Oct. 7. There's no acknowledgment that Israel offered a ceasefire in return for the release of hostages seized by Hamas. A statement by the Harvard Undergraduate Palestine Solidarity Committee originally co-signed by 33 other Harvard student organizations held Israel "entirely responsible for all unfolding violence."

South Africa has accused Israel of genocide before the International Court of Justice. The term "genocide" is defined by the United Nations 1948 Genocide Convention as "acts committed with intent to destroy, in whole or in part, a national, ethnical, racial or religious group." Gaza's population in 1970 was 345,000 people. Its population is now 2.1 million. That's hardly evidence of genocidal intentions toward Gaza. On the other hand, the Hamas Covenant calls for Islam to "obliterate" Israel and to "vanquish" all Jews. As President Joe Biden said of Hamas, "Its stated purpose is the annihilation of the State of Israel and the murder of Jewish people."

Why is South Africa accusing Israel and not Hamas? And why is there such international focus on Israel's actions as contrasted to true genocide elsewhere in the world? Russia is abducting Ukrainian children and bringing them to Russia. The U.S. State Department has reported on genocide in Burma where the government "launched a brutal campaign against Rohingya — razing villages, raping, torturing, and perpetrating large-scale violence that killed thousands of Rohingya men, women, and children." The United States has also determined China is guilty of genocide for subjecting Uyghurs to imprisonment, forced labor, torture, rape and sterilization.

The only reason I can come up with for that focus on Israel is the fact that 74% of Israel's population is Jewish, making it the only majority Jewish state in the world. Israel's Declaration of Independence guarantees "freedom of religion, conscience, language, education and culture." Could Israel do better? Of course. So could the United States. Remember the Trump administration's Muslim bans?

What if Israel is indeed considered a Jewish state? Should that take away its right to exist? The Islamic Republic of Iran and the Islamic Republic of Pakistan are the official names of those countries. Heck, King Charles III is the head of the Church of England. Again, it seems the Jewish state is being singled out. Again, antisemitism and anti-Zionism are blended.

When I defend Israel's right to exist, the response is often to attack the policies of Israeli Prime Minister Benjamin Netanyahu. I am no fan of his. But I was no fan of many policies of the Trump administration and disagree with President Biden on numerous issues as well. I don't think that takes away the United States's right to exist as an independent, democratic nation.

When demonstrators chant, "From the river to the sea, Palestine shall be free," they, knowingly or not, are calling for erasing the State of Israel and eliminating its people. What could be more antisemitic and anti-Zionist?

Despite all, I look forward to a future where Hamas rule in Gaza has ended, where peace reigns in the Middle East and where Palestinian Arabs have set forth on the road to justice and democracy. And where antisemitism and anti-Zionism are no more.

Did Judges, Legislators and Presidential Candidates Play Hooky During History Class?

February 21, 2024

The late Sam Cooke sang, "Don't know much about history" in his classic "Wonderful World." He was a great artist, so we'll give him a pass, but the rest of us need to learn more history. We need to ensure that political campaigns, judicial decisions, education and laws are based on fact, not myth.

When asked the causes of the Civil War, Republican presidential candidate Nikki Haley did not mention slavery. She's the former governor of South Carolina, which declared back in 1860 it was leaving the Union because of "an increasing hostility on the part of the nonslaveholding States to the institution of slavery." Of the four states that spelled out why they were seceding, all proclaimed their support of slavery.

Florida legislators have another approach. They simply outlaw the teaching of facts they don't like. The Stop WOKE Act requires history to be taught in a way that students not "feel guilt, anguish, or any other form of psychological distress" due to their race, color, sex or national origin. Anyone who can teach about slavery without conveying distress ought not be teaching at all.

Members of the Supreme Court apparently need a history lesson, too. In striking down affirmative action at a private university, Chief Justice John Roberts offered what he called "an originalist defense of the colorblind Constitution" based on the 14th Amendment's Equal Protection Clause. That amendment was passed by the Senate on June 8, 1866. Ten days later, the Senate reaffirmed a law establishing a Freedmen's Bureau to benefit newly emancipated African Americans. As Justice Sonia Sotomayor futilely pointed out to Justice Roberts, laws like that one were anything but colorblind and leave "no doubt that the Equal Protection Clause permits consideration of race to achieve its goal."

Supreme Court justices have twisted the historical record time and again. Its 2008 decision that the Second Amendment protects an individual's right to bear arms ignores precedent, too. As former Chief Justice Warren Burger, appointed by Richard Nixon, said: "The Framers clearly intended to secure the right to bear arms essentially for military purposes." Justice Samuel Alito's decision striking down Roe v. Wade cites the opinion of a 17th century English judge regarding abortion but doesn't mention that Sir Matthew Hale also sentenced women to death for witchcraft. In a 1997 case, then-Chief Justice William Rehnquist wrote, "We begin, as we do in all due process cases, by examining our Nation's history, legal traditions, and practices." Wouldn't it be nice, then, to get the history right? It might do some good to have a few Supreme Court justices with Ph.D.s in history sitting on the bench along with the law school grads.

When it comes to American policy in the Middle East, too, historical understanding is at a low ebb. Yes, 700,000 Palestinian Arabs left or were expelled from Israel during and after Israel's 1948-49 War of Independence. But it's seldom mentioned that in the aftermath of the war, 900,000 Jews left or were expelled from Arab and other Muslim lands. The slogan "from the river to the sea, Palestine shall be free" is often chanted at anti-Israel demonstrations. UC Berkeley professor Ron Hassner conducted a survey that showed almost half of those chanting could not identify the river and sea being referred to.

In a December 2021 interview on Newsmax, former presidential advisor Peter Navarro said, "With respect to the issue of Ukraine, I think a little history at least is useful." He went on to assert, "Ukraine is not really a country." I doubt that did much to discourage the Russian invasion two months later. Here is one historical fact: Ukraine became part of the Soviet Union only after losing the 1917-21 Soviet-Ukrainian War. And another: Over 90% of Ukrainian voters backed independence in 1991. Last month, Navarro was sentenced to four months in jail. Perhaps he could use the time to learn a little more East European history.

Now in the interests of full disclosure, I admit to studying history in college myself. But I also lament that we history majors are well on our way to becoming an extinct species. The percentage of history majors in American universities sunk by more than two-thirds between 1971 and 2018. You don't have to be a history major or a college graduate to know history. But you do need to know some to be a good citizen.

If we're going to rely on history to dictate policy, law and teaching, we need more people learning historical facts and fewer spouting what Trump advisor Kellyanne Conway called "alternative facts." Here's a paraphrase of what another presidential advisor, Bernard Baruch, said way back in 1946: Everyone has the right to an opinion, but no one has a right to be wrong in their facts.

A Pro-Russian U.S. President Moves From Fiction to Reality

February 28, 2024

Way back when, I served as senior counsel to the Senate Intelligence Committee. That experience provided background for my 2011 novel "Drop By Drop." In it, top U.S. officials conspire with the Russian government to reelect an American president.

Just after the 2016 election, friends teased me and said Russian President Vladimir Putin must have read my book before he launched his plot to win the presidency for Donald Trump.

What plot? Of course, former President Trump called the investigations into Russian involvement in the 2016 election "the single greatest Witch Hunt in American history." Nevertheless, a report by the Republican-majority Senate Intelligence Committee found that "the Russian government engaged in an aggressive, multi-faceted effort to influence, or attempt to influence, the outcome of the 2016 presidential election."

It is ironic Trump says the 2020 was stolen from him based on no evidence, while it appears the 2016 election may well have been stolen from Hillary Clinton. In her book "Cyberwar," University of Pennsylvania professor Kathleen Hall Jamieson concludes it's "highly probable" Russia affected the outcome of the race. Secretary Clinton has moved on. Former President Trump has not.

"Drop By Drop" was meant to be a work of fiction, not a blueprint for Russian action. A pro-Russia American president was meant to be a character in a thriller novel, not the real-life resident of the White House. And there's no doubt that Donald Trump was the most pro-Russian U.S. president of the past century.

As far back as 2007, Trump told CNN's Larry King that Putin was "doing a great job in rebuilding the image of Russia and also rebuilding Russia period." Just after launching his presidential campaign in 2015, Trump said, "I think I'd get along very well with Vladimir Putin." At the GOP convention in the summer of 2016, Trump's staff weakened a plank supporting military aid for Ukraine. During the fall campaign, Trump beseeched the Russians to hack Hillary Clinton's emails. Apparently, they were listening. Hours later the Main Intelligence Directorate in Moscow attacked over 70 Clinton campaign accounts.

Once in office, Trump backed Putin's "extremely strong and powerful" denial of interference in the 2016 election over concrete evidence supplied by U.S. intelligence agencies. In a 2017 Oval Office meeting, Trump shared highly classified intelligence with the Russian foreign minister. To the horror of his aides, he often brought up the prospect of dropping out of NATO.

Now seeking to recapture the White House, Trump has refused to condemn Putin for the death of opposition leader Alexei Navalny in a Russian prison. Trump has said he would ignore treaty obligations and encourage Russia to "do whatever the hell they want" to any NATO country that didn't pay their dues. (In fact, NATO doesn't require dues.) European Council President Charles Michel described Trump's comments as "reckless," saying they "serve only Putin's interest." Surprise, surprise.

Right now, Ukraine is suffering from a munitions shortage in combating Russian aggression. Congressional Republicans refused to fund more military aid for Ukraine unless their demands for dealing with the Mexican border were met. They were met. And then Trump intervened to stop any compromise. He wanted to use immigration as an issue in his campaign to take back the White House. Support for Ukraine also fell by the wayside as Trump knew it would. Nikki Haley, his Republican rival for the presidency, said,

"Trump is siding with Putin, who has made no bones about wanting to destroy America."

Former Republican presidents Dwight Eisenhower and Ronald Reagan must be turning in their graves. Eisenhower was the first military commander of NATO. As president, he called the alliance "essential to world peace." Reagan said his policy toward Russia was simple: "We win, they lose."

Trump says if he's reelected president, he'll end the war in Ukraine in "24 hours," noting he "got along great" with Russian president Vladimir Putin. That could only mean he would abandon support for Ukraine and accept Russian aggression. Such a move would mean the death of the robust foreign policy embraced by Republicans in the Cold War and a return to the isolationist policy of the party before World War II. In the 1930s, America stood by as the Nazis marched into Poland and the Japanese army invaded China. We know how well that worked out. If there is one thing World War II and the Cold War should have taught us, it is that appeasement of aggression by major powers only encourages more aggression.

I'd thought about writing a sequel to "Drop By Drop" where the hero would be confronted by more threats to the U.S. But given what's happened on the world stage in the 13 years after its publication, I did decide to come up with something else.

McConnell's Judicial Gamesmanship Clears Path for Trump Second Term

March 7, 2024

Mitch McConnell has announced he will step down from his leadership of Senate Republicans at the end of the year. Democratic Majority Leader Chuck Schumer wished McConnell the very best. I do not. Instead, I scorn him for undermining the Senate's role in American democracy.

On Feb. 13, 2021, then-Senate Majority Leader McConnell declared to his colleagues that insurrectionists attacked the U.S. Capitol on Jan. 6 "because they had been fed wild falsehoods by the most powerful man on Earth — because he was angry he'd lost an election." McConnell went on to say, "There is no question that President Trump is practically and morally responsible for provoking the events of that day."

And yet, because of how McConnell reengineered the process for confirming federal judges, Trump may never suffer any consequences for his actions. Judges ushered through the Senate confirmation process by McConnell may hand the November election to Trump.

Let me explain.

Three members of the Supreme Court — Justices Neil Gorsuch, Brett Kavanaugh, and Amy Coney Barrett — owe their seats to how McConnell gamed their confirmations. Gorsuch took over the seat on the court left vacant by the 2016 death of Justice Antonin Scalia. An hour after Scalia's death was announced, McConnell announced, "This vacancy should not be filled until we have a new president." A nomination that, under the Constitution, belonged to President Barack Obama, went nowhere in the 11 months remaining in his term. Obama's nominee then-Chief Judge Merrick Garland did not even get a hearing.

In his 2016 memoir, McConnell wrote, "The Senate is the only legislative body on earth where a majority is not enough — most things require sixty votes to pass." McConnell had the 60-vote requirement for Supreme Court justices eliminated in the first months of Trump's term so that Trump's nominee Gorsuch could be confirmed by a majority 54-45 vote.

McConnell's hypocrisy was shown when Ruth Bader Ginsburg died with only four months left in Trump's term. He rammed through Amy Coney Barrett's confirmation only one month after her nomination. In his memoir he'd called the Senate "a place where nothing is decided without a good dose of deliberation and debate."

Without the abolition of the 60-vote requirement, there's no way Brett Kavanaugh would be on the Supreme Court. Accused of lying under oath and of sexual assault, Kavanaugh was confirmed by a 50-48 vote.

By all rights, then, the seat held by Gorsuch should have been Merrick Garland's, the seat held by Kavanaugh should have been held by someone who could have garnered 60 confirming votes and the one held by Barrett by someone nominated by Joe Biden.

How much difference would that have made?

The Supreme Court has just rejected a major threat to another Trump term. Judges in Colorado ruled that Trump should be taken off the state's ballot because of the 14th Amendment's bar on candidates who have "engaged in insurrection or rebellion" against the United States or "given aid or comfort to its enemies." Upon review, five members of the U.S. Supreme Court, including Gorsuch and Kavanaugh, held that a statute must be passed by Congress for such a disqualification to take effect. The Supreme Court ruled less than three months after appeal and less than a month after oral argument.

While the court moved at lightning speed in a case that would keep Trump on the ballot, the Supreme Court is moving molasses-slow in the Washington, D.C. case where Trump has been indicted for a "criminal scheme" to obstruct Joe Biden from taking office. Trump claims absolute immunity for any actions he took as president. His attorney has argued that unless convicted in a Senate trial first, a president would not face criminal charges in the courts even for ordering Navy Seals to assassinate a political rival. There is little chance Trump will win this argument. Trump's appeal was in December, and the oral hearing is not until April. Who knows when the decision will come and the trial can proceed?

Current polls show Donald Trump leading incumbent President Biden in the presidential race. However, an NBC poll released in February shows Biden pulling into the lead if Trump is convicted of a felony before the election. The Supreme Court's procrastination may mean the D.C. case is not decided by then. Trump's strategy is to delay. If he does win the presidency, he can have the Justice Department drop all federal charges.

It sure appears as though the current Supreme Court with its three Trump appointees moves quickly when it will help Trump and slowly when that suits him.

McConnell's influence has reached beyond nominations to the Supreme Court. Of 678 authorized federal district court judgeships, McConnell ensured the confirmation of 179 Trump nominees. Confirmed by a lame duck session of the Senate after Trump was defeated for reelection in November 2020, Judge Aileen Cannon was assigned the case where Trump was indicted for hiding top secret documents at his Mar-a-Lago residence. Federal prosecutors want the case to begin in July. Trump's lawyers argue that it should be postponed until next year. Cannon thus far has shown little urgency in moving forward.

In 2021, McConnell said Trump "kept repeating election lies and praising the criminals" even "with police officers bleeding and broken glass covering Capitol floors." And yet he has just endorsed him for a new term in 2024. Why not? It's his machinations and hypocrisy that might put Trump back in the White House.

Alas, what a legacy.

The Israel-Hamas War Woke Me Up

March 13, 2024

I'm not the youngster I thought I was.

During the school year, I live in an apartment tucked into a college dorm. I eat most of my meals in the dining hall with undergraduates. We discuss everything from classes and life's meaning to vacation plans and Taylor Swift. It's exciting and energizing to hang out with them.

We've always been pretty sympatico when it comes to political views. Women should have control over their own bodies; diversity among its citizens is an American strength; we need to confront climate change; Biden won the 2020 presidential election; etc.

No longer. I wised up in the wake of the murderous Hamas attack on Israel on Oct. 7.

Here's an example of what I'm talking about: Last week at dinner, two brilliant undergraduates encouraged me to express my views on the Israel-Hamas war. I plunged into the troubled waters. After a few minutes, one of them asserted Israel had instigated the attack as an excuse to invade Gaza. They believed there was no other explanation for the success of the attack given Israeli superiority in military power and intelligence assets.

Dumbfounded, I pointed out that over 1,200 Israelis had been murdered in the attack. As a percentage of population, that's equivalent to 30-plus 9/11 attacks. Would Israel really be complicit in the murder of so many of its citizens? I also brought up the Israeli withdrawal of its troops from Gaza in 2005. Why would they want to come back? These arguments and others were received by eyes rolled at my naivete.

I shouldn't have been surprised. In the hours after Hamas violated a ceasefire and attacked Israel on Oct. 7, a statement written by the Harvard Undergraduate Palestine Solidarity Committee held the "Israeli regime entirely responsible for all unfolding violence." Ryna Workman, president of NYU's Student Bar Association, wrote in a student newsletter that the Hamas atrocities were Israel's "full responsibility."

According to a recent poll, 60% of college-aged Americans (18-24), agree that the Hamas attack was justified, compared to only 9% of those over 65, Moreover, some two-thirds of these college-aged Americans see Jews as oppressors. Now, mind you, that's Jews, not just Israelis. The number of antisemitic incidents in the U.S. rose 361% in the three months following the Oct. 7 attack. Apparently, American Jews are being held responsible for the actions of a foreign country.

Facts just don't seem to matter. NYU's Workman and others condemn Israel's "settler colonialism." Jesus, a Jew, was preaching to his co-religionists there 2,000 years ago. Referring to Jesus, the Gospel of John reads, "Rabbi, we know that you are a teacher come from God." Jews were in the Holy Land before Christians or Muslims. They were there when the land was conquered and colonized by the Babylonians, Seleucids, Romans, Crusaders, Ottomans and British.

There are cries to send the Jews back to where they came from. About half of all Israeli Jews trace their ancestry to Arab and other Muslim-majority countries where they were forced out after the founding of the State of Israel.

A United Nations report found Hamas committed "rape and gang rape" in its Oct. 7 attack There was credible evidence of "genital mutilation, sexualized torture" along with "mutilation of corpses, including decapitation." Young American progressives, who supported the #MeToo movement against sexual abuse and who condemned Donald Trump when a jury found him a rapist, said nothing in response. Rep. Rashida Tlaib (D-Mich.) refused to vote for a House condemnation of "countless instances of rape, gang rape, sexual mutilation" perpetrated by Hamas.

Young Americans concerned about racism in this country (count me in) try to apply their American-centric views to Israel. "We are also freedom fighters who have been grossly mislabeled and violently targeted for standing up against injustice to our people," said Black Lives Matter Phoenix on social media. Those who are raping and murdering refugees from Arab countries, members of families that have lived in Israel for centuries, and American citizens at a music festival are civil rights protesters?

There's a certain racism involved, too, in supporting Hamas. Hamas attacks are validated without reservation, and Israel's responses are condemned without nuance. Palestinian Arabs do have agency. They have rejected opportunities to set up a Palestinian homeland. For example, in 1947, the United Nations voted to partition the British mandate in Palestine into majority-Arab and majority-Jewish states. The Jews accepted and declared the independence of the State of Israel. Palestinian Arabs and neighboring countries tried to conquer the entire territory.

In 2000, Yassir Arafat, chairman of the Palestinian Liberation Organization, rejected the Israeli proposal for a Palestinian Arab state. Former president Clinton stated, "I regret that in 2000 Arafat missed the opportunity to bring that nation into being and pray for the day when the dreams of the Palestinian people for a state and a better life will be realized in a just and lasting peace." As noted, in 2005, the Israeli Defense Forces left Gaza. In 2006, Hamas, whose charter calls for the elimination of the State of Israel and for the death of all Jews, took over Gaza. Students do not seem to know all this history.

My goodness, there is a need for peace and humanity in the Middle East. There is an urgent need for the end of violence and the replacement of Hamas by Palestinian Arabs who want peace.

Support for Israel's right to exist does not mean support for the current Netanyahu government. As the poet John Dunne knew, every death "diminishes" us all.

I will keep expressing my views when asked and hope students reach their own conclusions based on facts and study, not reflex and prejudice.

Justice Clarence Thomas Is a Great Candidate — for Impeachment

March 20, 2024

"I can resist everything except for temptation," the Irish poet and playwright Oscar Wilde wrote in one of his plays.

The Constitution gives the House of Representatives the sole power to impeach all civil officers of the United States. The Republican majority in the House apparently cannot resist the temptation of using it — even when it means doing so as political theater and not as a constitutional duty.

First, they impeached Alejandro Mayorkas, the Homeland Security secretary, for "the high crime or misdemeanor" of failing to fix the immigration mess on our southern border. The real high crime was the failure of the House to give Mayorkas the tools and authority to address the crisis. A bipartisan bill laid out a solution but was pulled back at the behest of former President Donald Trump. House Republicans were, Homeland Security spokesperson Mia Ehrenberg said, "trampling on the Constitution for political gain rather than working to solve the serious challenges at our border."

Nor could House Republicans resist the urge to begin impeachment proceedings aimed at President Joe Biden. GOP Rep. Matt Gaetz and his colleagues voted to investigate the Biden family for taking "bribes from corrupt foreigners." To make these accusations, they relied on the testimony of an informant with ties to Russian intelligence who was eventually arrested and charged with lying to the FBI. As Gaetz admitted to CNN, "A few of those characterizations might have been a little oversauced."

Perhaps I can make a suggestion to House Republicans: Why not use your constitutional power to impeach a high official who secretly took funds not from foreigners, but from Americans?

Members of the House, may I introduce you to the longest-serving member of the Supreme Court, Justice Clarence Thomas?

According to an investigation by the independent nonprofit ProPublica, Thomas accepted "at least 38 destination vacations, including a previously unreported voyage on a yacht around the Bahamas; 26 private jet flights, plus an additional eight by helicopter; a dozen VIP passes to professional and college sporting events, typically perched in the skybox; two stays at luxury resorts in Florida and Jamaica; and one standing invitation to an uber-exclusive golf club overlooking the Atlantic coast."

Texas real estate billionaire Harlan Crow was especially generous in funding Thomas' vacations, private jet flights, gifts, the purchase of his mother's house in Georgia and tuition payments to his grandnephew. In 1997, Thomas reported the gift of a private plane flight from Crow. After the gift became public in 2004, Thompson stopped disclosing gifts, including Crow's. Unsurprisingly, in the Supreme Court case Citizens United v. FEC, Thomas provided the decisive vote in permitting widespread use of "dark money" in political campaigns by undisclosed donors.

Thomas also borrowed over a quarter million dollars to buy a luxury RV from a friend. According to the Senate Finance Committee, it appears the principal on the loan was forgiven. Ron Wyden, the chair of the committee, said on the Senate floor, "I am working to learn whether he paid the taxes he was supposed to — taxes that any American is legally required to pay. Justice Thomas refuses to respond."

While Thomas accepted gifts and vacations worth millions and failed to report them, his colleague on the bench Justice Elena Kagan turned down lox and bagels from her high school classmates for fear of any appearance of corruption.

Thomas's wife, Ginnie, wrote to Wisconsin state legislators to reject Biden's victory in the state after the November 2020 election. She urged the appointment of fake electors. "Please stand strong in the face of political and media pressure ... And then please take action to ensure that a clean slate of Electors is chosen for our state." A D.C. grand jury has charged that Trump and his coconspirators organized a "fraudulent" slate of electors in Wisconsin and other states. Thomas shows no signs of recusing himself from motions and decisions that could affect his wife's status as one of those coconspirators. As Hofstra professor of law James Sample said of Justice Thomas: "He could be ruling on a case that could determine whether or not the events his wife participated in amounted to an insurrection against the United States of America."

The stench surrounding the Supreme Court is not only due to Thomas. The wife of Chief Justice John Roberts has allegedly made more than $10 million from her services to prominent law firms. At least one of them argued a case before the court. Justice Brett Kavanagh's nomination was rammed through the Senate without a thorough investigation of whether he lied in his testimony regarding allegations of heavy drinking and sexual assault. Nominee Amy Coney Barrett was confirmed for a seat on the Supreme Court by the Senate with three months left in the term of Donald Trump, after the GOP Senate had refused to confirm nominee Merrick Garland because Barack Obama's term had only 10 months left.

No wonder the Gallup Poll shows disapproval of the Court has doubled from 29% in 2000 to 58% in 2023. Laws or even constitutional amendments setting forth term limits, strong ethical rules, procedures for the investigations and hearings of nominees and strict standards for conflicts of interest are all needed, even if not imminent.

Hearings on the impeachment of Thomas would be more than theater. They would be justice. It's time to clean up the Supreme Court, and the best place to start is impeaching Clarence Thomas.

Things Are Great, but They're Miserable, Too

March 27, 2024

"It was the best of times, it was the worst of times." In rereading the opening lines of Charles Dickens' "A Tale of Two Cities," I had the sense they were written last week, not almost two centuries ago.

Scanning the book's next few lines, I'm even more convinced Dickens is describing 2024 America: "It was the spring of hope, it was the winter of despair, we had everything before us, we had nothing before us."

I'm a news junkie who pores over magazines, newspapers and websites every day. Minutes after being buoyed by a report of more equality, better health, expanding rights, growing prosperity and increased justice, my mood will sink into the depths when I realize how far we have to go.

The number of Americans without health insurance decreased from 14.5% in 2008 to 8.0% in 2022. That's progress! But the life expectancy of Black Americans is still more than five years shorter than for white Americans. For American Indian and Alaska Native citizens, the difference is 11 years. Sigh. We do have a long way to go.

The American economy grew faster last year than that of Canada, Germany, France, the UK or Japan. At the same time, the distribution of America's wealth is more unequal than in any of those five countries. The wealthiest 10% holds 79% of this country's wealth.

American democracy survived an attempt to keep Donald Trump in office even after he lost the 2020 election. Still, despite being indicted on 91 criminal counts, most polls show him ahead in the upcoming November contest.

The right of women to reproductive freedom was stripped away by a 6-3 Supreme Court vote in the 2022 Dobbs case. Three members of the majority were appointed by Trump, who lost the popular vote in 2016. Those three justices along with Clarence Thomas were confirmed by senators who also represented only a minority of the American electorate. But since 2022, voters have made their opinions known. Each of the seven states that voted on reproductive rights in the wake of Dobbs, including red states such as Kentucky, Ohio and Kansas, have resolved to protect them.

By one important measure, racism in the U.S. is declining. Only 5% of Americans approved of interracial marriages in the 1950s. The number in this decade is 94%. On the other hand, antisemitism in the United States is on the rise. Jews are just 2% of the American population, but they are victims of 60% of religious-based hate crimes according to the FBI. Moreover, the number of white supremacist propaganda incidents last year increased to 7,567 cases, a 12% increase from 2022.

In his last speech as president, Ronald Reagan declared, "Thanks to each wave of new arrivals to this land of opportunity, we're a nation forever young, forever bursting with energy and new ideas." Nobel prizewinner Paul Krugman showed the validity of the statement when he wrote last week, "Overall, then, immigration appears to have been a big plus for U.S. economic growth, among other things expanding our productive capacity in a way that reduced the inflationary impact of Biden's spending programs." Bravo for immigrants? Not necessarily. Trump wins applause from supporters when he says immigrants are "poisoning the blood of our country."

Thank goodness for the fast delivery of COVID-19 vaccines. UCLA professor Andrew Atkeson estimates the availability of the vaccines had saved 748,600 American lives by June 2023. Being current on my vaccinations might have even saved me. I caught

COVID-19 at my family's Thanksgiving dinner last November. It was no worse than a mild cold. And yet fewer than a quarter of American adults are up to date on their COVID-19 shots. Robert F. Kennedy Jr. has used his anti-vax rants as a springboard to run for president as an independent.

Ten of the world's 12 largest companies by market cap are American. Seven of them are tech companies founded since 1975 and headquartered in either Silicon Valley or Washington state. I'm not saying there aren't problems, lots of problems, with a free market system, but the dynamism of American capitalism improves the standard of living and provides good jobs to tens of millions. Will this continue? A 2021 poll showed over half of 18- to 24-year-olds have a negative view of capitalism. I live on a college campus and would bet the number has only increased.

The first federal gun safety law in 30 years was passed in 2022. On the other hand, there were 39 mass shootings in 2023, the highest number ever.

There's a lot more I could add to the list, but that's enough for now. If Dickens' words speak to me across two centuries, what the Talmudic sage Tarfon said two millennia ago calls out to me even more strongly: "It's not your duty to finish the work, but neither are you free to neglect it."

What is the work Tarfon is talking about? To make the world a better place for us and future generations. He is reminding us that the world will never be perfect, but we should all do our share in improving it.

The Sioux in the U.S. and the Jews in Israel Are Both Indigenous Peoples

April 3, 2024

The Sioux Nation stretched over much of the Great Plains before the westward push of settlers after the Civil War encroached on their lands. Given that history, it's natural enough for the Oglala Sioux Tribe to back the Indigenous people in the currently raging Gaza War.

But in the upside-down world where we live, the tribe declared its support for Palestinian Arabs, not the Israeli Jews who are the Indigenous people in the land known across the centuries as Canaan, Judea, Palestine and Israel.

Archeological evidence shows the descendants of King David ruled over a Jewish state with its capital in Jerusalem 2,800 years ago. Led by the Maccabees, the Jews of Judea threw off the rule of the Seleucid Empire 2,200 years ago, an event commemorated by the annual Hanukkah holiday. In 131 C.E., the Roman Emperor Hadrian expelled Jews from Jerusalem and its environs and renamed the province of Judaea "Syria Palaestina," which is where the name Palestine comes from.

In exile, Jews did not forget Jerusalem, also referred to as Zion. The 12th century poet Judah Halevi, living in Muslim Spain, wrote these lines to reflect his yearning for the Holy Land: "My heart is in the East and I am at the edge of the West." The traditional Passover service ended with the words: "Next year in Jerusalem."

Over the centuries, Jews trickled back into Jerusalem. By 1896, the Jewish population of Jerusalem had grown to over 28,000, more than the number of Muslims and Christians combined.

Modern Zionism, calling for a return to the Holy Land by all Jews, grew in response to late 19th and early 20th century antisemitism in Europe.

During World War I, the British government declared its support for the "establishment in Palestine of a national home for the Jewish people." The declaration was supported by Arab leaders including Emir Faisal, later the first king of Iraq, who said, "No true Arab can be suspicious or afraid of Jewish nationalism." In 1922, then-Colonial Secretary Winston Churchill explained that Jews were returning to Palestine "as of right and not by sufferance, and that this was based on their ancient historical connection." He also noted, "The Jews had Palestine before (the Arabs) came in and inhabited it."

The League of Nations entrusted rule over Palestine to the British. Despite Churchill's sympathy to Jewish return, just five years after the Balfour Declaration, he broke off over three-quarters of the Palestinian mandate to establish Arab-ruled Transjordan.

In 1947, the newly established United Nations voted to divide Palestine into Jewish and Arab states. The Jewish land would have included only 13% of the original mandate's territory. The Arab inhabitants of Palestine and the governments of the surrounding Arab countries nevertheless fought for the entire territory of the mandate. The Arabs lost the war, and the state of Israel was established on May 17, 1948.

If any Indigenous people should sympathize with the Jewish attachment to the land of Israel, it should be the Sioux. They entered into a treaty in 1868 where the United States designated a large swath of land including the Black Hills for their "absolute and undisturbed use and occupation." When gold was discovered in the Black Hills, the U.S. reneged on the treaty. In the 1980 case United States v. Sioux Nation of Indians, the U.S. Supreme Court awarded $600M in damages to the Sioux. They have refused to accept the money, demanding instead the return of the land including the Black Hills where the Mount Rushmore National Memorial stands.

The Sioux continue to demand their land back through governmental processes, not by the slaughter of non-Indigenous Americans. It is Hamas who has declared its aim to be genocide against the Indigenous people of Israel. The Hamas Covenant calls for Islam to "obliterate" Israel and to "vanquish" all Jews. As Biden said of Hamas, "Its stated purpose is the annihilation of the State of Israel and the murder of Jewish people."

Why don't the Sioux then regard the establishment of the state of Israel as an inspiration? The Jews are the only Indigenous people in world history who maintained their ties to their ancient land while in exile and then returned to restore their language and religion there. No American Indigenous peoples have done so. Neither have the Maoris in New Zealand, nor the Aboriginal Australians, nor the Ainu in Japan.

One leader of an exiled people does find the story of the Jewish return inspiring. True settler colonials from China are today taking over the Dalai Lama's country of Tibet. The Chinese government has ignored then-President Barack Obama's plea "to take steps to preserve the unique cultural, religious and linguistic identity of the Tibetan people."

In looking to the situation of the Tibetans in exile, the Dalai Lama, head of Tibet government-in-exile, has said, "We have to learn from the experiences of our Jewish brothers and sisters."

I'd recommend the Sioux do the same.

After a Year of Column Writing, I Still Have Plenty to Say. Unfortunately.

April 17, 2024

My first journalism job was long ago, covering events at my high school for the local paper. Writing this column is the second. I've been at it since last April, and that first anniversary has put me in a reflective mood.

Last year, I worried about coming up with a topic each week. I have five published novels, which made me more anxious, not less. When I finished each of them, I had to figure out what topic was compelling enough to keep me engrossed for a year or more of writing the next book. Given the months that took, how was I going to come up with a topic for a column every seven days?

I needn't have worried. It turns out there's a big difference between coming up with 80,000 words a year and 800 words a week. For better and mostly for worse, I am flooded with column ideas. My notes and thoughts for future columns are stored on a document that runs over 30 pages! I will not run short of topics so long as any of these things continue:

— Politicians shedding principles for the sake of reelection

— Schools neglecting their educational mission

— Vladimir Putin yearning to rebuild the Russian Empire through conquest

— Americans declining to stand against overseas aggression

— Lawless, would-be authoritarians seeking the White House

— Voters wishing to "make America great again" by returning to a world with more poverty, more racism, more sexism, more illiteracy, less equality and shorter lifespans

— Terrorists committing unspeakable atrocities

— Elected representatives responding to mass shootings with nothing more than prayers

— People despoiling the Earth's land, sea and air

— Individuals living without adequate food, housing or health care

— Nonwhite, nonmale and non-Christian citizens being denied equal protection

— Supreme Court justices flouting the Constitution

— Whiners complaining about the state of the country but failing to vote

— So-called conservatives failing to support democracy

— So-called progressives closing their ears to any policy offered by opponents, while opening them to any antisemitism offered by allies

Given this list, which could be longer, I've been surprised to discover that writing the column is good for my mental health. I am not happy with the state of the planet, as you might have gathered from the daunting inventory above. Just reading papers and websites all day would only make me more despondent. The act of writing a draft column one day each week and a final draft the next day helps keep my brain from exploding with anger and frustration. I'm venting on a regular schedule.

In the mornings of the other five days of the week, I can work on a novel. Then I'm lost in a fictional world where I control what happens. Unsurprisingly, I have set the book I am currently finishing up in a different era. It's good to escape the here and now, or at least to try to. The problem is that when writing about 1960s America, so many of the issues are the same, and so many of the political speeches could have been given last week. Sometimes I think we humans are "captive on the carousel of time" as Joni Mitchell, the troubadour of those times, sang in 1966's "The Circle Game."

Still, even while despairing about the state of the world, I see I am a lucky man. I have my family and friends. I devour great books, watch terrific movies and stare at breathtaking art. I live during the school year on a college campus where undergraduates give me hope for the future.

And I have you, dear readers, who soften my sense that I am just spitting into the wind when I turn in my column each week. Thank you. Onward and upward to another year.

Muslim Civilians Didn't Volunteer To Be Martyrs for Hamas and Iran

April 24, 2024

On April 13, Iran fired hundreds of drones, rockets and missiles at Israel.

"So, let's be straight," said White House national security spokesperson John Kirby two days later. "Given the scale of this attack, Iran's intent was clearly to cause significant destruction and casualties."

I did notice in news photos that many of the Iranian projectiles were intercepted right over the Dome of the Rock and the Al-Aqsa Mosque on Jerusalem's Temple Mount. If Israel, with critical help from the United States and Jordan, had not blown up the incoming bombs, the Temple Mount might well have suffered significant destruction. Judging from the photographic evidence, Iran seemed ready to rain significant destruction down on what's often called Islam's third-holiest site.

While Jerusalem stands as its capital, Israel consents to the Muslim holy places on the Temple Mount being managed and controlled by the "Waqf," an 18-member committee appointed by the king of Jordan. When the Jordanian King Hussein wanted to replace the gold plates that cover the Dome of the Rock in the early 1990s, Israel agreed. Judging by actions taken, Israel values the sanctity of the Dome of the Rock and the Al-Aqsa Mosque far more than Iran.

Apparently, Iran intended its missiles to cause significant casualties, as well as destruction, within Israel. Thanks to formidable air defenses, the only serious casualty in the Iranian attack was not a Jew but a 7-year-old Muslim Bedouin girl. (At last report, Amina Hassouna is breathing on her own but remains in intensive care.)

Iran's disdain for Arab and Muslim lives carries over to Hamas, the terrorist group in Gaza it influences, finances and largely controls. Iran deemed the Hamas attack on Israel that killed over 1,200 people on Oct. 7 as a triumph of its "axis of resistance" strategy. That murder spree included Arabs as well as Jews among its casualties. It breaks my heart to see photographs of murdered children such as the four Alkra-an siblings and cousins who ranged in age from 11 to 14.

In Gaza itself, a critical part of Hamas' strategy is to promote Arab civilian deaths. A recent U.S. State Department report declares, "We have repeatedly condemned Hamas' abhorrent misuse of civilians and civilian infrastructure as human shields." Hamas understands full well that its policy of hiding armed combatants among the general populace and on or under schools and hospitals will lead to civilian deaths. Five years ago, a NATO report warned that Hamas' tactic of using civilians as human shields is intended to have Israel viewed in the world "as an aggressor that indiscriminately strikes civilians."

It serves Hamas' strategy, then, to have Arab Muslims civilians living in Gaza killed. They are not mere pawns in the game. They are involuntary martyrs.

While Iran and Hamas support the sacrifice of Arab and Muslim holy places and lives, Jordan, Egypt and Saudi Arabia do not. Jordan's government stated it shot down Iranian drones and missiles crossing over its territory on the way to Israel in order to defend "the nation, its citizens, and its airspace and territory."

Egypt borders on the Gaza Strip and in fact controlled it from 1948 to 1967. While Egypt still controls an access point for supplies to enter Gaza, the government steadfastly refuses to allow Gazans to take refuge in Egypt even amid the current war. It has even deployed tanks and troops to prevent it. The Egyptian government fears admitting Gazan refugees will allow Iran and Hamas to carry their brand of death and destruction across the border into Egypt.

Saudi Arabian Crown Prince Mohammed bin Salman has said that if Iran obtains nuclear weapons, his country will seek to do the same. Saudi Arabia rejects what Iran stands for and sees it as an existential threat. Therefore, it provided intelligence to Israel to aid in fending off the Iranian air attack.

Those who advocate for Iran and Hamas are supporting their disregard for Muslim lives and holy places. Jordan, Egypt and Saudi Arabia know better.

It's Time To Make the U.S. House of Representatives More Representative

May 8, 2024

Way back in 1929, the number of House members was set at 435 by the Permanent Apportionment Act. Little did those voting to pass the law realize how permanent it was to be.

In 1929, the population of the U.S. was about 122 million. Each member of the House represented about 280,000 constituents. Today, with a population of about 336 million, each member represents 773,000 — almost triple as many.

The U.S. is an outlier when it comes to the size of districts for the lower house of its legislature. For example, Germany, with a population about a quarter the United States', has 300 more members in its Bundestag than sit in the House of Representatives. The United Kingdom's House of Commons has 215 more members than the House of Representatives with a population about a fifth of ours.

The fewer members of the U.S. House don't appear to act with greater efficiency than their European counterparts, that's for sure. Germany and Britain's parliaments do a far better job at passing budgets and keeping the government running smoothly than the American Congress.

It's not the first Sunday in November, but it's still time to turn the clock back. It's time to return to the days of fewer people in each House district.

It's a tough job for members to represent today's populous districts. The kind of door-to-door campaigning instrumental in Jack Kennedy's 1946 congressional victory has largely disappeared. The successor to Kennedy's seat in 1953, old-time politician Tip O'Neill, would regularly go back to the district to get his hair cut, have shoes repaired and hang out with constituents at "Barry's Corner." Today's voters typically don't feel that connection with their representative, don't have the sense that the member is representing them in the national capital. Closer connections matter. Each vote matters more. At a time when trust in Congress is at record lows, polling shows locally elected officials are more popular with constituents than members of Congress.

House members have turned to performance rather than representation, to fundraising from contributors outside their district rather than staying in touch with those inside. More districts would make it less expensive to run for Congress. In advocating for more members of the House, Harvard professor Danielle Allen has pointed out, "The ever-growing size of districts reinforces the power of incumbency and money."

It doesn't take a constitutional amendment to change the number of representatives, just a law passed by Congress and signed by the president. Oregon Rep. Earl Blumenauer believes the growing population of congressional districts "makes it more difficult for members to be responsive to the will of the people, and voters are more likely to sit out elections when their voice and input are not fully represented in government." He has introduced H.R. 622, a bill that would add 150 seats to the current 435. It's a start.

There's plenty of room in the House chamber for those members. At State of the Union addresses, House members are joined on the floor by senators, members of the joint chiefs of staff, Supreme Court members, Cabinet secretaries and foreign ambassadors. Allen has worked with an architect to show how the House floor could easily accommodate double the current 435 members and almost four times more with a little crowding.

Not only would passage of Rep. Blumenauer's bill or one like it make the House members more responsive to their constituents, but it would also make presidential elections more responsive to the national will.

In this country, we don't elect the president by a popular vote. Instead, the winner is the candidate who gains a majority in the Electoral College. Each state gets two electoral votes for its senators and then an additional vote for each member it has in the House of Representatives. This favors smaller states because they get the "Senate bump," two seats no matter their population. Thus, in the last presidential election, the least populous state, Wyoming, had one elector per 180,000 people, while California, the most populous, had one per 700,000.

The current formula contributes to anomalies such as the 2016 election where Donald Trump was elected president by the electoral college 304-227, even while losing the popular vote by over 3 million. Adding more representatives would make that Senate bump less significant and increase the chances that the candidate with the most popular votes would also win the Electoral College.

Unfortunately, a bill such as Rep. Blumenauer's has little chance of passing in the current Congress. Republicans would see the change as diluting their chances in the Electoral College. There's a certain irony there since back in the 19th century, Republicans lobbied successfully to have the Dakota Territory divided into two states, North and South Dakota. This was in no small part to gain their party six electoral votes rather than the three if the territory had been admitted as a single state.

Would increasing the size of the House help one party more than the other now? Maybe, but that really shouldn't matter. It would make the United States government both more responsive and more democratic (with a small d).

Call me naive, but I still believe support for American democracy should trump partisanship every time.

When It Comes to the Middle East, Slogans Mean Nothing Without Understanding History

May 15, 2024

After a year as a professor at Columbia University, former Secretary of State Hillary Clinton probably knows what she's talking about when she says young people "don't know much at all about the history of the Middle East."

As an example, she pointed to the often overlooked rejection by the Palestinian Authority of a peace deal with Israel in 2000. Under its terms, a Palestinian Arab state would have been established in 96% of the West Bank and Gaza plus some ceded territory from Israel. In a recent interview, Clinton said Yassir Arafat, then the head of the PA, said he intended to agree with the proposal but in the end declined for fear of his life. "It's one of the great tragedies of history that he was unable to say yes," she lamented.

Clinton warned that to fully understand the situation in the Middle East, one had to go back "thousands of years." There's not room to do that in this column. Still, here are eight more historical elements, beginning in ancient days, that protesters on today's college campuses should know.

1. Jews are indigenous to the Holy Land. A 1993 archeological discovery confirmed the existence of a King David and successors who lived in what's now Israel 3,000 years ago. And 2,000 years ago, Jesus was preaching there to his fellow Jews.

2. After World War I, the British were awarded a mandate over Palestine by the League of Nations, the forerunner of today's United Nations. The mandate called for "conditions as will secure

the establishment of a Jewish national home." Jews and Arabs alike carried Palestinian passports. In the early 1920s, 77% of the mandate's original territory was broken off from Palestine to become Transjordan ruled by an Arab emir.

3. In 1947, the United Nations voted that the remaining 23% of the original mandate's territory should be divided again into two states, one majority Arab and one majority Jewish. The Jewish settlers accepted the plan, but the Arabs did not. According to the U.S. State Department, "Fighting began with attacks by irregular bands of Palestinian Arabs... against Jewish cities, settlements, and armed forces." As soon as British troops left Palestine, the new state of Israel was invaded by Arab armies from Lebanon, Syria, Iraq and Egypt.

4. No Palestinian state was established after the Israeli War of Independence concluded in 1949. The West Bank and East Jerusalem were occupied by Transjordan, which was renamed Jordan, and the Gaza Strip was occupied by Egypt. Even with the existence of the state of Israel, over 85% of the original Palestine mandate's territory was Arab-ruled.

5. During and after the war, all Jews who'd lived in the West Bank and East Jerusalem were expelled by Jordan. In contrast, about one-sixth of the population of Israel remained Arab. During the 1947-49 war, between half and three-quarters of a million Arabs left Israel or were expelled from it. Over 800,000 Jews left or were expelled from Muslim lands in the years following Israel's independence. Since most of these refugees settled in Israel, Jews tracing their ancestry to non-European countries came to form a majority of Jews in the country.

6. Egyptian President Anwar el-Sadat and Israeli Prime Minister Menachem Begin signed a peace treaty between their two countries in 1979. Fifteen years later, the Jordan-Israel Peace Treaty was signed by King Hussein of Jordan, Prime Minister Yitzhak Rabin and President Bill Clinton.

7. In 1993 and 1995, the Oslo Agreements were signed between Israel and the Palestine Liberation Organization. The PLO recognized the state of Israel, and Israel recognized the PLO as the representative of the Palestinian Arab people.

8. In 2005, Israel shut down its civilian settlements and withdrew its military forces in the Gaza Strip. In 2007, Hamas overthrew the Palestinian Authority in Gaza after a civil war. According to Human Rights Watch, it established control with killings, abductions and beatings of opponents. There have been no elections in Gaza since 2006. Hamas is currently on the U.S. Department of State and the European Union's list of terrorist organizations.

Recently, pro-Palestinian Arab protesters in Harvard Yard displayed a poster of the acting university President Alan Garber with horns and a tail sitting on a toilet, with a caption stating, "Alan Garbage funds genocide." Do the protesters even know the meaning of genocide as defined by the UN in 1948?

Like so many, I'm deeply saddened by the loss of life on both sides in the current war, but sloganeering is not understanding. If protesters want to advocate for Palestinian Arabs, they need to do so on the basis of facts, not catchphrases. How can the state of Israel be illegitimate when it was established by a vote of the UN? How can it be a nation of white settler colonials when a majority of its citizens are Arabs, Druze and Jews indistinguishable in appearance from Egyptians, Jordanians, Yemenis, Iraqis, Moroccans, Syrians and Iranians?

I blame American universities in part for what's happening. They should be teaching their students critical thinking, not unquestioning acceptance. I find it commendable that students care enough about what's happening in the world that they are willing to demonstrate, but embracing trendy slogans isn't the same as learning the complexities of the past.

Protesters, whether pro-Israel or pro-Palestinian Arab, should go and study. They should be able to support their positions with history, not just gut feelings.

As Secretary Clinton said, "Propaganda is not history."

The Green Party's Jill Stein, a Good Friend of the Environment and a Better Friend of Russia

May 22, 2024

Who is Jill Stein? Is she a naive environmentalist, Donald Trump's secret weapon or Vladimir Putin's pal?

In November 2016 as the presidential nominee of the left-wing Green Party, Stein picked up 1.1% of the national vote. Those 1.45 million votes in 2016 don't seem like a lot when compared to the 130 million that were cast. But what if Stein, ideologically far closer to Hillary Clinton than to Donald Trump, hadn't run?

Let's take a closer look at the 2016 results. In Michigan, Trump edged Clinton by 11,000 votes, while Stein garnered 51,000. In Wisconsin, Trump beat Clinton by 23,000 votes, while Stein collected 31,000. In Pennsylvania, Trump won by 44,000, while Stein picked up 49,000. If Clinton had won Stein's votes in those three states, she would have won a majority in the Electoral College. Clinton, not Trump, would have been sworn in as president in January 2017. Oh, would a different world it would be.

While all eyes seem to be on Robert F. Kennedy Jr.'s fumbling, futile, feckless run for the presidency, it's unclear whether his candidacy will hurt Biden or Trump more. Why isn't more attention then being paid to Stein? She might have been the reason Donald Trump won in 2016. She appears to be planning a redo in 2024.

On her website, Stein says she's running this year to "put a pro-worker, anti-war, climate action agenda front and center in this election." It doesn't look that way. Trump favors cutting taxes for the wealthy, while AFL-CIO President Liz Shuler calls Biden "the most pro-union president in our lifetime." While Biden is calling for a ceasefire in the Middle East, Trump has told Israel to "get it done. Get it over with and get it over with fast." Trump has asked oil executives for $1 billion in campaign contributions so he could reverse Biden's clean energy initiatives to cut pollution from coal plants and support a transition to electric vehicles.

Clearly, if policy were Stein's main goal, she would be supporting Biden in 2024 and not running again herself.

Of course, no one who runs for president has a small ego. Stein ran for the presidency on the Green ticket in 2012 and 2016 and is running again in 2024. She may just enjoy the attention, the limelight and the sense only she can set the country moving down the right path.

There's a more nefarious explanation, though. In 2015, Stein dined with Vladimir Putin in Moscow. Also at the table was General Michael Flynn, Trump's future national security adviser who was convicted of a felony for lying about his discussions with a Russian diplomat. Stein says she was there to "lift up a different point of view" on U.S. foreign policy. A pro-Russian point of view?

The U.S. Senate Intelligence Committee, chaired at the time by Republican Sen. Marco Rubio, reported that the online propaganda and influence operations conducted by Russia's Internet Research Agency during the 2016 campaign promoted Stein: "The IRA's left-leaning accounts focused their efforts on denigrating Clinton and supporting the candidacy of either fellow Democrat candidate Bernie Sanders or Green Party candidate Jill Stein, at the expense of Hillary Clinton." There were, for example, postings by the IRA aimed at Black voters arguing, "A Vote for Jill Stein is Not a Wasted Vote."

In her first run for the presidency in 2012, Stein received 0.36% of the vote. Then she hung out with Putin in 2015, received illegal Russian support for her candidacy the next year, and tripled her vote percentage. She did not run in 2020 when Trump was the incumbent, but she is running again while Trump tries to regain office.

Recent polls show that in her third run, Stein is picking up about the same 1% as she did in 2016. She just might well be what Trump needs to win the White House again. Hmm. This brings to mind the remark Ian Fleming's villain Goldfinger made to James Bond: "Once is happenstance. Twice is coincidence. Three times is enemy action."

I must admit with some chagrin that Jill Stein and I were college classmates. To the best of my recollection, I did not know her and thus have no special insights into what she is up to. It is clear to me nevertheless that she is doing Russia's work. She is pulling votes away from Biden and enhancing the chances of Trump, again Putin's favored candidate. (How could Trump not be when he's described Russia's invasion of Ukraine as "genius" and invited Russia "to do whatever the hell they want" to NATO members who do not spend enough on their military?)

During the Cold War, those in the West who supported Soviet goals for idealistic reasons were known as "useful idiots" by the KGB. One of my favorite novelists, Doris Lessing, visited Russia in 1952. Over half a century later, she recalled, "I was taken around and shown things as a 'useful idiot' ... that's what my role was. I can't understand why I was so gullible."

It took Nobel Prize winner Lessing over 50 years to admit how misguided she was in serving Russian aims. I can only hope Green Party candidate Stein wakes up in the next 50 days.

Manhattan District Attorney Bragg Follows in Footsteps of Racket Busting Predecessor

June 5, 2024

New York prosecutors and judges are showing up their federal counterparts. It's not the first time a New York prosecutor picked up the baton when other agencies failed to pursue justice.

The legal system in New York City in the early 1930s was corrupt. Organized crime ran rampant. Officials and politicians were on the take. More than 90% of the arrests made for gambling never came to trial. The New York governor intervened and appointed Thomas Dewey as a special prosecutor.

Dewey is best remembered now as Harry Truman's stilted opponent in the 1948 presidential race. But he first won national acclaim as a "racket buster" who took on New York City gangsters in the 1930s as a special prosecutor and then Manhattan district attorney. He famously sent crime boss Lucky Luciano, who'd seemed immune to successful prosecution, off to prison for 30-50 years for committing sex crimes — running a prostitution ring.

Let's compare Dewey's work way back then to the recent prosecution of former President Donald Trump for secret payments that violated campaign finance laws.

Michael Cohen pleaded guilty in 2018 to conspiring with Trump for paying off Stormy Daniels. Her story of a one-night stand with Trump would have hurt his chances of winning the 2016 presidential election.

Trump himself was not charged while in office because U.S. Department of Justice policies forbade the indictment of a sitting president. But that doesn't explain why the feds failed to move against Trump after he left office. Where's the fairness in charging the subordinate and not the boss who ordered the illegal actions?

Then Manhattan DA Alvin Bragg stepped in. He followed the example of his predecessor Tom Dewey by bringing to trial an alleged lawbreaker even when other prosecutors would not. On May 30 of this year, a unanimous jury of 12 New Yorkers found Trump guilty of falsifying records to hide information that would have influenced the 2016 presidential election.

Was Bragg indeed inspired by Dewey's example? Apparently so. Bragg recently said: "In the 1930s, District Attorney Thomas Dewey ushered in the era of the modern, independent, professional prosecutor. For now nearly 90 years dedicated professionals in this Office have built upon that fine tradition."

While Trump was found guilty in a New York state court, two federal cases against him remain mired in procedural quicksand thanks to the questionable actions of federal judges.

In the initial investigation of Trump's misappropriation of classified materials in Florida, federal Judge Aileen Cannon's rulings have dragged out the investigation and the case from the get-go. During the investigative phases, she paid deference to Trump because of the risk of "reputational harm." A federal appellate court overturned her decision, finding "the district court stepped in with its own reasoning," but the process still delayed the indictment by months. Since she was assigned to the criminal case, she's deferred the trial date and not set a new one. There's virtually no chance now for trial before this November's election.

In a District of Columbia federal court, Trump is facing charges of spreading false claims about the November 2020 presidential election, disrupting certification of President Joe Biden's victory, and seeking to "oppress, threaten and intimidate" people in their right to vote. When Trump's lawyers argued that he was immune to prosecution for these acts, the Supreme Court reached down to stop the progress of the trial. The justices could have made an immediate ruling, but they waited first for an appeals court to hear the case. That court ruled unanimously that the case could proceed. The Supreme Court then interceded and scheduled argument for the very end of its term. Justice Neil Gorsuch defended the foot-dragging by pronouncing, "We're writing a rule for the ages."

Are the federal courts unduly influenced by loyalty to Trump? Justice Gorsuch was appointed by Trump. Pro-insurrection flags flew over the home and beach house of Justice Samuel Alito. Virginia Thomas, wife of Justice Clarence Thomas, sent texts to Trump's chief of staff in November 2020 falsely claiming, "Biden and the Left is attempting the greatest Heist of our History." Judge Cannon, whose decisions favor delay, was nominated by Trump when he was president and confirmed by the Senate in the days after he had lost the election but before he left office.

It really doesn't matter whether the judges are in fact fair-minded. It can be reasonably argued they are not, and federal law says, "Any justice, judge or magistrate judge of the United States shall disqualify himself in any proceeding in which his impartiality might reasonably be questioned."

After his New York conviction, Trump said, "The real verdict is going to be November 5, by the people." He is correct. If he wins the presidency, he will appoint DOJ officials who will drop both the Florida and D.C. cases against him.

Bravo to Tom Dewey's successor Alvin Bragg who ensured Trump faced a New York state jury verdict in 2024. Shame on the judges who are enabling Trump to avoid the same consequence in federal courts.

Putin and Hamas: Two Contemptible Peas From the Same Rotten Pod

June 12, 2024

Russia's aims and tactics in its war against Ukraine and Hamas' in its war against Israel are remarkably similar.

Russia's troops poured across its border with Ukraine on Feb. 24, 2022. It was the largest invasion of an independent country in Europe since World War II.

Hamas terrorists crossed into the United Nations-recognized state of Israel on Oct. 7, 2023. Over 1,200 Israeli citizens and residents and foreign visitors were murdered. It was the largest loss of Jewish life on a single day since World War II.

President Vladimir Putin justified the invasion by saying the U.N.-recognized state of Ukraine was an "artificial" state that historically belonged to Russia. On top of that, he charged, Ukraine is a hotbed of "neo-Nazism."

The Hamas Covenant says the organization's purpose is to "obliterate" Israel and to capture "Islamic land." The covenant, in a cruel twist on history, accuses Israel of "Zionist Nazi activities."

Russia is shelling power plants and apartment houses to undermine Ukraine's will to resist. Oxfam has estimated an average of 42 Ukrainian civilians have been killed each day since February 2022.

Hamas regularly shells cities, farms and kibbutzim in southern Israel. But even more fundamental to its strategy than killing Israeli civilians is provoking the death of Arab civilians in Gaza. Armed Hamas fighters hide among noncombatants and use them as shields. The ensuing bloodshed is effective as a tactic; it's leading the West to turn against Israel and encouraging protests in Israel itself. Six years ago, Yahya Sinwar, the military commander of Hamas in Gaza, said: "We make the headlines only with blood. No blood, no news." More recently, he said deaths of civilians in Gaza "are necessary sacrifices."

Rape and sexual violence are also key elements of both Russia's and Hamas' strategy. A 2023 U.N. report found, "During Russian armed forces' initial control of localities in Ukraine, many of the ... rapes, and sexual violence were committed in the context of house-to-house searches." These crimes continue.

A report by Pramila Patten, special representative of the U.N. secretary-general, described "rape and gang rape" during Hamas' Oct. 7 attack on Israel. Her investigation "found that several fully naked or partially naked bodies from the waist down were recovered — mostly women — with hands tied and shot multiple times, often in the head."

Hostage-taking and kidnapping are other common tactics of Russia and Hamas. Ukraine accuses Russia of kidnapping over 19,000 children. The New York Times managed to trace what happened to 46 children abducted from a Ukrainian foster center at the outset of the war. Many were adopted by Russian families.

Hamas abducted over 240 civilians and soldiers from Israel on Oct. 7. Those hostages, according to the U.N., were also subject to rape and sexual abuse. Forty-three of them have died in captivity according to Israeli estimates. A Hamas spokesperson said that a consequence of the recent rescue of four Israeli hostages will be "negative impact" on the conditions for the 100-plus remaining hostages.

Putin has called for a permanent ceasefire which would leave his troops in control of 18% of Ukraine. Hamas has called for a permanent ceasefire that would leave it in power in Gaza. To both Putin and Hamas, "permanent" means until ready to launch another attack. Knowingly or not, they wish to follow in the footsteps of Germany before World War II.

In 1938, Nazi Germany demanded the annexation of German-speaking parts of Czechoslovakia, promising no further claims on the country. British Prime Minister Neville Chamberlain said acceding to this demand and appeasing Germany meant "peace for our time." Six months later, German troops invaded what was left of Czechoslovakia. After another six months, German troops invaded Poland, and World War II had begun.

Ukrainian President Volodymyr Zelenskyy understands the ceasefire Putin wants would mean only a delay in Russian ambitions. To Zelenskyy, the only acceptable ceasefire is one where Russia withdraws from all Ukrainian territory and Russian war criminals are tried. In a January speech to the World Economic Forum in Switzerland, he reminded listeners: "After 2014, there were attempts to freeze the war in (the Ukrainian province) Donbas. There were very influential guarantors of that process ... But Putin is a predator who is not satisfied with frozen products."

Israeli Prime Minister Benjamin Netanyahu says Israel's No. 1 goal in the Israel-Hamas war is "the destruction of Hamas." To leave it in power would only mean more attacks on Israel in the future. Despite well-publicized disagreements between Netanyahu and President Joe Biden, they agree on this. As national security adviser Jake Sullivan reported earlier this month, Biden has "explicitly said that the path forward is a Gaza where Hamas is no longer in power."

In a January 1940 radio speech, future British Prime Minister Winston Churchill denounced appeasers in his own inimitable way: "Each one hopes that if he feeds the crocodile enough, the crocodile will eat him last. All of them hope that the storm will pass before their turn comes to be devoured. But I fear — I fear greatly — the storm will not pass. It will rage and it will roar, ever more loudly, ever more widely."

The only outcome that can lead to long-term peace between Ukraine and Russia is the end of Putin's regime. The only outcome that can lead to peace in Gaza and Israel is Hamas' overthrow.

As Churchill also declared, "No pact with unrepentant wrong."

The Handwriting on the Wall for Religion in the Classroom and Gay Marriage

June 26, 2024

On June 20, the governor of Louisiana signed into law a requirement that the Ten Commandments be posted in public school classrooms throughout the state. The statute applies to the rooms where kindergartners are taught their ABCs as well as to the LSU Health New Orleans School of Medicine where prospective doctors learn anatomy.

The law sure appears to be unconstitutional on its face. In 1980, the U.S. Supreme Court ruled in Stone v. Graham that posting the Commandments in the classroom violates the First Amendment's prohibition on government establishment of religion. And yet, it's not hard to see why Louisiana is giving it another go 44 years later.

In the 1973 case of Roe v. Wade, the Supreme Court held that the 14th Amendment gave women a right to an abortion in the first six months of pregnancy. In the 2022 case of Dobbs v. Jackson Women's Health, the court overturned Roe, returning to the states the authority to regulate abortions. Why not see if the court will follow a similar path in overturning Stone?

The First Amendment begins, "Congress shall make no law respecting an establishment of religion..." In the early days of the republic, the amendment was understood to prohibit federal interference in a state's establishment of religion. For example, the Congregational Church remained the state religion in Massachusetts until the 1830s.

Only in 1947 did the Supreme Court rule the 14th Amendment extends the prohibition on establishing a religion to state and local governments. Louisiana is hoping, à la Dobbs, that the Court will ignore the 14th Amendment and return the question of establishment of religion to the states.

And, without doubt, the Louisiana law establishes a state religion.

Of course, what's posted in the Louisiana classrooms will be in English, not the original Hebrew. The source of the wording appears to be an early 1950s poster of the Youth Guidance Commission of the Fraternal Order of Eagles. At that time, the Eagles excluded non-Caucasians. In a case of history being stranger than fiction, the wording was used in a marketing campaign for the 1956 epic film "The Ten Commandments" starring Charlton Heston. In any case, the exact words are prescribed in a form that's been shortened, edited and even mistranslated from the Bibles I consulted.

For example, the Louisiana/Eagles version of the commandments contains only eight words pertaining to the Sabbath: "Remember the Sabbath day, to keep it holy." The King James translation of the Bible includes an additional 86 words that go into far greater detail. Also posted will be the injunction, "Thou shalt not kill." Biblical scholarship says the commandment should be translated to read "Thou shalt not murder." As Professor Berel Lang of Trinity College wrote: "The original Hebrew, lo tirtsah, is very clear, since the verb ratsah. means 'murder,' not 'kill.' If the commandment proscribed killing as such, it would position Judaism against capital punishment and make it pacifist even in wartime. These may be defensible or admirable views, but they're certainly not biblical."

The Ten Commandments appear in the Hebrew Bible (often referred to as "the Old Testament"), which is held sacred by Christianity and Judaism. However, what's being posted in Louisiana are not the holy words of either. Nor are they in any manner, shape or form from the holy writings of Islam, Buddhism, Hinduism or the multitude of other religions practiced in the state.

Why then post the Louisiana/Eagles version of the Ten Commandments? Governor Jeff Landry explains, "If you want to respect the rule of law, you've got to start from the original law giver, which was Moses."

That might be according to the Louisiana Bible, but the original lawgiver in my Bible is not Moses. He is simply transmitting God's word to the Hebrews. In the King James version, Exodus chapter 20 begins, "And God spake all these words."

On top of that, from a historical perspective, there were other laws before the time of Moses. For example, the Babylonian King Hammurabi, who lived at least two centuries earlier, set down a legal code. It predates the Bible in saying if one person "should blind the eye of another, they shall blind his eye."

I guess Louisiana state officials cannot resist fighting a rearguard action to maintain their own beliefs as supreme. In 1972, 90% of adults in the United States were Christians, while in 2022, it was 63%. According to Pew Research, over 80% of Americans older than 75 are Christian, while only about 50% of those 20-34 are.

A futile fight against a demographic tidal wave is underway. First, the decision on whether to ban abortion was returned to the states. And now, the federal ban on establishment of religion is being challenged.

Next on the list looks to be the constitutional right to gay marriage. Justice Clarence Thomas wrote in the Dobbs decision that the Supreme Court has a duty to "correct the error" and give the states back the authority to ban gay marriages. According to a recent Gallup poll, Republican support for gay marriage has fallen from 55% in 2022 to 46% today.

The question today is how this Supreme Court will follow up on its decision to return legislating on abortion back to the states. Is the responsibility to legislate on whether to establish a state religion and whether to allow gay marriage going to return to the states, too?

As is written in the Bible's Book of Daniel, "the handwriting is on the wall."

It's Time To Save the Republic From This Supreme Court

July 3, 2024

The Supreme Court's decision in the presidential immunity case Trump v. United States issued on July 1 has made clear what's at stake in the November elections. It's whether the American republic survives.

Sanford Levinson of the University of Texas Law School has written: "The Constitution is simply whatever the Supreme Court says it is." A majority of the current justices show the truth of the professor's words. To reach their desired result, sometimes they ignore words that are in the text of the Constitution, and sometimes they rely on their imagination to insert words that are not.

In Dobbs v. Jackson Women's Health Organization, the Court overturned Roe v. Wade, by a 6-3 vote, and abolished the constitutional right to an abortion. Why? Because a right to abortion has "no firm grounding in constitutional text, history, or precedent."

It didn't matter to the same six justices in the Trump case that they were granting presidents sweeping immunity without the so-called "firm grounding" they'd required in Dobbs. Writing for the majority, Chief Justice John Roberts concludes "the President is absolutely immune from criminal prosecution for conduct within his exclusive sphere of constitutional authority." In the "outer perimeters" of their authority, presidents receive a "presumption" of immunity.

The majority apparently reached the conclusion they desired and only then found the reasoning to back it up. Inconsistency did not matter. In her scathing dissent, Justice Sonia Sotomayor writes, "The majority ... invents an atextual, ahistorical, and unjustifiable immunity that puts the President above the law."

She goes on to point out the Founders were well acquainted with the concept of immunity. The Constitution grants it to senators and representatives "for any Speech or Debate in either House." They did not grant any immunity at all to the president. Sotomayor notes that in "The Federalist Papers," Alexander Hamilton makes "an important distinction between 'the king of Great Britain,' who was 'sacred and inviolable,' and the 'President of the United States,' who 'would be amenable to personal punishment and disgrace.'"

So, Sotomayor asks what happens under the majority's holding if a president "orders the Navy's Seal Team 6 to assassinate a political rival? Immune. Organizes a military coup to hold onto power? Immune. Takes a bribe in exchange for a pardon? Immune. Immune, immune, immune." Richard Nixon would have been immune for everything he did during Watergate.

Back when in office, Trump said, "I have the right to do whatever I want as president." As a current candidate, he promises that when once again in office, he will order Justice Department investigations of "every Marxist prosecutor in America" and take on the role of "a dictator on Day One." Under the Supreme Court's ruling, he will not have to answer for such acts in the courtroom.

Justice Sotomayor finds "a twisted irony in saying, as the majority does, that the person charged to 'take Care that the Laws be faithfully executed' can break them with impunity." Congressional Republicans see no need to fret about that. "Today's ruling by the Court is a victory for former President Trump and all future presidents," says Speaker Mike Johnson (R-La.).

Especially disconcerting is the illegal participation of Justices Samuel Alito and Clarence Thomas in Trump v. United States. Thomas was in the majority on the Trump case. His wife Ginni Thomas texted Trump's chief of staff seven days after the 2020 election: "Help This Great President stand firm, Mark!!! ... The majority knows Biden and the Left is attempting the greatest Heist of our History." After the storming of the Capitol on Jan. 6, 2020, the

American flag flew upside-down at the home of Alito, a signal usually understood to support Trump in his claim the 2020 election was stolen.

Rep. Jamie Raskin, a constitutional law professor, has pointed to Section 28 of the U.S. Code which holds: "Any justice, judge or magistrate judge of the United States shall disqualify himself in any proceeding in which his impartiality might reasonably be questioned." Who can believe that Alito and Thomas' impartiality cannot be questioned? In their own minds, then, the two justices get some immunity from the laws of the land, too.

After the drafting of the Constitution was completed in 1787, Benjamin Franklin was asked, "Well, Doctor, what have we got, a republic or a monarchy?" He replied, "A republic, if you can keep it." In their ruling in Trump v. United States 237 years later, six justices of the Supreme Court decided they did not wish to keep it. "In every use of official power, the President is now a king above the law," Sotomayor noted in her dissent.

What to do? The only practicable way to overturn the Supreme Court's decision in the next decade is to appoint additional justices who will provide a majority to uphold fundamental constitutional values. The number of nine justices is not engraved in stone. In fact, it isn't even written in the Constitution. A law enacted in 1869 increased the number from seven to nine. Let's increase it to 15. To pass a law to do that and appoint six more justices, Democrats will have to win control of both houses of Congress and the White House in the November election.

Last year, President Joe Biden said, "If we start the process of trying to expand the court, we are going to politicize it maybe forever, in a way that is not healthy." Even if that were the right position then, it is not now, when the republic is on life support.

All Democratic candidates, whether running for the White House or Congress, must run against a court that has run amok. And it's critical that we voters defend our republic at the ballot box this November.

A Letter to Joe: You've Had a Great Run. Now It's Time To Pass the Baton.

July 10, 2024

Dear Joe,

On the wall of my office is your letter thanking me for my help in passing a bill which protects national security. That's from when you were a member of the Senate Intelligence Committee, and I was counsel to the committee.

If a vote had been taken in the 1980s by Capitol Hill insiders on who was the fastest-on-his-feet elected member, you would have won. At a hearing on that bill mentioned above — or was it a press conference? — my House of Representatives counterpart sighed with envy, "I wish I worked for someone that smart and articulate."

When Robert Hur, the Republican special counsel investigating charges for mishandling classified information, called you a "well-meaning, elderly man with a poor memory" last March, I blamed it on partisanship. When the Wall Street Journal ran a story in early June headlined "Behind Closed Doors, Biden Shows Signs of Slipping," I attributed it to the paper's well-known anti-Biden bias.

I was wrong.

I watched your debate with Trump on June 27. This was not the Joe Biden I once knew, not even close. You excused your performance by saying that you had "a really bad cold," that you needed to sleep more, that you'd been affected by international travel completed 11 days before the debate. On July 7, I watched your television interview with George Stephanopoulos. It was a performance reminiscent of the debate — often fumbling and inarticulate.

In a 1933 Marx Brothers movie, Chico asks, "Well, who ya gonna believe, me or your own eyes?" Sorry, Joe. I am going to believe my own eyes.

Your campaign aides point to your strong performance the day after the debate in North Carolina. Even granting that, I'm reminded of an elderly father's children who say, "He has good days and bad days."

Throwing you under the bus isn't fair. If anyone should be denied a major party nomination, it's the ex-president, not you, the current one.

Trump's performance in the debate undercuts his pitch to be president far more than any stumbles you made. He lied when he said that during his presidency, we had "the greatest economy in the history of our country and we have never done so well." The top year of growth in the gross domestic product under Trump was 2.9% in 2018, far short of Truman's top year of 8.7%, Johnson's 6.6%, Clinton's 4.8% and your 5.9%. Trump accused you of allowing "millions of people to come in here from prisons, jails and mental institutions to come into our country and destroy our country" and boasted that "Every legal scholar throughout the world" wanted to overturn Roe v. Wade. Both these assertions and many more he made during the debate were, in one of your favorite words, "malarkey."

On the campaign trail, Trump called the nation of Argentina "a great guy" who "loves Trump." Last month, he suggested migrants on the Southern border form a "fight club" to challenge the Ultimate Fighting Championship. On trial for a criminal conspiracy to cover up a potential sex scandal ahead of the 2016 presidential election, Trump fell asleep multiple times. And to know Trump is not to love him. His former Defense Secretary Mike Esper called him "a threat to democracy," his former chief of staff General John Kelly denounced him as "a person that has nothing but contempt for our democratic institutions" and his former vice president, Mike

Pence, refused to endorse him because he puts himself "over the Constitution."

I've always thought what matters most in life is not what one says, but what one does. On that basis, you trounce your predecessor. You rallied support for Ukraine and oversaw passage of an infrastructure law. More Americans are working today than ever before, and the stock market has reached all-time highs. In the three weeks after you restricted asylum on the U.S.-Mexican border at the beginning of June, illegal entries dropped by 40%. In the three years after 2020, annual job growth in just under 1,000 of the nation's poorest counties grew more than five times faster than in the previous three years.

And yet you still trail in the polls. As I wrote in a column last December, "If Biden cannot tell a better story than the one he is telling, he will lose." And you have fallen further behind since the debate.

With Presidents Vladimir Putin in Russia, President Xi Jinping in China, leader Kim Jong Un in North Korea and supreme leader Ayatollah Ali Khamenei in Iran, we face a dangerous world. We don't want a president like Trump, who according to General John Kelly "admires autocrats and murderous dictators," to be the one who faces them.

The pollster Nate Silver estimates you have at most a 29% chance of winning in November. American voters apparently prefer a blustering liar with meager accomplishments over one who gets stuff done while stumbling and hesitating. It's as if the economy, Supreme Court appointments, NATO, democracy and civil liberties don't matter.

Joe, I am so proud to have worked with you back in the day. I am proud to be one of the Americans who voted for you in 2020. I want you to be remembered as the president whose accomplishments rival those of Lyndon Johnson and Franklin Roosevelt — not as the person who enabled a second term for Donald Trump, who was found by a New York trial court to be a rapist and by the Colorado Supreme Court to be an insurrectionist.

Nancy Pelosi stepped down as speaker at age 82, the same age you'll be at the end of your current term. She's said that time is running short for you to make a final decision whether to run.

It is indeed time for you to yield the Democratic nomination to a candidate who can articulately and energetically carry on your admirable legacy.

With deference, respect and gratitude,

Keith

Trump Continues To Break the Laws of Probability

July 17, 2024

In 2009, Patricia Demauro held the dice at a craps table in Atlantic City for a record 154 rolls. Given the stakes involved, Ms. Demauro's lucky streak doesn't amount to much compared to the roll former President Donald J. Trump is on.

On July 13, an assassin fired an AR-15 style semiautomatic rifle at presidential candidate Trump that nipped his right ear. Move the shot over 3 inches to his left, and he would have died instantly. Lifesaving luck. If the bullet that killed the less fortunate Robert Kennedy during his 1968 presidential campaign had been shifted a few inches, he could have survived, too.

Three days later came another stroke of luck for the former president. He had been indicted in June 2023 on 37 counts for unlawful possession of classified documents. Photographs show he'd hidden some of the material from the FBI in a bathroom at his Mar-a-Lago residence in Florida. U.S. district court judge Aileen Cannon, a Trump appointee, had previously made a decision in his favor where she'd "abused" her "discretion" according to an appeals court. Cannon had a one in four chance of being assigned as trial judge in the classified documents case. Trump won that roll of the dice. Then on July 15 of this year, Judge Cannon threw out the case against him based on reasoning that had been explicitly rejected by the Supreme Court a half-century ago in U.S. v. Nixon.

Trump received another gift from the current Supreme Court this month. His attorneys had argued the former president could not be tried for his attempts to overturn the 2020 election result unless he was first convicted by the Senate in an impeachment trial. The court gave him much more than that. A majority of six justices handed him a gift of absolute immunity from prosecution for actions "within his exclusive sphere of constitutional authority" and a presumption of immunity for actions "within the outer perimeter of his official responsibility." Neither the historical record nor the plain language of the Constitution gave the president such immunity. Merry Christmas in July, Donald J. Trump!

That wasn't the first time during the current presidential campaign the Supreme Court majority relied on their imagination to insert words into the Constitution. The document's Fourteenth Amendment prohibits anyone from taking federal or state office who "shall have engaged in insurrection or rebellion" against the United States, or "given aid or comfort to the enemies thereof." Colorado courts found Trump had done just that. In March of this year, the U.S. Supreme Court waved its wand, and, poof, there was a new rule saying Congress had to pass a law to enable the amendment's provision. O lucky man, Trump kept his place on the Colorado ballot.

Trump's record of good fortune stretches much further back than 2024.

Of course, he was born lucky. A 2018 article from The New York Times put this into perspective: "By age 3, Mr. Trump was earning over $200,000 a year in today's dollars from his father's real estate empire. He was a millionaire by age 8."

In the last half-century, at least 25 women have accused Trump of nonconsensual kissing or groping. He admitted to this type of behavior when he was caught on tape in 2005 saying, "And when you're a star, they let you do it. You can do anything. ... Grab 'em by the (private parts)." He suffered no consequences in the courts for such behavior until he was found to be a rapist in E. Jean Carroll's defamation suit last year. But he lucked out there, too. That was a civil trial for defamation — the statute of limitations had run out on bringing a criminal case.

There were 57 presidential elections prior to 2016. In 53 of them, or about 93%, the winner of the popular vote also won the Electoral College. Again, Trump defied the odds. Although former Secretary of State Hillary Rodham Clinton outpolled Trump by about 3 million votes in 2016, he prevailed in the electoral vote 304-227.

In early April of this year, a YouGov poll found more than two-thirds of respondents, including a majority of Republicans, believed a person convicted of a felony should not be allowed to become president. The next month, a unanimous jury of 12 New Yorkers did find Trump guilty of 34 felony counts for falsifying records to hide information that would have influenced the 2016 presidential election. Trump is lucky enough to have some kind of magic wand that showered amnesia over the electorate. He currently leads in the presidential polls.

I could go on and discuss the record of Trump's businesses of discriminating in housing and declaring bankruptcies and of Trump himself encouraging violence, belittling the handicapped, defending white nationalists and much more, but why bother? Suffice it to say he had the luck to get away with all of it.

The German chancellor Otto von Bismarck reputedly said there is "special providence for fools, drunkards, and the United States of America." Of course, that doesn't apply to all Americans, but it does certainly seem to apply to Donald J. Trump.

Or as my wife asked me the other day, "Do you think he has a guardian devil?"

Despite Political Rhetoric, America Does Not Encourage Couples To Have Children

July 31, 2024

Iowa's Gov. Kim Reynolds recently stated there is "no cause more worthy than protecting innocent unborn lives." Please allow me to suggest one. How about supporting innocent *born* lives?

It certainly does appear the Hawkeye State governor cares more for the unborn than children living outside the womb. Last January, she was one of 16 Republican governors who turned down federal aid for children's food aid this summer. A failure to get enough nutrition may lead to short height, behavior problems and developmental delays in a child. Iowa Hunger Coalition Board Chair Luke Elzinga noted Iowa has "food banks and food pantries across the state assisting record-breaking numbers of people."

Republican vice presidential nominee Sen. J.D. Vance also believes in families with children. Maybe what he called "childless cat ladies" would decide to have kids if they were bearing them in a country where the government supported their choice. Did it occur to Vance, Reynolds or the other governors who refused federal aid that women who worry about feeding potential offspring would be less likely to have them?

But the concerns of couples contemplating parenthood go beyond providing nutrition. According to a Pew Research poll, 36% of adults under 50 without children cite the expense of raising children as a deterrent to having them. The fact the average American house costs $501,700, up $236,400 in constant dollars over the last two decades, has to be a major deterrent to enlarging family size. The Republican response? A proposed House budget for 2025 that cuts support for housing and transportation by 4.3% and rejects President Joe Biden's proposal for a tax credit for first-time homebuyers and for building or preserving 2 million housing units.

Daycare runs an average of around $16,000 for a child in 2024. According to Bank of America, these high costs may be driving women out of the workforce. Logic dictates they also deter couples from having children at all. How do other countries handle this problem? In 2021, Norway contributed $30,000 per year for a young child's care, and Spain contributed $10,000. The U.S. coughed up $500, the lowest among 16 rich countries.

Costs are scary, too, for prospective parents once any children reach their late teens. At a time when a bachelor's degree is seen as a key to economic success, prospective parents must fear the burden of paying college tuition, which has gone up more than three times in constant dollars since 1963. The provision for free community college in Biden's 2025 budget proposal has little chance of passing over Republican opposition.

It's not just a matter of money, either. The year 2023 was the hottest on record, and chances are 2024 will be hotter still. I contacted Dr. Lise Van Susteren, a psychiatrist who specializes in the physical and mental health effects of climate disruption. She told me the young adults she sees are "struggling with whether it is ethical to bring a child into the world when climate change will create chaotic life-threatening conditions."

At a Mar-a-Lago dinner this past April, former President Donald Trump told energy executives from ExxonMobil and other companies that they should donate $1 billion to his campaign since he was committed to undoing Biden administration clean air policies. His running mate is also supporting repeal of electric vehicle tax credits and pollution regulations. Dr. Van Susteren says, "Nothing makes young adults feel more betrayed than when politicians know there is a problem and do nothing about it."

What does it say about American support for having children when the United States offers no nationally paid maternity leave?

The other six countries in the United Nations that do not are the Marshall Islands, Micronesia, Nauru, Palau, Papua New Guinea and Tonga.

No wonder the number of U.S. adults younger than 50 without children who say they aren't likely to ever have them rose from 37% to 47% between 2018 and 2023. The fertility rate per woman of childbearing age in the U.S. has fallen from 2.05 kids to 1.79 in the past 30 years.

The way to encourage couples to have children in the United States is not through criticism, nor is it declaring sympathy only for the unborn. Common sense dictates that a United States with support for nutrition, housing, daycare, parental leave and education will lead to more American families with children. Voters who care about these issues might want to listen carefully to candidates between now and Election Day.

Harris Makes Good Choice for Running Mate, but Not the Best

August 7, 2024

Minnesota Gov. Tim Walz seems bright, articulate, genuine and a solid selection as Kamala Harris' running mate. But he's not the best one.

Pennsylvania Gov. Josh Shapiro would have made a better choice for two important reasons. First and foremost, he would have given her a better chance to win in November. Secondly, if Harris had tapped Shapiro, she would have won approval for standing up to left-wing antisemitism in her party.

Of course, job No. 1 for Harris is winning the White House.

In earlier days, her opponent, former President Donald Trump, would have disqualified himself for the presidency on numerous grounds. He's been judged a rapist by a civil jury and a felon by a criminal jury. He's vowed to pardon insurrectionists currently in jail for attacking police officers at the Capitol's Jan. 6 insurrection. He's threatened to give Russian President Vladimir Putin a free hand in Europe. He's advocating pushing for the repeal of the Affordable Care Act, which helps provide medical insurance to 45 million Americans. He's appointed three judges to the Supreme Court who voted to overturn half a century of voting protection for minorities and of bodily autonomy for women.

Critical to a Harris victory in November 2024 is carrying Pennsylvania. The Keystone State won that nickname due to its position in the middle of the original 13 colonies. The tag is apt now for a second reason. The candidate who carried the state has won the last four presidential elections. According to polling maven Nate Silver, Harris has only a 4% chance of winning the presidency if Trump carries Pennsylvania.

As I write, The Washington Post's average of polls shows a dead heat in Pennsylvania. That's no surprise. Trump carried the state by a razor-thin 0.72% in 2016 and President Joe Biden by a similar 1.17% in 2020.

A Fox News poll last month shows 61% of Keystone State voters approve of Shapiro with 32% disapproving, while 49% approve of Harris with an identical 49% disapproving. Here's the arithmetic, then: If Shapiro on the ticket changes the vote of even 1 in 50 Pennsylvanians from Republican to Democratic, Harris is bound to carry the state. With Shapiro on the ticket, I'd tell Harris she should call Mayflower now to reserve a van to move her family's belongings into the White House on Jan. 20.

Harris does not need Walz in order to carry his home state of Minnesota. The Gopher State has gone Democratic the past 12 presidential elections, including 1980 when it was the only state in the union to do so. Harris's choice of Walz followed a version of the Hippocratic oath: First, do no harm. Trump's choice of JD Vance failed on that score. Harris' choice of Walz with his Midwestern charm and backstory as a high school coach will not.

Now on to the second reason Harris should have chosen Shapiro.

No issue is more contentious among Democrats than the Israeli-Hamas War. Shapiro's strong support of Israel's right to exist matches that of most of the party. A March poll showed Americans believe Israel's reasons for fighting Hamas were valid by 61% to 15%. Two anti-Israel Democratic representatives have lost primaries this election cycle including Missouri's Cori Bush who accuses Israel of "war crimes." Shapiro was out front when he called Israeli Prime Minister Netanyahu "one of the worst leaders of all time" last January. Senate Majority Leader Chuck Schumer called for Netanyahu to step down two months later.

Americans oppose violent protests against the war. As President Biden said, "Violent protest is not protected. Peaceful protest is." Shapiro has taken the same position, stating, "What we're seeing in some campuses across America, where universities can't guarantee the safety and security of their students, it's absolutely unacceptable."

Nevertheless, left-wing congressional staffers along with members of the Democratic Socialists of America have been working to deny Shapiro the vice presidential nomination. The website nogenocidejosh.com urged supporters to "Tell Kamala and the Democrats now: Say no to Genocide Josh Shapiro for Vice President!"

Here, the simplest explanation is most likely to be true: Shapiro is being singled out for his support of Israel because he is Jewish. As Rep. Ritchie Torres, D-N.Y., said: "Every potential nominee for Vice President is pro-Israel. Yet only one, Josh Shapiro, has been singled out by a far-left smear campaign calling him 'Genocide Josh.' The reason he is treated differently from the rest? Antisemitism."

Vice President Harris is no antisemite. Her husband is Jewish. Her stepchildren call her "Momala," a play on her name and "Mamaleh," Yiddish for "Mommy."

Still, choosing Shapiro did provide Harris with a golden opportunity to firmly reject left-wing antisemitism. In the wake of 1992 race riots in Los Angeles, the artist and activist Sister Souljah asked, "Why not have a week and kill white people?" At a time when Jesse Jackson had strong support on the left wing of the Democratic Party, candidate Bill Clinton denounced Souljah as a racist and extremist, which reassured voters and gave impetus to his candidacy. What worked for Clinton would have worked for Harris. She could have had her Sister Souljah moment in choosing Shapiro.

When it comes to vice presidential nominees, JD Vance said: "My attitude is, it doesn't really matter. ... People are going to vote primarily for Donald Trump or for Kamala Harris. That's the way these things go." Now that Harris has selected Walz rather than

Shapiro, I am in the uncharacteristic position of agreeing with Vance.

If Harris loses Pennsylvania, she will almost certainly lose the presidency. Her choice of Walz over Shapiro means the burden is all on her shoulders.

In a Topsy-Turvy Campaign, Dems Support Freedom, Foreign Affairs, Flag and Football

August 28, 2024

It's no surprise that one party is staking a claim on the White House based on freedom, foreign affairs, family and football. The surprise in 2024's topsy-turvy campaign is that it's the Democrats, not the Republicans, who are embracing those four pillars.

1. Freedom

Running on their "Contract with America" in the election of 1994, Republicans won a majority in both the House and Senate for the first time in over four decades. Grover Norquist, a key engineer of that strategy, boasted "the imperial city of Washington will fall to the forces of freedom."

While Norquist dedicated himself to building the "Leave Us Alone" coalition back in the 1990s, Republicans now seem determined to interject the federal government into the doctor's examining room, the marital bedroom and the school library. It's Democratic vice presidential nominee Tim Walz who declares, "We respect our neighbors and the personal choices they make. And even if we wouldn't make those same choices for ourselves, we've got a golden rule: Mind your own damn business."

Freedom has definitely become the byword of this year's Democratic campaign. In her address at the Democratic National Convention, Vice President Kamala Harris accused her opponent former President Donald Trump of taking away "reproductive freedom" from American women. She went on to tick off her support for the freedom "to live safe from gun violence," "to love who you love openly," "to breath clean air and drink clean water," and "to vote."

2. Foreign Affairs

Republican presidents have a tradition of support for NATO and standing against Russian aggression. Two years before his run for the White House, Dwight Eisenhower took an indefinite leave as president of Columbia University to become the commanding general of NATO. In 1987, President Ronald Reagan stood at the Brandenburg Gate dividing West and East Berlin and told Russian leader Mikhail Gorbachev to "tear down this wall." By contrast, Trump as president threatened to leave NATO. After the Russian invasion of Ukraine in 2022, current Republican vice presidential candidate JD Vance said: "I gotta be honest with you, I don't really care what happens to Ukraine one way or another." Eisenhower and Reagan must be spinning in their graves.

In the 2024 campaign, Democrats are supporting an active and muscular foreign policy based on opposition to Russia and China. Regarding the Russian attack on Ukraine, Harris declared, "I helped mobilize a global response — over 50 countries — to defend against Putin's aggression. And as president, I will stand strong with Ukraine and our NATO allies." She also promised to see "that America, not China, wins the competition for the 21st century and that we strengthen, not abdicate, our global leadership."

3. Flag

Every Republican president since World War II has served in the military except Trump. In a 1993 interview, Trump said avoiding sexually transmitted diseases in the 1980s was "the equivalent of a soldier going over to Vietnam" and called women's vaginas "potential landmines." In 2018, then-President Trump skipped a visit to an American military cemetery in France, reportedly saying, "Why should I go to that cemetery? It's filled with losers."

Now the Democrats have nominated a man as vice president who spent 24 years in the Army National Guard and who, unlike all those Republican presidents, was an enlisted man, not an officer. On the campaign trail, Walz declared, "I'm proud to have served my country and I always will be." Delegates at the Democratic convention waved flags and chanted "USA." This summer, Harris condemned flag-burning during anti-Israel protests as "despicable," writing, "That flag is a symbol of our highest ideals as a nation and represents the promise of America."

Embracing the flag could prove good politics. A YouGov poll in June showed 30% of independent voters thought of the Republican Party as "patriotic" while only 13% thought the same of Democrats. There are votes to be won there. Former GOP Rep. Adam Kinzinger was invited to address the Democratic convention, where he said, "I've learned something about the Democratic Party, and I want to let my fellow Republicans in on the secret: The Democrats are as patriotic as us."

4. Football

Republican President Eisenhower played college football for Army and Gerald Ford for Michigan. Reagan was known as "the Gipper" for playing Notre Dame football great George Gipp on the silver screen. Trump urged football legend Herschel Walker to run for a Georgia Senate seat in 2022.

Now it's Democratic vice presidential nominee Walz who's the candidate most strongly identified with America's favorite sport. The party plays up his role as defensive coordinator at Minnesota's Mankato West High School, which won the 1999 state football championship. "I like to call him Coach Walz," Harris says. The campaign's website is offering a Coach's Collection that includes a football-shaped patch with the words "Team Harris Walz." At the convention, Walz leaned into past glory: "It's the fourth quarter. We're down a field goal, but we're on offense, and we've got the ball. We're driving down the field, and boy, do we have the right team."

The Trump team has fumbled the ball regarding a proven strategy. Harris' team has scooped it up and are speeding toward the goal line with it securely held.

Who Cares What the Calendar Says? Happy New Year!

September 4, 2024

We don't need to wait for January. I say a new year has just started.

The sweltering days of summer are gone. Memories of the visit to the beach, to Disney World and to grandmother's house are fading fast. The last morsel of leftover potato salad from the Labor Day picnic has been eaten. The scent of autumn is already wafting through the air. Classes are starting at elementary schools, high schools and universities from Hartford to Honolulu, from Juneau to Jacksonville.

As F. Scott Fitzgerald wrote in "The Great Gatsby," often cited as *the* great American novel, "Life starts all over again when it gets crisp in the fall." Yep, it's the start of a new year.

From the time we waddle off to kindergarten at age 5, we're trained to believe a new year starts with the first day of school. By the end of 12th grade, the cycle of the school year has been imprinted on our impressionable brains. If and when we have children, it all floods back.

My own life has come full circle. Seven years ago, my wife and I returned to campus life. In the cafeteria and around the dorm, we speak to fresh-faced undergrads anticipating new challenges, both academic and personal. As Dr. Seuss wrote: "If you keep your eyes open enough, oh, the stuff you will learn! The most wonderful stuff!" (I must admit to a twinge of envy.)

It is indeed the time for new beginnings. The 105th National Football League campaign is just kicking off. Speaking of campaigns, I recently came across a 2016 piece by columnist Dahleen Glanton headlined: "The real presidential campaign begins after Labor Day — God help us." That sentiment seems just as appropriate this September in Trump's third run for the presidency as in his first.

Some of the ancients did have it right. The Assyrians, Egyptians and Phoenicians all believed the year started in what we now call September. For Jews, Rosh Hashanah, literally "the head of the year," usually falls in September (but in October this year). That starts a 10-day period of contemplating the past year and deciding how to do better in the next.

Having the new year begin in January is arbitrary. Pope Gregory XIII moved it there for Catholic countries in 1582. Only in 1750 did the British parliament pass a law that shifted the start of the year in the 13 colonies to Jan. 1 from March 25.

I'm not such a cockeyed optimist to call for any kind of federal legislation to again reset the year's start date. We cannot count on Congress for timely passage to feed hungry children, to defend the borders or to support an ally under attack, so for this? Not a chance in a million. Nevertheless, even without action from Capitol Hill, we can continue to treat this time of the year as the season to embark on new voyages.

A favorite quote from the monk and theologian Thomas Merton inspired the title of my novel "A Fine and Dangerous Season," which of course was set in the fall. He calls the time of year when school starts, "a fine and dangerous season in America. It is dry and cool and... you are full of ambition. It is a wonderful time to begin anything at all."

Amen.

It's Time To Stop the Use of Military-Style Weapons Against Our Schoolchildren

September 11, 2024

The beginning of the school year is indeed the season of glorious end-of-summer weather, learning and new challenges.

It also begins another season of innocent young lives lost to assault rifles.

On Sept. 4, two teachers and two students were gunned down by another student using an AR-15-style rifle at Apalachee High School in Winder, Georgia.

We're not talking about typical handguns or hunting rifles here. An AR-15-style weapon is a close relative of the military-issue M16 rifle designed to kill enemy soldiers. Its bullets carry three to four times the energy of a typical 9 mm handgun. A single bullet can explode a victim's skull. The damage to children is especially devastating.

Sen. Tammy Duckworth, an Iraq war veteran, has asked, "Have you imagined how it would feel when authorities told you that you could not view the body of your murdered child —because there was nothing left of your baby to visually identify?"

In the wake of the Sept. 4 shooting, presidential candidate Donald Trump offered only this consolation: "We are going to make it better and heal our world." Last January, he said people needed to "get over" an Iowa school shooting that left a sixth grader dead. For Trump's running mate JD Vance, school shootings are a "fact of life."

What about legislation to protect school children from military-style weapons? Well, last February, Trump pledged to members of the National Rifle Association that "no one will lay a finger on your firearms" if he is elected president and that "every single Biden attack on gun owners and manufacturers will be terminated on my very first week back in office, perhaps my first day.

In contrast, Democratic presidential candidate Kamala Harris has promised to work for a ban on the sale of assault weapons. Her running mate Tim Walz tweeted in July, "I'm a veteran, a hunter, and a gun owner. But I'm also a dad. And for many years, I was a teacher. ... It's about keeping our kids safe. I had an A rating from the NRA. Now I get straight F's. And I sleep just fine."

In a 6-3 June decision, the Supreme Court overturned a federal ban on using "bump stocks" which enable an AR-15-style weapon to fire continuously when the trigger is held down. Bump stocks were used to fire the over 1,000 rounds that killed 60 people at a 2017 Las Vegas concert. Bump stocks cost a few hundred dollars and are readily available.

Justice Sonia Sotomayor wrote for the three justices in the minority: "Today's decision ... will have deadly consequences. The majority's artificially narrow definition hamstrings the Government's efforts to keep machineguns from gunmen like the Las Vegas shooter. I respectfully dissent."

I myself respectfully dissent from the last three words of Sotomayor's opinion. Why should she "respectfully" dissent from a decision that will cost so many lives? She should have "angrily" or "accusingly" dissented instead.

In addition to the shootings at Apalachee High and the Las Vegas concert, AR-15-style weapons were used at the 2022 Uvalde school shooting (19 students and two teachers murdered), the 2018 Parkland High shooting (14 students and three teachers killed), the 2016 Orlando nightclub shooting (49 deaths with the youngest victim aged 18) and the 2012 Sandy Hook Elementary School shooting (20 students and six teachers killed).

Back in 1993, Congress passed the federal assault weapons ban (the Public Safety and Recreational Firearms Use Protection

Act) that prohibited the purchase and possession of "certain semiautomatic assault weapons," including AR-15-style rifles. In 2003-2004, the two years before the ban expired, there were 16 shooting deaths in K-12 schools. In 2021-22, there were 92.

Now, Americans have over 24 million AR-15-style and similar Russian-style semiautomatic rifles. The ease of acquiring them and bump stocks will inevitably lead to more deaths of children and teens in schools, on streets and at concerts. Some, but not all, members of Congress and justices of the Supreme Court have decided that allowing people to purchase and own military-grade weapons outweighs the value of those lives. In my opinion, they are guilty of reckless homicide.

CNN reports that the Georgia school murders on Sept. 4 were "at least the 45th school shooting in 2024."

It's time for voters to take action at the ballot box to support candidates who take a stand against this slaughter of our children and fellow Americans by military-grade weapons. Otherwise, morally even if not legally, we will be accomplices in their deaths.

Right and Left Both Want To Cancel Books They Don't Like

September 18, 2024

Both the right and the left are waging a war against books.

The right is focusing on schools. According to a PEN America analysis, there were 4,349 instances of U.S. schools banning books in the second half of last year. Utah has banned books by beloved children's author Judy Blume. Stephen King lamented, "Florida has banned 23 of my books. What the f***?"

Under an Arkansas statute passed last year and currently being challenged in the courts, teachers and librarians can be sent to prison for "furnishing a harmful item to a minor." Red states Indiana, Missouri, Oklahoma and Tennessee have also passed such legislation. More than a dozen other mostly red states have similar bills under consideration.

Speaking of the law in his state, Keith Gambill, president of the teachers union in Indiana, told The Washington Post, "It will make sure the only literature students are exposed to fits into a narrow scope of what some people want the world to look like. ... We are entering a very frightening period."

Progressives are fighting the bans. For example, the authors' organization PEN America, which says it stands for protection of "free expression in the United States and worldwide" joined with parents, students and publishers to sue a Florida school board. Their action maintains books were removed from library shelves "based on an ideologically driven campaign to push certain ideas out of schools" in violation of the First Amendment.

Yet while PEN America fights book bans in schools, its members are advocating the suppression of authors based on their political views. Over 1,000 authors signed an open letter dated Feb.

3 that condemned PEN America for sponsoring a conversation between comedian Moshe Kasher and actor Mayim Bialik, who is on the record for believing that "Israel as a homeland for Jews has a right to exist." In its sponsorship, the letter continued, PEN is "offering tacit approval for the Zionist, racist and genocidal regime."

Both presidential nominees have expressed support for Israel's right to protect itself against the terrorist Hamas organization, which murdered over 1,200 people and which, according to the U.N., also committed "rape and gang rape" in its Oct. 7, 2023 attack. Harvard professor and bestselling author Steven Pinker, who wrote a chapter on genocide in his "Better Angels of Our Nature," tweeted, "What Israel is doing may be criticized, but it is in no way 'genocide'; this is a blood libel."

Last May, @moyurireads on X published a spreadsheet classifying 200 authors according to her shaky take on whether the author is pro- or anti-Zionist. The list, which garnered over a million views within a few days of the posting, recommended books by alleged pro-Zionist authors not be "purchased or promoted on social platforms." Taylor Jenkins Reid, author of "Daisy Jones and the Six," should be shunned for posting a photo of a Hamas hostage's father who says, "I want there to be peace, but I also want my daughter to return."

Chicago bookstore City Lit Books removed "Tomorrow and Tomorrow and Tomorrow," one of the 100 best books of the century according to the New York Times, as a potential choice for its monthly book club. According to a news report, assistant manager Charlie Schumann wrote to members, "It was brought to my attention that the author Gabrielle Zevin is a Zionist and I am not comfortable having us reading something by her, especially knowing people would buy it from the store and she would receive monetary support from us."

So where are we now? Red state legislatures want to ban children's access to books based on their version of what's harmful, not that of professional librarians and teachers. Members of the McCarthyite left call for boycotts of authors who do not support their views on the Hamas-Israel war.

So where am I amid all this furor? I don't support either side. As in the classic 1972 song by Steelers Wheel, I am "stuck in the middle" with "clowns to the left of me" and "jokers to the right."

When it comes to school libraries, I'm with Judy Blume, who said, "Let children read whatever they want and then talk about it with them. If parents and kids can talk together, we won't have as much censorship because we won't have as much fear."

When it comes to banning and shunning books based on who wrote them, I'm with President John Kennedy, who said, "We must know all the facts and hear all the alternatives and listen to all the criticisms. Let us welcome controversial books and controversial authors."

I stand for free expression.

Trump Must Wish Only White Men Could Vote (Like in the Good Old Days)

September 25, 2024

It's the job of a conservative to stand before history "yelling stop," said the late political commentator William F. Buckley. Former President Donald Trump and his supporters appear to want to go even further.

They are screaming at history to go backward in order to "make America great again."

Two centuries ago, only white men could vote. If we went back to those days, Trump would not be trailing Harris in the polls but leading by more than 20%.

Before the Civil War, the Supreme Court held that Black people were "so far inferior, that they had no rights which the white man was bound to respect." Only with the 15th Amendment, which took effect in 1870, was the right to vote extended to people of color, at least in theory. When Jim Crow laws continued to block access to the polling booth, Congress passed the Voting Rights Act of 1965. An amendment to the act in 1975 prohibited voting discrimination against non-English-speaking citizens which led to widespread voter registration among Hispanics.

Women did not obtain a constitutionally guaranteed right to vote until the 19th amendment was passed in 1920. Only in 1943 did Congress pass a law giving Chinese immigrants access to citizenship. The door for Asian Americans was opened further by the Immigration and Nationality Acts of 1952 and 1965.

Trump's rhetoric, past and present, does little to hide his disdain for each of these new groups that have been added to the electorate. He's called Black Lives Matters protesters "thugs," "terrorists" and "anarchists." In his debate against Kamala Harris,

Trump lied in accusing legal Black immigrants in Ohio of eating their neighbors' cats and dogs. Researchers have found that white people who resent Black people are even more likely to vote for Trump than those who agree with him on economic issues.

Women? Trump infamously boasted they let allow him to do anything to them including grabbing them by their private parts. He has referred to his current female opponent as "dumb as a rock" in public and reportedly as a "bitch" in private. He has called other women who opposed him "a dog" and "disgusting." His choice of a running mate refuses to retract his attack on prominent Democrats as "childless cat ladies."

In announcing his candidacy for the presidency in 2015, Trump labeled Mexican immigrants as "rapists." Trump claims illegal immigrants, "not just (those from) South America," are "poisoning the blood of our country." At a rally this month, he issued a warning about Hispanic immigrants, declaring that "A vote for Kamala Harris means 40 or 50 million more illegal aliens will invade across our borders, stealing your money, stealing your jobs, stealing your life."

Trump's persistent designation of the COVID-19 virus as the "China Virus" fueled anti-Asian rhetoric, according to a study in the American Journal of Public Health. He insulted his own former labor secretary, the Chinese American Elaine Chao, as "Coco Chow" and denounced her as "crazy."

If actions speak louder than words, voters who are not white males have even more to worry about. Trump's appointments to the Supreme Court have been decisive in undermining the protections of the Voting Rights Act, women's rights to reproductive freedom and Black student access to selective colleges.

Polling indicates Black people, women, Hispanic people and Asian Americans know Trump's record. In a recent New York Times poll, Trump trails his opponent by 12 points among women, by 64 points among Black people and by 12 points among Hispanic people. In a poll focused on Asian Americans and Pacific Islanders, Trump lags by 38 points.

Trump's electoral strategy of focusing on a core of white men while attacking other segments of the electorate is futile in the long run. The census in 1970 showed the U.S. to be 87.5% white. In 2022, the Census Bureau estimated that non-Hispanic white people were 57.7% of all Americans, and about 2 million more women than men voted in the November election.

In a matter of weeks, we'll see whether Trump's strategy to make America great again can win one last time. Or if it will be Harris's proclamation "We won't go back" that carries the day.

Last October's Surprise Attack by Hamas Was Israel's Pearl Harbor

October 2, 2024

In a surprise attack on Dec. 7, 1941, Japanese planes and submarines attacked American forces on Hawaii, killing about 2,400 persons. The next day, the United States declared war on Japan.

In a surprise attack on Oct. 7, 2023, the terrorist group Hamas crossed the border into Israel and killed about 1,200 persons. The next day, Israel declared war on Hamas.

Given the difference in population between 1941 America and 2023 Israel, the Israeli death toll would be equivalent to 17,000 killed at Pearl Harbor.

Japanese aircraft and submarines attacked U.S. naval ships and military bases on Dec. 7, so civilian casualties were less than 5%. In its Oct. 7 attack, Hamas targeted civilians including those at a music festival. Moreover, a United Nations report found Hamas committed "rape and gang rape" including "genital mutilation, sexualized torture" against its victims.

Four days after the attack on Pearl Harbor, Japan's ally Germany declared war on the United States. One day after the Hamas attack on Israel, Hezbollah, like Hamas an Iranian-backed terrorist group, began firing missiles into Israel from its bases in Lebanon.

In April 1943, United States fighter aircraft shot down a plane known to be carrying Japanese Admiral Isoroku Yamamoto, the planner of the Pearl Harbor attack. This Operation Vengeance resulted in his death along with the crew and other passengers. In September 2024, Israeli planes bombed the Hezbollah headquarters in Lebanon resulting in the death of Hassan Nasrallah. It was he who ordered the daily barrage of missiles to be launched from Lebanon into Israel, including the one that killed 12 Israeli Druze children on a soccer field.

The United States signed the Potsdam Declaration in July 1945, which called on "the government of Japan to proclaim now the unconditional surrender of all Japanese armed forces. ... The alternative for Japan is prompt and utter destruction."

In a speech in July 2024, Israeli Prime Minister Benjamin Netanyahu echoed the Potsdam Declaration in calling for victory over Hamas. He told the U.S. Congress, "Like December 7th, 1941... October 7th is a day that will forever live in infamy." He continued, "The war in Gaza could end tomorrow if Hamas surrenders, disarms and returns all the hostages. But if they don't, Israel will fight until we destroy Hamas' military capabilities and its rule in Gaza and bring all our hostages home."

It's difficult to estimate the Japanese World War II casualties caused specifically by the United States as distinguished from those inflicted by allied countries. In any case, overall Japanese military casualties were estimated at 1.7 million while the U.S.'s were 109,000. In perhaps the most destructive bombing raid in history, the March 1945 attack on Tokyo by U.S. bombers is estimated to have killed 100,000 civilians and left over a million homeless. The atomic bombs dropped on Hiroshima and Nagasaki by American bombers killed at least 150,000 more, mostly civilians. Before all three attacks, the U.S. dropped leaflets warning civilians to leave.

Casualties in the war in Gaza are hard to measure. The Gaza Health Ministry cites a number of over 40,000. Numbers from this source, an arm of Hamas, have been criticized as inflated and may include over half combatants. Like the U.S. in World War II, Israel drops leaflets warning civilians of bombings before attacking.

I am no fan of Netanyahu on account of his embrace of the religious right, the charges of corruption and his attempt to undermine his country's Supreme Court. Of course, I am also no fan of former and perhaps future President Donald Trump for the exact same reasons. That doesn't mean, however, that I think either Israel or the U.S. surrenders its right to defend itself against attacks whether on military personnel or civilians.

If the U.S. went to war in 1941 over an attack on Hawaii, then a territory 2,500 miles away from the nearest state, how can Israel be condemned for protecting itself against enemies directly on its border? The Japanese feared American interference in expansion of their empire. The Hamas Covenant calls for the elimination of the state of Israel and for a "holy war" against Jews. Japan never was an existential threat to the United States. Hamas and Hezbollah are such a threat to Israel.

Hamas' stated aim is to destroy Israel and kill Jews. That goal appears to take priority over saving Palestinian Arab lives. Hezbollah attacks on Israel further the aims of Iran. As with Japan and Germany in World War II, the goal of Israel and the United States must be victory over these dark forces. Without doubt, each death is a tragedy. A thousand deaths are a thousand tragedies. Nevertheless, failure this time will lead only to more attacks and more thousands of deaths in the coming years.

Recently, the American government has shown the strongest signs yet of understanding this viewpoint. President Joe Biden called the death of Hezbollah leader Hassan Nasrallah "a measure of justice for his many victims." The United States joined with Israel in protecting the country from 200 ballistic missiles launched on Oct. 1 by Iran, the sponsor and financial backer of Hezbollah. State Department spokesperson Matt Miller declared, "This was a brazen, unacceptable attack by Iran, and every nation in the world must join us in condemning it. ... We will continue to stand with the people of Israel at this critical moment."

The attack on Pearl Harbor led first to the defeat of the attackers and ultimately to peace and prosperity. What should be the end goal in the Middle East war today then? Again defeating the attackers and subsequent peace and prosperity.

Donald Trump, 2024's 'Beetlejuice' Candidate

October 16, 2024

It's not often that Donald Trump engages in understatement, but he did in his oft-repeated statement back in January 2016. "I could stand in the middle of Fifth Avenue and shoot somebody, OK, and I wouldn't lose any voters, OK?" he marveled just before that year's Iowa caucuses. "It's, like, incredible."

To my knowledge, the ex-president has never actually shot anyone. However, he has taken actions that led to the deaths of innocent people and to his conviction on 34 felony counts. And no one seems to care.

At the outset of the COVID-19 pandemic in 2020, then-president Trump reassured the public that things were "under control," although he had multiple reports from his advisers to the contrary. He went so far as to speculate publicly whether bleach or ultraviolet light were suitable treatments for the virus. Later, he admitted to The Washington Post's Bob Woodward, "I wanted to always play it down." A Columbia University report estimated between 130,000 and 210,000 Americans unnecessarily died in the first 10 months of the pandemic due to decisions made by Trump and his administration.

In May 2024, a jury of 12 New Yorkers found Trump guilty of 34 felony counts for falsifying records to hide damaging information that would have influenced the 2016 presidential election. Manhattan District Attorney Alvin Bragg explained, "Mr. Trump went to illegal lengths to lie repeatedly in order to protect himself and his campaign."

Neither the high COVID-19 death rate nor the felony conviction appears to have affected the public's view of Trump. The "incredible" result he predicted has come to pass. He is more popular now just before next month's election than he was eight years ago. On the eve of the 2016 election, the Gallup Poll found him with a favorability rating of 36%. Last month, his rating hit 46%.

As the metaphor goes, Trump can just about get away with murder. Weeks before the November 2016 election, a tape emerged in which Trump said he could grab women by their private parts without repercussions. While some called for him to withdraw from the race, he won the presidency nevertheless. Last year, a New York court found Trump had raped E. Jean Carroll "as many people commonly understand the word 'rape.'" Trump went on to win the Republican nomination for the presidency this year with little opposition.

It's recently been disclosed that Trump reacted to rioters calling "Hang Mike Pence" on Jan. 6 by saying, "So what?" If anything, his polling numbers have since risen.

Polls and commentators alike agree that Trump was crushed by Kamala Harris in their Sept. 10 debate. Trump lied when he said tariffs are paid by foreign countries, not U.S. consumers, and again when he said, "millions of people (are) pouring into our country from prisons and jails, from mental institutions and insane asylums." His rambling, deceitful performance cost him... nothing. According to 538.com's poll averages, Trump was 2.6% behind Harris the day before the debate and 2.6% behind four weeks afterwards.

Trump's threats to turn the American military on his "evil" enemies, his lies about the efforts of FEMA in the wake of the hurricanes in the Southeast and his refusal to acknowledge the results of the last presidential election do not seem to affect the polls either.

Nothing seems to matter. Not even the endorsement of Kamala Harris by superstar Taylor Swift. According to an ABC News/Ipsos poll, only 6% of potential voters said it made them more likely to vote for Trump's opponent. Thirteen percent said it made them more likely to vote for Trump.

In 1983, former representative Patricia Schroeder said on the House floor that Ronald Reagan "has been perfecting the Teflon-coated presidency: He sees to it that nothing sticks to him."

In 2021, scientists harvested a lubricant from the legs of beetles that's even more slippery than Teflon. Is Donald Trump, then, the "Beetlejuice" candidate? After all, he can twirl heads away in response to almost any charge.

Trump Faces His Own Battle of Waterloo on Election Day

October 23, 2024

Some of the cost for Donald Trump's room and board after the November election will be borne by taxpayers. The key question is whether they'll be paying to accommodate him in the 132 rooms of the White House or the one room of a prison cell.

Last May, a New York state jury found Trump guilty on 34 felony counts of falsifying records to hide information that could have influenced the 2016 presidential election. New York Judge Juan Merchan postponed sentencing until Nov. 26 "to avoid any appearance — however unwarranted — that the proceeding has been affected by or seeks to affect the approaching Presidential election."

Why would the judge have delayed passing down a sentence for probation or for a fine? No reason — Trump had already been found guilty. Only a sentence including imprisonment had a realistic chance of affecting the election. I'm guessing, then, that Merchan does intend to sentence Trump to a prison term. But if Trump wins, the sentence will be suspended by either Merchan or the federal courts.

Federal prosecutor Jack Smith has put together a compelling narrative of Trump's efforts to retain the presidency even after losing the 2020 election. Among other violations of the criminal code, the indictment Smith filed on Aug. 27 argues Trump's unofficial actions as a candidate constituted an illegal attempt to obstruct the counting of electoral votes. Should Trump win in November, he will certainly appoint an attorney general who will drop the case. If he loses, it will go to trial after Trump has run out of appeals. A prison sentence is certainly one possible outcome.

The case against Trump for theft of classified documents after leaving office was thrown out by Judge Aileen Cannon, a Trump appointee. Photos show compelling evidence of the crime, but Cannon held that prosecutor Jack Smith had been illegally appointed. She based her decision on reasoning rejected by the Supreme Court a half-century ago in U.S. v. Nixon. If Harris wins the presidency, the special prosecutor's appeal to reinstitute the case will proceed with a high chance of success. If Trump wins the presidency, again his newly appointed attorney general will drop the case. In fact, Cannon herself may get the chance to drop the appeal. ABC News reports she is being considered as attorney general in a second Trump administration.

Trump still faces state charges for leading a conspiracy "to unlawfully change the outcome" of the 2020 presidential election in Georgia. Four of his co-defendants have already pleaded guilty. If he should lose the presidency, Trump will be appealing procedural rulings for years before facing trial with the potential for a prison sentence. If he wins, his participation in the case would almost certainly be suspended until he completes his term of office.

Of course, Trump faces a bucketful of civil cases as well. Whether he wins the presidency or not, Trump will be dealing with appeals in two cases that awarded the writer E. Jean Carroll civil judgments for defamation and sexual abuse adding up to over $88 million before interest. However, should Trump win back the presidency, the civil suits against him by members of Congress and injured Capitol Hill police officers stemming from his behavior on Jan. 6, 2021, will almost certainly be suspended since the causes of action arose while he was in office. In contrast, a newly filed defamation suit accuses Trump of falsely claiming in his debate with Kamala Harris that the so-called Central Park Five were guilty of assault. That suit should proceed no matter the result of the election because the Supreme Court held in Clinton v. Jones (1997) that there was no temporary immunity for a president's behavior while not in office.

There's more at stake in the upcoming election for Trump himself than potential prison sentences, court appearances and civil fines. There are billions of dollars in stock market gains or losses. Trump owns 114.75 million shares of Trump Media & Technology Group, which operates Truth Social, his social media platform. Each share was worth $12.15 on Sept. 23 and $36.41 on Oct. 23, which means the value of Trump's holding increased by $2.7 billion. Why did the price triple? Because investors believed the odds of Trump being re-elected increased over the month. If he wins, it will zoom up again. If he loses, it will crash. That could be a swing of $4 billion or more.

In 1815, the Battle of Waterloo was fought to determine whether Napoleon would reacquire the crown of Europe's most powerful country or whether he would be imprisoned on a rocky island in the middle of the Atlantic. This November, Trump's fate will be decided not by French soldiers shooting muskets but by American voters casting ballots.

Trump Dresses Up as a Fascist for Halloween and It Sure Is Scary

October 30, 2024

In this Halloween season, it's clear what costume former President Donald Trump has donned. He is frightening millions in his getup as a fascist.

What makes him so scary is not just his white shirt, blue suit, orange hairdo and floppy red tie — it's the sound effects that go with them. No werewolf's growl, witch's cackle or ghost's boo could be as menacing as the rhetoric emerging from Trump's mouth.

Let's take a look at how Trump playing a fascist matches up against the criteria for the real thing.

Umberto Eco, the Italian philosopher and novelist born in 1932, actually won a prize at age 10 for his essay on "Should we die for the glory of Mussolini and the immortal destiny of Italy?" The antifascist adult Eco wrote in 1995, "The first appeal of a fascist... is an appeal against the intruders."

In announcing his candidacy in 2015, Trump warned that immigrants from Mexico "were bringing drugs, they're bringing crime. They're rapists." This October, he played that tune of untruths again: "Kamala has imported criminal migrants from prisons and jails, insane asylums and mental institutions from all around the world, from Venezuela to the Congo. A lot of people are coming from the Congo prisons."

Eco also points to "machismo" and "disdain for women" as fundamental facets of fascism. Trump recently admiringly cited Arnold Palmer's physique as "all man." And of course, the thrice-married Trump was caught on videotape boasting he could grab beautiful women by their private parts because "when you're a star they let you do it. You can do anything."

In 2019, the late Secretary of State Madeleine Albright said, "The important thing is that fascists aren't actually trying to solve problems; they're invested in exacerbating problems and deepening the divisions that result from them." When Republican Sen. James Lankford won bipartisan support for a tough border bill, Trump made a call or two and deep-sixed it. GOP Sen. Mitt Romney of Utah lamented Trump's message "that he doesn't want us to solve the border problem because he wants to blame Biden for it...."

Albright went on to say a fascist rejects the free press. Trump has denounced the press as "truly the enemy of the people."

Trump's former chief of staff Gen. John Kelly called fascism a "movement characterized by a dictatorial leader." Trump said that the results of the 2020 election allowed "for the termination of all rules, regulations, and articles, even those found in the Constitution." He's threatened to be a dictator on "Day One" of a second term. He told a crowd to "get out and vote, just this time." He continued, "It'll be fixed, it'll be fine, you won't have to vote any more, my beautiful Christians." Hitler suspended elections, too.

Fascists hark back to days of glory. For Mussolini, it was to the grandeur of the Roman Empire. Hitler was drawn to the rule of Charlemagne over much of Europe in medieval times. And Trump, of course, wants to "make America great again," implicitly promising a return to an era of white, male, Christian predominance.

Trump didn't have to fly to Rome or Berlin to get the right background for his cosplay as a fascist. On Oct. 27, he held a rally at Madison Square Garden in New York City. Eighty-five years earlier, 22,000 Americans had filled the Garden with pro-Nazi cheers and salutes. Fritz Kuhn, "national Fuehrer" of the American fascist movement, thundered that members of his organization were determined "to protect themselves, their children and their homes against those who would turn the United States into a Bolshevik paradise." At his rally, Trump promised to "protect our great families. And I will protect the birthright of our children to live in the richest and most powerful nation on the face of the Earth."

Trump sure is playing his Halloween role as a fascist up to the hilt, isn't he?

Remember that Trump was once a pro-abortion registered Democrat. He made contributions to Hillary Clinton's campaign for the New York senate in 2002, 2005, 2006 and 2007 and also invited her to his 2005 wedding to Melania at Mar-a-Lago. Heck, he even donated $6,000 to Kamala Harris's campaign for reelection as California attorney general.

And now we're supposed to believe he's a true-red fascist? Well, Gen. Kelly, his former chief of staff, says he does fit "the general definition of fascist." Former Secretary of Defense Mike Esper spoke out in support of Kelly's statement. Dr. Benedetta Carnaghi, a historian of totalitarianism in Italy, France and Germany at England's University of Durham, wrote that "Trump would act as fully-fledged fascist if he could."

So this Halloween, I am wondering: Is Trump a true fascist or is he just acting? Does it matter if he implements his policies as someone playing a role or as someone committed to deeply held beliefs?

No, I don't think it really does.

In This Topsy-Turvy World, Authors Call for a Boycott of Books

November 6, 2024

I am troubled, disappointed and shocked that so many of my fellow authors wish to suppress books based on the nationality of their author.

Over 3,000 "writers, translators, illustrators and book workers" have signed a petition to boycott books printed or distributed by Israeli publishers. They also refuse to have their own works translated into Hebrew by these publishers for the Israeli market.

The petition says this is about the situation in the Middle East: "The current war has entered our homes and pierced our hearts." Yes, mine, too. I am a novelist and columnist and still have difficulty finding the words to convey my distress.

But what makes the signatories think that a boycott will bring peace nearer? Are the signatories afraid of what Israeli authors write? Last spring David Grossman, one of Israel's preeminent novelists, wrote, "Neither side is capable of viewing the other's tragedy with a shred of understanding — not to mention compassion." Should his opinions be squelched? Israel is a nation with a free press. Doesn't it make sense to ensure Israelis have access to all books including those telling Palestinian Arab stories and conveying all views on the Israel-Hamas War?

In trying to suppress free expression, the petition's signatories use McCarthyite tactics, embrace sloppy history, ignore terrorist violence and turn toward antisemitism.

The petition calls for a boycott of Israeli "publishers, festivals, literary agencies and publications" unless they have "publicly recognized the inalienable rights of the Palestinian people as enshrined in international law." This is reminiscent of the loyalty oaths required during the McCarthy era of the early 1950s.

In 1950, the University of California fired faculty member Erik Erikson, the author of the classic "Childhood and Society," for refusing to sign an oath promising he would support and defend the United States and the state of California against all enemies foreign and domestic. Texas required that textbook authors sign anti-communist oaths and ensure their writing reflected "our glowing and throbbing history of hearts and souls inspired by wonderful American principles and tradition."

Aren't the 3,000 signatories asking for the same kind of loyalty oath, pledging to boycott publication of the works by authors who will not publicly vow to take a specific political stand?

In 1953, the American Library Association issued a "Freedom to Read" statement that said "We Americans ... to make their own decisions about what they read and believe." Charles Muscatine explained why he wouldn't sign the University of California's oath: "As a young assistant professor, I had been insisting to the kids that you stick to your guns and you tell it the way you see it and you think for yourself and you express things for yourself and I felt that I couldn't really justify teaching students if I weren't behaving the same way."

Evidently there are over 3,000 signatories in 2024 who do not share those sentiments.

The petitioners not only wish to limit free expression, but they also put forward a shamefully one-sided view of the facts behind the Israel-Hamas War. There is not one word in the petition about the Hamas attack that started the current war on Oct. 7, 2023. Over 1,200 civilians died in the attack, including 40 Americans. The attack was found by a U.N. report to have comprised "a catalogue of the most extreme and inhumane forms of killing, torture and other horrors" including "rape and gang-rape." There is no mention either of the Hamas Covenant that calls for the elimination of the state of

Israel and a jihad against "the warmongering Jews." I could go on, but this column has a word limit.

The petition calls the war going on in the Middle East "the most profound moral, political and cultural crisis of the 21st century." How do you measure it against the Russian invasion of Ukraine where Russia has inflicted over 57,000 military deaths, displaced 3.7 million civilians and kidnapped 20,000 children? In the last two years, Sudan's civil war has killed as many as 150,000 people with over 10 million displaced. The Department of State reports the Chinese government has detained more than 1 million Uyghurs, ethnic Kazakhs, Kyrgyz and other Muslims in reeducation or detention centers in its western province of Xinjiang.

The fact these are going on is no reason to overlook the horrors that the Middle East war has inflicted on Israelis and Palestinian Arabs. But why a petition aimed only at the majority Jewish state of Israel and not one at Russia, Sudan or China? Could the answer be antisemitism?

In response to the petition, over 1,700 authors, critics, movie directors, screenwriters, publishers and others have signed a letter calling for "support of freedom of expression and against discriminatory boycotts." It goes on to say, "Over the past year, planned bookstore appearances by Jewish authors have been canceled, ads for books about Israel have been rejected, book readings have been shut down, literary groups have been targeted and activists have publicized lists of 'Zionist' authors to harass."

I myself have signed that letter along with Lee Child, whom I know and admire and whose Jack Reacher thrillers have sold over 100 million copies. Lee says this: "Politically targeting novelists, authors, and publishing houses based on their nationality is misguided. ... The written word, and the dissemination of it, must always be protected, especially in times of heightened tension. And to achieve peace, we must humanize one another and build bridges across communities through the open exchange of ideas. Literature allows for that. Boycotts hinder it."

Words to live by. Thank you, Lee.

Trump Again in Driver's Seat, Slams Country into Reverse

November 13, 2024

The election is over. So where are we? The calendar says we're in 2024. But the history books say 1924, give or take a few years.

Under the Johnson-Reed Act, aka the Immigration Act of 1924, immigrants from Asia were banned. Entry into the U.S. by Jews and Catholics from Poland, Italy and other countries in Southern and Eastern Europe was severely restricted. "White" immigrants from the British Isles and Northern Europe were favored. Overall, legal immigration into the United States plummeted by 80%.

Having retaken the White House, Trump is harking back to those days. During his first term, he said he wanted to restrict Black and Hispanic immigration from "shithole countries." During the recent campaign, he said Black immigrants from Haiti were eating pets. Now he seeks popular and congressional support in rounding up and deporting undocumented residents, potentially using the U.S. military. Juan Proano, CEO of the League of United Latin American Citizens, warns mass deportations "will rip parents from their children, destroy businesses and livelihoods, and devastate the fabric of our nation and our economy." There are an estimated 11 million undocumented residents in the U.S., roughly the population of Ohio or Georgia.

A century ago, the nation was recovering from a worldwide pandemic. The Spanish flu killed 675,000 Americans. Resistance to wearing masks popped up around the country. On a single day in November 1918, 1,000 were arrested in San Francisco. In the past five years, COVID-19 has killed 1.2 million in the U.S. Resentment toward public health measures such as mask-wearing and vaccinations boosted the 2024 Trump election campaign especially among evangelical Christians.

In the wake of World War I, America abandoned its allies and refused to join the League of Nations. Former President Woodrow Wilson decried America's refusal "to bear any responsible part in the administration of peace" and its withdrawal into "sullen and selfish isolation." One hundred years later, former and future President Trump has threatened to ignore obligations under the 1949 NATO Treaty to defend European allies against aggression and has even encouraged the Russians "to do whatever the hell they want."

The Smoot-Hawley Tariff, passed by Congress and signed by President Herbert Hoover in 1930, raised tariffs on 20,000 imported goods and sparked retaliatory tariffs from American trading partners. U.S. exports to Europe dropped by two-thirds from 1929 to 1932. Economists including Nobel Prize-winning Milton Friedman assigned partial blame to the "infamous" Smoot-Hawley for the Great Depression. President-elect Trump has vowed to impose a tariff of up to 20% on all imports with a rate of 60% or 100% on goods from China.

Back in 1938, Adolf Hitler demanded that Czechoslovakia cede a chunk of its territory to Germany where German-speakers constituted a majority. In 2021, Russian President Vladimir Putin published an essay "On the Historical Unity of Russians and Ukrainians" which deemed Ukraine "historically Russian lands." In both cases, an invasion ensued the next year. President-elect Trump has repeatedly said he could end the war between Ukraine in one day, presumably by allowing Russia to keep the border lands of Ukraine it illegally seized.

On the eve of World War II, Charles Lindbergh, spokesperson for the America First movement, called for isolationism. He attacked "the groups who advocate foreign war" in opposing German aggression in Europe. President-elect Trump has announced plans to nominate Fox News host Pete Hegseth as defense secretary in his new administration, calling him "tough, smart and a true believer in America First." JD Vance, Trump's choice as vice president, has said: "I gotta be honest with you, I don't really care what happens to Ukraine one way or another."

Almost all the 20th century stances mentioned above were eventually reversed. The 1965 Immigration Act removed discrimination against potential immigrants from Asia and Southern and Eastern Europe. And the Immigration Reform and Control Act of 1986, supported by the Reagan Administration, established a pathway to citizenship for undocumented residents who'd entered the U.S. before 1982. The Salk and Sabin vaccines ended the polio epidemic that had killed over 3,000 Americans and infected 20,000 in the peak year of 1952. Czechoslovakia regained its land after the defeat of Germany in the Second World War. The isolationism of the America First movement was replaced by bipartisan support of NATO and the United Nations after the war. Free trade flourished after the 1947 General Agreement on Tariffs and Trade lowered trade barriers and U.S. exports to other countries increased almost 200 times in dollar value between 1950 and 2023.

And yet, Trump argues that to make America great again, we must flip the pages of the calendar back to a time of racism, high tariffs, pandemics and isolationism. The next four years will see whether Congress, the Supreme Court and voters will support such a reversal of the past century of American history.

Mirror, Mirror on the Wall

November 20, 2024

What does Donald Trump see when he looks at his choices for attorney general, secretary of defense, director of national intelligence and secretary of health and human services?

Himself.

To head the Department of Justice, the president-elect has tapped former member of the House of Representatives Matt Gaetz. Witnesses have testified to the House Ethics Committee that Gaetz had sex with a 17-year-old in his home state of Florida. That's statutory rape. By nominating Gaetz, Trump is saying commission of rape does not disqualify Gaetz from being attorney general. After all, we already know Trump does not believe a New York civil jury's finding that he raped E. Jean Carroll disqualifies him from being the nation's chief executive and the attorney general's boss.

Trump has picked Pete Hegseth to command the Defense Department. Hegseth's primary qualification for the post is his tour of duty as a Fox News host. He's never run a big complex organization. The resemblance to Trump's own story is striking. The 45th president won election to the White House in 2016, having come to national prominence for his stint on TV's "The Apprentice." He had no significant business experience beyond running a family real estate firm. The fact Hegseth paid hush money to a woman who accused him of sexual assault makes him even more like his potential boss, who reached a notorious hush money agreement with adult film actor Stormy Daniels.

Former Rep. Tulsi Gabbard, Trump's choice for director of national intelligence, has attacked American aid to Ukraine as a threat to global security. About the Russian aggression against Ukraine in 2022, she tweeted, "This war and suffering could have easily been avoided if Biden Admin/NATO had simply acknowledged Russia's legitimate security concerns." At that time, Sen. Mitt Romney (Rep-Utah) accused Gabbard of "parroting fake Russian propaganda," and her former House colleague Rep. Adam Kinzinger (Rep-Ill) called her comments "traitorous." Also in 2022, Trump declared the Russian invasion of Ukraine to be "genius" and "pretty savvy." Romney voted twice to convict in both Trump's impeachment trials, and Kinzinger served on the House's Jan. 6 Committee. Trump and Gabbard then share common enemies as well as a soft spot for Putin.

Robert F. Kennedy, Jr., a member of the royal family of American politics, won notoriety as a vaccine denier. In 2021, Kennedy called the COVID-19 vaccine the "deadliest vaccine ever made." A 2022 note in The Journal of Paediatrics and Public Health estimated the vaccine saved over 14 million lives worldwide. Kennedy's willingness to disregard proven science jibes with the instincts of a boss who suggested that the injection of bleach into the human body might be a means of fighting COVID-19. The stance of Kennedy's siblings against their brother's fake science is a plus in Trump's book — they'd endorsed Harris in this month's election.

Trump is not overlooking the questionable credentials of Gaetz, Hegseth, Gabbard and Kennedy. He is choosing them because pieces of their backgrounds reflect pieces of his own — whether sexual misconduct, TV celebrity, obeisance to Russia or support for medical nonsense. As they'd say in the software world, those aspects of his picks' resumes are not bugs; they're features.

What will matter among these selections is not competence nor is it allegiance to the Constitution. It will be their reflection of some part of Trump's own image back at him. Trump wishes to confirm that the American people don't care much about the alleged crimes, sins, blips or fallacies he has in common with them.

Alas. All this does not bode well for the administration of justice, the national defense, the capabilities of the intelligence community or the health of Americans over the next four years.

Rooting for Middle Eastern Peace, But Not Betting on It

November 27, 2024

I stood next to the border between Israel and Lebanon on a hot day in the summer of 2008. When I approached the fence of a lemon grove on the Israeli side, one of my colleagues yanked me back. Look, he said, pointing to a dirt road a few hundred yards away where I could make out the white vehicles of the United Nations Interim Forces in Lebanon (UNIFIL). I could also see the glint of binoculars and rifles aimed my way by members of Hezbollah, the Iranian-sponsored terrorist militia.

UNIFIL's mission was to establish a demilitarized zone of 15-20 miles between the Hezbollah forces in Lebanon and the northern border of Israel. It never really worked. UNIFIL looked the other way as Hezbollah stored missiles and other arms in homes and tunnels in the DMZ. The day after the Hamas terrorist attack launched from Gaza at southern Israel on Oct. 7, 2023, Hezbollah began launching missiles at northern Israel from Lebanon, some from the area ineffectually patrolled by UNIFIL.

Israel showed itself willing to ignore this history in its acceptance of the Nov. 27 ceasefire with Hezbollah in Lebanon brokered by President Joe Biden and his administration. Hezbollah again is promising to move away from the border with Israel. It may be a step toward peace in the region, but it's only a baby step.

While a ceasefire is being implemented on Israel's northern border, there's no ceasefire in Gaza. Just as importantly, there's been no stoppage of antisemitic and anti-Israeli attacks in the rest of the world.

On the night of Nov. 7, marauding crowds in Amsterdam went on a "Jew hunt," cruising the city on motorbikes and assaulting any Jews they could find. Israel sent planes to pick up its citizens who were in town for a soccer match.

It was just this type of riot against Jews in European capitals over a century ago that gave birth to modern Zionism — support for a Jewish homeland in the Promised Land of the Bible.

The Austro-Hungarian journalist Theodore Herzl reported on anti-Jewish riots in Paris and Vienna in the 1890s. He was horrified by the notorious Kishinev Pogrom in Czarist Russia, which began on Easter Sunday in 1903, during which 49 Jews were murdered. The founder of the World Zionist Congress, Herzl came to believe Jews could only be safe in a homeland of their own, not in Europe where two-thirds of the world's Jews lived. In 1923, a major step toward Herzl's goal was taken by the League of Nations when it set up temporary British rule in what was to become "a national home for the Jewish people" — now known as Israel.

During the Second World War, Herzl was proven correct that Jews in Europe were not safe. The United Nations partitioned Palestine in 1947 between a Jewish state and a prospective Arab one. Israel became the 59th member of the United Nations in 1949. (Much of the land that was supposed to become an Arab state was seized by Egypt and Jordan.)

So then, who are the Jews of Israel? Just under half trace their ancestry to Europe and are alive because their forebears left Europe before the Holocaust or survived it. And there's another half descended from the 900,000 Jews who fled neighboring Arab and Muslim countries.

Given that national DNA, Israeli Jews know they cannot rely on the goodwill of the world's non-Jews. One-time allies such as Russia and Turkey no longer support Israel. Arab leaders, who were willing to contemplate peace with Israel, such as King Abdullah I of Jordan and Anwar Sadat of Egypt, were assassinated. The Hamas Charter does not call for an independent Palestinian Arab state alongside a Jewish one. It calls for the obliteration of the state of Israel and adds a call for the extermination of all Jews.

What are Israelis to think when within hours after the Oct. 7 massacre of 1,200 civilians by Hamas, 33 student organizations at Harvard held "the Israeli regime entirely responsible" for the violence? The International Criminal Court has indicted the Israeli prime minister and former Defense Minister Yoav Gallant for war crimes in Gaza, even though, according to the Wall Street Journal, Israel's military "may have achieved the lowest ratio of civilian-to-combatant deaths in the history of urban warfare."

The casualties in Israel, Lebanon and Gaza are tragic indeed. But even in the midst of the fighting, Israelis know they can only count on themselves.

On his way out of office, President Bill Clinton tried to leave a Middle East peace as a lasting legacy. He blamed head of the Palestine Liberation Organization Yasser Arafat for "miss(ing) the opportunity to bring a (Palestinian Arab) nation into being." U.S. negotiator Dennis Ross explained Arafat wanted "a one-state solution. Not independent, adjacent Israeli and Palestinian states, but a single Arab state encompassing all of Historic Palestine."

Will President Biden be able to establish the peace in his last months in office that Bill Clinton could not?

Damon Runyon, that chronicler of New York gamblers and wise guys, used to say, "The race is not always to the swift, nor the battle to the strong, but that's the way to bet." I'm rooting for Biden's peace efforts with all my heart, but my brain tells me that betting on their long-term success is a 100-1 shot.

Don't Count On Trump Draining the Swamp This Time Either

December 11, 2024

As the saying goes, even a stopped clock is right twice a day. And even in the river of lies pouring from the mouth of President-elect Donald Trump, occasional truths flow by. He's repeatedly accused Washington, D.C., of being a "swamp" of corruption. That resonates with the American people because they can see evidence of the corruption at every turn.

The Supreme Court made pro-business decisions as its senior member, Justice Clarence Thomas, accepted gifts worth millions from billionaires. Texas real estate mogul Harlan Crow, whose holdings could be affected by court rulings, was especially generous in funding Thomas's vacations, private jet flights, gifts, purchase of his mother's house and grandnephew's tuition payments.

The CEO of Nvidia, one of the world's two most valuable companies, is using loopholes in the federal tax code to avoid $8 billion in taxes. That's about the same amount as 1 million average taxpayers pay in federal income tax each year. Eight billion dollars is enough to pay for the whole federal court system for a year, for the National Park Service for over two years or for the state of Mississippi's K-12 education system for two and a half years. Warren Buffett, one of the 10 richest people in the world, once said he paid taxes at a lower rate than his secretary. Tax loopholes for the rich, while legal, do carry the whiff of the swamp.

Trump has tapped the world's richest person, Elon Musk, to co-head a "Department of Government Efficiency." Well over $100 billion of Musk's wealth stems from his ownership position in the electric vehicle manufacturer Tesla. Trump has vowed to impose tariffs of up to 60% on imports from China. Such taxes would protect Tesla's U.S. market position from Chinese-manufactured electric vehicles. Musk also owns 42% of Space X, which makes the Falcon 9 rocket that has become the go-to rocket for U.S. government agencies including NASA. Since the DOGE, despite its name, is not an official government body, Musk will not be subject to government conflict-of-interest laws.

Campaign finance records show Musk contributed $277 million to support Trump and other Republican candidates in last month's election. In the two weeks after the election, Musks's net worth climbed by over $70 billion, about 250 times his contribution total. Not a bad return on investment.

Electing Trump to drain the swamp of corruption is like installing Al Capone as head of an anti-organized crime strike force. A unanimous New York criminal jury found Trump guilty on 34 felony counts for his attempt to influence the 2016 election through a six-figure payoff to adult film star Stormy Daniels. Also, a staff report from the House Committee on Oversight and Accountability found Trump's "businesses received, at a minimum, $7.8 million in foreign payments from at least 20 countries during his presidency" in violation of the Constitution. The homepage of World Liberty Financial, a cryptocurrency firm, features a picture of Trump and the tagline "sponsored by Donald J. Trump." Steve Witkoff, Trump's designee as Middle East envoy, is a co-founder of WLF. Eric Trump is calling for "sensible" regulation by his father's incoming administration of the cryptocurrency industry that he and his father participate in.

Other Trump family members stink of the swamp, too. After serving as a Middle East adviser in the first Trump administration, Trump son-in-law Jared Kushner raised $2 billion for his firm Affinity Partners from Saudi Arabia's Public Investment Fund. The Saudi government invested despite objections from its fund's advisers about "the inexperience" of Affinity's management and a management fee that "seems excessive." The chair of the Senate

Finance Committee, Sen. Ron Wyden, wrote to Affinity in July asking whether its "investors may not be motivated by commercial considerations but rather the opportunity to funnel foreign government money to members of President Trump's family, namely Jared Kushner and Ivanka Trump."

There are too many other examples of unethical behavior, favoritism and greed in the swamp to list here. We do know, however, that Supreme Court justices should adhere to an enforceable ethics code, that tax loopholes favoring billionaires and burdening average taxpayers should be closed and that self-dealing by the nation's chief executive and his family and associates should be outlawed.

Donald Trump is right: In order to preserve the faith of Americans in their national government, the swamp should be drained. But as for counting on an administration headed by him to end D.C. corruption? I don't think so.

In fact, the American people have elected the Swamp King as their president. Whatever Trump drains will be more than offset by the new streams of sewage he generates and proliferates.

Today's Best Getaway Vehicles Have Pages, Not Wheels

December 18, 2024

In 1966, Timothy Leary, the psychedelics guru, famously told a crowd of 30,000 hippies in San Francisco to "tune in, turn on, and drop out." In the wake of last month's election, an awful lot of my friends and colleagues are following his advice. After tuning in and turning on to the news before the election, they are now dropping out.

"I can't watch what's happening in Washington," a friend told me at dinner last Friday. "I just can't take it." He is not alone. News channels CNN and MSNBC lost half their viewers in the weeks following the election.

I sympathize with anyone who is tuning out. It's painful for me, too, to watch an anti-vaxxer being tapped to head the Department of Health and Human Services and an apologist for Putin being nominated as director of national intelligence. I do encourage them, though, to tune back in. Let's not give up actively participating in our country's democracy. As the abolitionist Wendell Phillips said in 1852, "Eternal vigilance is the price of liberty."

And yet, I don't think critics of Trump's policies and motives can or should be truly vigilant every hour of every day. We all need time to work, tend to family and friends and take care of ourselves. Plus, I would like to recommend one more item for your to-do list in these turbulent times — reading novels.

Reading a work of fiction allows one to flee this fraught world and enter another created through the magic of an author's words. As the poet Emily Dickinson put it, "There is no Frigate like a Book to take us Lands Away."

After being battered by the post-election news, I've turned to novels that offer me an escape to lands faraway. In the last few weeks, I finished a murder mystery set along the Seine in Paris, a thriller that plays out at an English airfield, a recounting of a lonely man's last days, a narrative of a chase through Canadian forests, a classic whodunnit unspooling in an L.A. courthouse and a suspense novel sprawling across an Australian sheep ranch. In each, the protagonist finds the inner resolve to rise up against what life throws at them.

It's deeply satisfying to lose oneself in a fictional world where sexual offenders, supporters of authoritarianism, corrupt officials and advocates of fake science do not prevail. I finished each book renewed and ready to engage in what gamers and digerati call IRL — in real life.

An article in the journal Social Cognitive and Affective Neuroscience suggests science supports what I get from my reading. The authors suggest readers of fiction "make good citizens because reading may improve one's ability to empathize with and understand the thoughts and feelings of other people." Fiction readers "demonstrate greater civic engagement, including higher levels of volunteering, donating and voting, than non-readers."

As is well-known, there's a dichotomy on the political views of women and men. Can some of this be attributed to women's proclivity for reading fiction vis-a-vis that of men? In a 2017 survey, the National Endowment for the Arts found half of all women had read fiction in the previous 12 months. Only a third of men had. As the celebrated author Ian McEwan said, "When women stop reading, the novel will be dead."

On top of all that, it appears reading fiction is good for your cognition. In his "The Book of Memory," Richard Restak, a professor of neurology at George Washington University, prescribes fiction to keep one's brain sharp. Reading novels requires an investment of time and attention that "provides an especially helpful exercise in working memory" which nonfiction does not.

So where does all this leave us? Reading fiction not only provides a refuge from the fraught world we live in, but it also apparently encourages us to empathize with our fellow citizens and provides hope for a happy ending. It's even good for our minds.

I've just signed up for a college class next semester on the epic novel "War and Peace." (The book is 1,200 pages long!). I'm bound to learn something from how Leo Tolstoy's characters deal with justice, love, villainy, conflict and courage that will help me grapple with the same issues IRL.

In the next couple of days, I'll be putting a few more novels on my holiday gift list. I invite you to do the same.

Will the Empires Strike Back in 2025?

January 1, 2025

Donald Trump has won the American presidency twice while vowing to make America great again. He's not the only national leader who seeks policy guidance by looking back at his country's past glories.

Russian President Vladimir Putin has called the breakup of the Soviet empire "the greatest geopolitical catastrophe of the century." As the head of the largest of the 15 countries established after the dissolution of the Soviet Union, Putin believes his mission is to reestablish "what had been built up over a thousand years." A major step was the invasion of Ukraine which he has stated "is historically Russian land." If Russia wins that war, which parts of the former Soviet Union will he turn to next? Estonia, Latvia, Lithuania, Georgia and Moldova are on notice.

According to estimates, the Chinese economy represented about 30% of the world's output in 1600. Today it is 19%. China was humiliated by Britain in the Opium Wars of the mid-19th century. Japan seized Taiwan in 1895. Chinese President Xi Jinping has told Putin: "Right now, there are changes, the likes of which we have not seen for 100 years. And we are the ones driving these changes together." Xi seeks to reclaim Chinese economic primacy in the world and undo American protection of Taiwan's current democratic government. He's out to restore his country's greatness by undoing what he sees as the "all-around containment, encirclement and suppression of China" led by the U.S.

The state of Israel was established under a 1947 United Nations resolution. Hamas, which had ruled Gaza since 2007, launched its terrorist attack against Israel on Oct. 7, 2023, with the objective of reversing the U.N. vote. As the Hamas Covenant says,

"Israel will exist and will continue to exist until Islam will obliterate it, just as it obliterated others before it." The covenant goes on to call for holy war "until liberation is achieved, the invaders vanquished and Allah's victory comes about." So, Hamas stands for turning back the calendar by three-quarters of a century or more.

At one time, the Ottoman Empire ruled over what is now the state of Israel as well as Southeastern Europe, Lebanon, Syria, northern Iraq, Cyprus, North Africa and the holy city of Mecca. For years, Turkey, the Ottoman successor state, was a firm ally of the United States and Israel. No longer. The current Turkish president, Recep Tayyip Erdogan, has taken to harking back to Ottoman times. His party calls its supporters "grandchildren of Ottomans." He declared in 2020 that "our civilization is one of conquest. Turkey will take what is its right in the Mediterranean Sea, in the Aegean Sea, and in the Black Sea." Turkish troops are occupying parts of Syria and Cyprus as Erdogan continues to seek influence and leadership in the lands of the former Ottoman Empire.

And to the retrospective, expansionist policies of Putin, Xi and Erdogan, we must add those of incoming U.S. President Donald Trump. The United States grew in the 19th century by displacing Indigenous peoples in its Western expansion, by war against Mexico and by buying land from other nations. About 40% of the territory in the current United States stems from purchasing the Louisiana Territory from France in 1803 and Alaska from Russia in 1867. Now Trump and his team speak of wanting to make America great again through territorial growth.

There's the demand that Denmark sell the self-governing territory of Greenland to the United States for strategic reasons. Trump says making Canada the 51st state is "a great idea." (I wonder if he knows the U.S. tried to conquer Canada in the War of 1812 and failed miserably.) He threatens to retake the Panama Canal Zone despite a 1977 treaty turning it over to Panama.

Trump ought to cut out his bullying rhetoric. His efforts to return to 19th century expansionism are bound to add to global instability and to encourage war. He is emboldening and excusing Russian, Chinese, Hamas and Turkish aggression in their attempts to reestablish past glories. Why should they hold back if the U.S. does not?

Where will it all end? Taken to its absurd extremes, Greece might as well claim Egypt, Iraq, Iran and western India as the successor to Alexander the Great's empire, while Mongolia claims Russia and China as the successor to Genghis Khan's.

The United Nations Charter states that "All Members shall refrain in their international relations from the threat or use of force against the territorial integrity or political independence of any state." Trump doesn't care. His disregard of the charter gives others permission to disregard it, too. But that's who Trump is. He's a destroyer of norms, a wreaker of havoc and an enabler of aggression.

Evidence Points to Supreme Court as Enemy of Democracy

January 8, 2025

American politics are a mess. Congress is so tied in knots that it can barely fund the federal government. What's lifesaving medical care for a pregnant woman in one state may be prosecuted as homicide in another. Too often policymakers rely more on pseudoscience than the real thing. Authoritarianism is on the upswing.

I want to take what I've learned as a reader and writer of mysteries to identify the villain here. Just who bears the most blame for the mangled machinery of American democracy? Is it Donald Trump? Joe Biden? Elon Musk? The right-wing House Freedom Caucus? The left-wing Squad?

No, too obvious. As happens so often in the best-crafted whodunnits, the story's roots are buried decades in the past. Let's go back to December 2000 when the vote count in Florida would determine the victor in the presidential election.

In a judicial coup d'etat, the Supreme Court intervened before the state count was certified and selected George W. Bush as the winner over Al Gore by a 5-4 vote. All the justices in the majority had been selected for the Court by Republican presidents and all four in the minority by Democrats. The road to the White House led through the nine justices of the Supreme Court and not the 101 million who'd cast ballots. Late in her life, then-Justice Sandra Day O'Connor regretted joining the majority in the case, suggesting the Court should have left the decision to Florida and Congress by holding, "We're not going to take it, goodbye."

In last summer's decision in United States v. Trump, a 6-3 majority of the Supreme Court conjured up a right to immunity for the president "from criminal prosecution for conduct within his exclusive sphere of constitutional authority." In a scathing dissent, Justice Sonia Sotomayor notes that the majority in the case "invents an atextual, ahistorical, and unjustifiable immunity that puts the President above the law." She goes on to point out that if a president "orders the Navy's Seal Team 6 to assassinate a political rival," he would be "immune."

In 2010, the Supreme Court overturned a century of restrictions on spending in elections in Citizens United v. FEC. A century before that case, Theodore Roosevelt denounced "the use of corporate funds directly or indirectly for political purposes." The Tillman Act, passed in 1907, prohibited monetary contribution by corporations. Ignoring precedent, the Court concluded "that independent expenditures, including those made by corporations, do not give rise to corruption or the appearance of corruption."

In the 2013 case of Shelby County v. Holder, the Supreme Court decided that a provision of the Voting Rights Act, passed by Congress in 1965 to protect the right of minorities to vote, was outmoded. A 2024 article in the Journal of Political Economy found evidence that the Shelby County holding "decreased relative turnout for minoritized registered voters" due to "voter suppression tactics that have occurred in the absence of federal oversight." In a 2018 case, the Court resolved to look the other way even as flagrant gerrymandering deprived tens of millions of voters of their voice in choosing representatives.

Overturning 40 years of precedent in last year's Loper Bright Enterprises v. Raimondo, the Supreme Court directed federal courts to apply their own judgments to interpreting laws rather than those of government experts. As Justice Elena Kagan notes in her dissent, the six-justice majority gives "the courts the power to make all manner of scientific and technical judgments" on climate change, artificial intelligence, healthcare, and any other area of federal regulation.

When it comes to overturning precedent, though, it's tough to outdo the Court's 2022 holding in Dobbs v. Jackson Women's Health Organization. Half a century after Roe v. Wade granted women a constitutional right to reproductive freedom, the Supreme Court waved its wand and made it disappear in Dobbs.

The evidence is overwhelming. The Supreme Court is seizing power that rightfully belongs to the legislative and executive branches while weakening individual rights. Chief Justice John Roberts and Associate Justices Brett Kavanaugh and Amy Coney Barrett learned their lessons well when they were lawyers on the Bush team in the Bush v. Gore case.

The first step in fixing a problem is recognizing there is one. Over the past quarter-century, then, the Supreme Court has set itself as the expert on all things, cut back on protecting the right to vote, diminished women's reproductive freedom, given the president a free hand in breaking the law and turned a firehose of corruption on to the electoral process. It's time to discuss solutions which might include setting fixed terms for justices, expanding the size of the Court or reformulating the Court's jurisdiction.

The Declaration of Independence was written in reaction to the British king's "history of repeated injuries and usurpations." After nearly 250 years, the villain of the story appears to have changed from a supreme monarch to a supreme court.

For Trump, Mission Accomplished Even Before Second Term Begins

January 15, 2025

Since Nov. 5, Trump has done something no president-elect has ever done. He's checked off the top three to-dos on his postelection agenda before taking the oath of office.

No question that staying out of jail was Trump's No. 1 priority.

Last May, a New York state jury found Trump guilty on 34 felony counts of falsifying business records as part of a scheme to unlawfully influence the 2016 presidential election. In 2018, Trump's lawyer Michael Cohen was sentenced to three years in prison for more or less the same activities undertaken at Trump's direction. This month, the trial judge acknowledged "the seriousness" of Trump's crimes but said imprisonment would interfere with Trump's duties as president and let him off with no prison time.

In 2023, Trump was indicted in two federal cases, one for stealing classified documents and the other for conspiring to overturn the 2020 presidential election results. Both cases were dismissed after this past November's election because Justice Department policy bans the prosecution of a sitting president. Trump crowed, "The voters have spoken." Yes, Trump is moving into the White House, not the Big House, this year.

Trump's next goal was to have former political opponents acknowledge his primacy and seek his favor.

Trump and his allies have long seen Big Tech as a part of the "deep state" that fought an underground war against his policies. Trump was kicked off Facebook, Meta's social networking app, after the 2021 insurrection. He was only allowed back on in 2023 but with "new guardrails to deter repeat offenses" in postings. Just after this past November's election, Meta CEO Mark Zuckerberg traveled to Mar-a-Lago for dinner with Trump. This month, Meta announced that it would no longer review Facebook posts for content and that it was replacing Nick Clegg, the former head of the UK's Liberal Democrat party, as president of global affairs with Joel Kaplan, a former Republican White House staffer.

Jeff Bezos, the founder of Amazon, bought The Washington Post in 2013. Four years later, The Post won a Pulitzer Prize for exposing Trump's untruths regarding his charitable giving. In 2018, the paper won for its investigation of the connections between the 2016 Trump presidential campaign and Russia, and it won in 2022 for its coverage of the Jan. 6, 2021, attack on the U.S. Capitol. None of these stories was close to favorable to Trump.

Amazon, the primary source of Bezos' fortune, does billions in business with the federal government and, of course, would like to do more. It also runs a streaming service which this month struck a deal to run a documentary about Melania Trump that she herself is executive producing. In addition, Blue Origin, another Bezos company, holds a $3.4 billion contract with NASA to build a lunar lander and is competing for a $5.6 billion contract to provide space launches for the Pentagon. On the same day executives of Blue Origin met with Trump, Bezos quashed a Post editorial endorsing Trump's opponent, Vice President Kamala Harris.

In the past month, prominent Post staffers including the Pulitzer-winning Ashley Parker, political cartoonist Ann Telnaes and popular columnist Jennifer Rubin have resigned from the paper. The motto of the new platform Rubin founded is a none-too-subtle "Not owned by anybody." The Post's masthead still includes the slogan "democracy dies in darkness," but it sure looks as though the paper's lights are dimming.

Last month, the Walt Disney Company agreed to pay $15 million to settle a defamation case brought by Trump for a statement made on its ABC Network even though Disney would probably have prevailed on the merits. Democratic attorney Marc Elias commented: "Ring kissed. Another legacy news outlet chooses obedience."

Mission accomplished here, too. Tech billionaires and media magnates are approaching Trump on bended knee. Last month, he boasted: "In the first term, everyone was fighting me. In this term, everybody wants to be my friend." Jeff Bezos and Mark Zuckerberg will be seated on the dais at Trump's inauguration along with Elon Musk, tech's wealthiest man.

What's third on Trump's Top 3 list? To show that being a sexual predator is no big deal, that everyone does it. Over two dozen women have accused Trump of sexual misconduct. In the infamous Access Hollywood tape, he was recorded as saying: "And when you're a star, they let you do it. You can do anything. Grab 'em by the (private parts)." A New York state judge found that according to the common understanding of the word, Trump raped author E. Jean Carroll.

Trump seems to regard accusations of sexual misconduct as a plus on a potential cabinet member's resume. In December, he nominated Matt Gaetz as attorney general despite credible evidence that Gaetz had committed statutory rape. Even after Gaetz withdrew his nomination, Trump's choice for the CFO of Florida, Joe Gruters, said, "Matt Gaetz continues to have a bright future in elected office." Trump's nominee for secretary of defense, Pete Hegseth, paid a woman to drop charges of sexual assault in return for her silence. Trump's nominee for secretary of health and human services, Robert F. Kennedy, Jr., texted an apology to a former babysitter who accused him of sexual assault.

Hegseth's confirmation hearings appear to confirm that for Republicans, sexual misconduct is not a disqualification from high office. Trump can put a checkmark by his goal to normalize harassing and assaulting women.

Between his election victory and moving into the White House, Trump has already gotten what he wanted most. And the American people are about to get the felonious, predatory, bullying, shameless president they elected.

Trump Finds His Inspiration in Failed Policies of the Past

January 22, 2025

President Franklin D. Roosevelt promised the American people a "New Deal," and President John F. Kennedy declared America stood on the edge of a "New Frontier." In contrast, the newly inaugurated Donald J. Trump wants to "make America great *again*," to go back to the good old days. In a flurry of executive orders and pronouncements, he embraced policy after policy rejected or abandoned years ago.

On the first day of the Trump presidency, the White House website posted a document stating, "the State Department will have an America-First foreign policy." When it comes to foreign policy, the phrase "America First" has a menacing connotation. Before the U.S. entered World War II, the aviator Charles Lindbergh spearheaded the America First Committee, which advocated an isolationist foreign policy that would give German aggression a free hand.

President Roosevelt told his Treasury secretary Henry Morgenthau: "If I should die tomorrow, I want you to know this: I am absolutely convinced Lindbergh is a Nazi." The isolationist America First organization is hardly an ideal model for 2025 as war rages in Ukraine, the Middle East seethes and China threatens Taiwan.

In his inauguration address, Trump said, "We will tariff and tax foreign countries to enrich our citizens." Trump is following in the footsteps of President Herbert Hoover, who signed a law raising tariffs on 20,000 imported goods which sparked retaliatory tariffs from American trading partners. U.S. exports to Europe dropped by two-thirds from 1929 to 1932. A poll of economists and historians shows over 80% believe the increase in tariffs worsened the Great Depression.

Trump has also pardoned or commuted the sentences of hundreds of insurrectionists who stormed the Capitol on Jan. 6, 2021. Enrique Tarrio, the leader of the Proud Boys, and Stewart Rhodes, founder of the Oath Keepers, both convicted of seditious conspiracy for their role in the attack, have been released from prison. This all brings to mind President Andrew Johnson's Christmas 1868 "full pardon and amnesty" for all those "who directly or indirectly participated in the late insurrection or rebellion." Included were Jefferson Davis, the former president of the Confederacy, and Nathan Bedford Forrest, a former Confederate general. Forrest led the Ku Klux Klan in a post-Civil War campaign of violence and intimidation directed against Black people. Referring to those released by Trump, Harry Litman, former Supreme Court clerk, former U.S. attorney and current law professor, writes, "As for the pardoned horde, it's hard to see why they wouldn't conclude they now have license, even duty, to intimidate Trump's opponents anytime they perceive a wink and nod from the boss."

The administration is prioritizing a "deportation operation" in which the military "will engage in border security, which is national security, and will be deployed to the border to assist existing law enforcement personnel." This evokes the infamous Executive Order 9066 issued by President Roosevelt in 1942 which allowed to military to round up whoever the appropriate military commander deemed "necessary." Under the authority granted by this order, about 120,000 persons of Japanese descent, including 70,000 citizens, were placed in detention camps. Forty-six years later, President Ronald Reagan signed an official apology to those incarcerated due to "race prejudice, war hysteria, and a failure of political leadership." Over $1 billion in reparations were paid.

Trump also issued an executive order that would give him the authority to fire tens of thousands of employees without the longstanding protections enjoyed by career civil servants. Everett Kelley, the president of the American Federation of Government Employees, said, "This unprecedented assertion of executive power will create an army of sycophants beholden only to Donald Trump, not the Constitution or the American people." Again, it is back to the past for the new administration. In the early days of the Republic, the spoils system reigned, where all positions in the federal government were held at the pleasure of the president until 1883 when the Pendleton Civil Service Reform Act became law. A quarter-century after passage of the act, almost two-thirds of the U.S. federal workforce gained their appointments through tests and could not be fired arbitrarily by a new president.

When it comes to turning back the clock, though, nothing beats Trump's executive order undercutting the right to citizenship granted by the 14th Amendment to all children born in the United States. That Amendment, ratified in 1868, states, "All persons born or naturalized in the United States, and subject to the jurisdiction thereof, are citizens of the United States and of the State wherein they reside." The essence of Trump's argument is that a baby born in the U.S. to unauthorized immigrants is not "subject to the jurisdiction" of the United States. The Supreme Court held otherwise in 1898 when it held that all babies born in the U.S. are citizens except for the children of diplomats or those born to noncitizens in "hostile occupation" of part of the U.S.

The attorneys general of over 20 states have sued to overturn this birthright executive order. Connecticut Attorney General William Tong, a citizen by virtue of his birth on U.S. soil, stated the fight was personal was for him: "The 14th Amendment says what it means, and it means what it says — if you are born on American soil, you are an American. Period. Full stop." Nick Brown, the Washington State attorney general, estimates Trump's order would deny citizenship to 150,000 newborn children each year.

All this is bad news for Americans. Even with the tremendous challenges facing the country today — aggression overseas, technology, climate change, unequal opportunity, education, pandemic threats and more — Trump is stubbornly focused on refighting the lost battles of the past.

Trump Just Took Office and I'm Already Mad as Hell

January 29, 2025

What was seen as outrageous during Trump's first term is seen as normal in his second. A Washington Post columnist recently wrote Trump's return to office "marked not just a political transition but the normalization of the man and his movement." The Hill, an insiders' D.C. paper, ran a story that began, "Welcome to Washington's new normal."

Don't buy such blathering. Trust your own common sense. What Trump is doing is not normal.

During the Jan. 6, 2021, assault on the U.S. Capitol, Daniel Rodriguez plunged a stun gun into the neck of a police officer multiple times. Judge Amy Berman Jackson said Rodriguez was "a one-man army of hate, attacking police and destroying property" as she sentenced him to a prison term of over 12 years. On his first day in office, Trump pardoned Rodriguez and over 1,500 others for their actions on Jan. 6. Pardoning those who attack police officers while storming the Capitol is not normal.

Trump tapped Pete Hegseth as defense secretary to manage a budget of $850 billion and lead 2.9 million employees including 1.4 million active-duty uniformed personnel. Having a man heading the Pentagon who faced allegations of mismanaging two veterans' advocacy groups, paying off a woman who accused him of rape, abusing his ex-wife and public drunkenness is not normal.

On the first day of his second term, Trump issued an executive order violating the 14th Amendment's grant of citizenship to anyone born in the U.S. and subject to U.S. laws. Judge John Coughenour, appointed to the bench by President Ronald Reagan in 1981, said: "I can't remember another case where the question presented is as clear as this one. This is a blatantly unconstitutional order." An attempt to overrule the Constitution hours after taking the oath of office to defend it is not normal.

Trump has appointed Elon Musk to head a committee to enhance government efficiency. Musk's recommendations on artificial intelligence, social media, electric vehicles, space exploration and tariffs are bound to affect his own personal wealth. Having the world's richest person and a huge contributor to the Trump presidential campaign in such a role is corrupt, not normal.

During last year's campaign, Trump labeled government employees "crooked" and "dishonest." On Jan. 24, he fired 18 inspectors general, the very officials tasked with looking for malfeasance in government departments. In so doing, the president ignored the federal statute requiring that he give 30 days' notice to Congress before removing an inspector general and provide substantive reasons for their removal. Mark Greenblatt, appointed inspector general of the Department of the Interior by Trump during his first term, explained to CBS News: "The most charitable interpretation is that he doesn't believe in our independence or our fairness. The least charitable interpretation is that he wants lackeys to rubber stamp what he's trying to do." Neither explanation would be normal.

On his first day in office, Trump said U.S. control over Greenland is necessary to national security. He has refused to rule out taking the territory from Denmark by force. The U.S. led opposition to territorial aggression against Ukraine by Russia. It's not normal for an American president to advocate it against a NATO ally.

In 2020, then-president Trump ordered a drone strike that killed Qassem Soleimani, an Iranian general reportedly responsible for hundreds of American deaths. Iran has threatened revenge against Mike Pompeo, Trump's former secretary of state, and John Bolton, his former national security adviser, among others.

Intelligence reports indicate the threat is ongoing. Nevertheless, Trump withdrew the security protection provided to Pompeo and Bolton by the Biden administration, explaining "When you have protection, you can't have it for the rest of your life." It's not normal for a president to express nonchalance toward a foreign power threatening former senior U.S. officials.

In his confirmation hearing on Jan. 16, Trump's nominee to head the EPA declared that addressing contamination by forever chemicals would be a "top priority." A week later, Trump withdrew plans to regulate discharge of those toxic contaminants in drinking water. Presidentially sanctioned poisoning of Americans is not normal.

At a national prayer service the day after his inauguration, Episcopal Bishop Mariann Edgar Budde addressed the new president: "In the name of our God, I ask you to have mercy upon the people in our country who are scared now." Trump responded: "She was nasty in tone, and not compelling or smart." The Bible says the Almighty requires each person "to act justly and to love mercy and to walk humbly with your God." An out-and-out rejection of mercy by a president claiming to be Christian is not normal.

Indeed, there are more examples of aberrant Trumpian actions. There are the refusal to spend funds already appropriated by law, the firing of career civil servants, the exploitation of cryptocurrency for personal gain, the cancellation of a 1965 order banning hiring discrimination in federal employment and the threatened violation of the Panama Canal Treaty. And then, too, there are the nominations of antivaxxer Robert F. Kennedy as secretary of Health and Human Services, alleged Russian sympathizer Tulsi Gabbard as director of National Intelligence and revenge advocate Kash Patel as FBI director. But enough.

What's going on under the Trump administration is not normal. Instead, it's unmerciful, vindictive, destructive, cruel, unconstitutional, illegal and un-American.

Have you ever seen the 1976 film classic "Network"? In it, a TV anchor tells Americans to protest this way: "I want you to get up right now and go to the window. Open it, and stick your head out, and yell, 'I'M AS MAD AS HELL, AND I'M NOT GOING TO TAKE THIS ANYMORE!'"

The anchor took the words right out of my mouth. What Trump is doing in the first days of his second administration is not normal, and I'm already as mad as hell.

Trump Demands Loyalty, Not Expertise

February 5, 2025

An old adage held that "At least Mussolini made the trains run on time." In other words, everyday convenience partially excused the authoritarian rule imposed by the Italian dictator a century ago.

At the outset of his second term, it appears Trump cannot even make the planes stay in the air. Nine days after the head of the Federal Aviation Agency was pushed to resign, a commercial airliner and a military helicopter collided over Reagan National Airport killing 67 people. Trump critics draw a connection between the two events. Trump himself blames the crash on DEI hiring of air traffic controllers.

Politically speaking, it doesn't much matter much whether either explanation has any validity. What matters is whether potential passengers will trust the Trump administration to keep the skies safe.

Recent polls show Trump is viewed favorably by about half of all Americans. What will undercut this support is not what columnists write nor what a Supreme Court opinion holds. It's the reaction of Americans to how the administration touches their everyday life.

Current Trump supporters won't change their favorable views of him because the Agency for International Development stops aiding the poor, diseased and hungry overseas nor because a bunch of tech bros have taken a peek at their tax returns. They will base their views on — among other things — whether it is safe to fly, whether Social Security payments show up on time, whether groceries cost more, whether the schools and streets are safe, whether they have access to quality health care, whether American military men and women are placed in mortal danger and whether the U.S. Postal Service delivers Amazon packages undamaged and on time.

My bet is the Trump administration will fail in dealing with at least some of these. The president is appointing inexperienced and unproven cabinet members while driving experienced experts out of their jobs.

With an anti-vaxxer like Robert Kennedy, Jr. as head of the Department of Health and Human Services, American children are in peril from outbreaks of measles, mumps and even polio. At the end of January, Medicaid portals were temporarily shut down in all 50 states. Sen. Ron Wyden (D-OR) wrote, "This is a blatant attempt to rip away health insurance from millions of Americans overnight and will get people killed." The fact that Trump tapped Dr. Mehmet Oz, the failed Senate candidate and promoter of questionable medical cures, as head of the $1.5 trillion Centers for Medicare and Medicaid Services is a disaster waiting to happen. As American seniors say, "Don't let the government mess with my Medicare."

Trump enforcer Elon Musk and his gang of tech bros are messing with the federal disbursement system. If Social Security payments are delayed by a single day, senior citizens are bound to blame Trump and his hapless team.

During the presidential campaign, Trump promised to get the price of groceries down on "Day One." Instead, egg prices have continued to climb, and the Department of Agriculture projects they will rise an additional 20% this year mainly due to bird flu. Rather than fighting bird flu, the Trump administration has blocked the release of scientific studies on how to deal with it.

Trump ordered the U.S. Army Corps of Engineers to open two California dams to demonstrate action in sending water to combat fires in the Los Angeles area. The water, however, will not reach any city and will dry out before it can be used for irrigation on the Central California farms where 40% of the U.S.'s fruits, nuts and other table foods are raised. Peter Gleick, a water scientist and senior fellow at the Pacific Institute, told The L.A. Times that "for a political photo op and a social media post, the Trump administration has thrown away billions of gallons of California water." That will only raise the produce prices shoppers see at the grocery store.

Who knows what's going to happen with tariffs? If tariffs on goods imported from Canada and Mexico are indeed imposed after the current 30-day waiting period, consumers will see higher prices on new houses, cars, fruits, vegetables, beer, tequila and oil. If his current tariffs for Chinese imports remain in place, prices on computers, shoes, toys and more will go up, too.

Trump was elected in no small part because of inflation during the first two years of the Biden Administration. If Trump's policies and appointees make the situation worse, the chances of a Democratic wave in the 2026 midterm elections jump.

In the 1920s, Mussolini said, "The truth is that men are tired of liberty." As the story goes, Italians gave up liberty back then in return for trains running on schedule. In the 2020s, Americans run the risk of giving up democratic norms for a lot less.

2025 Greenland and 1938 Czechoslovakia: Too Close for Comfort

February 12, 2025

History does not really repeat itself, not exactly. But with both a bachelor's and a master's in history, I can't help but make comparisons between current and past events. What Trump is doing with regard to Greenland sure does remind me of what was going on in Central Europe during the late 1930s.

In 1938, Germany declared its intention to annex the German-speaking portions of Czechoslovakia. Those areas, known as the Sudetenland, had never been part of the German Empire. Hitler believed in expansionism and called for "Lebensraum," or living space, for his country. Sudetenland was strategically located on the German border and contained valuable economic resources, mainly major industrial areas.

Germany threatened war to seize the territory by force of arms. At the infamous Munich conference, British Prime Minister Neville Chamberlain and French Prime Minister Edouard Daladier yielded to German demands.

OK. Now let's talk about Greenland. The world's largest island, it's about the same size as Alaska and California combined but has only 57,000 people. The two states have about 700 times more. Greenland is an autonomous dependency of the Danish crown which has promised it independence.

Like Hitler, Trump has embarked on a policy of expansionism. At his inauguration last month, he declared, "The United States will once again consider itself a growing nation — one that increases our wealth, expands our territory ... and carries our flag into new and beautiful horizons." He has an eye on not just Greenland, but also Canada, the Panama Canal and even the Gaza

Strip. In regard to a U.S. takeover of Greenland specifically, he has said, "I think we're going to have it" and has indulged in saber-rattling by refusing to rule out force in taking it. He explicitly said, "I'm not going to commit" to not using U.S. military forces.

Czechoslovakia was a member of the League of Nations, the predecessor to the United Nations. Hitler didn't care. His policy was to expand Germany's territory through threats or by invasion. Greenland is a dependency of Denmark, a U.N. member. The U.N. Charter states that "All Members shall refrain in their international relations from the threat or use of force against the territorial integrity or political independence of any state." Trump's threats have already violated that provision.

During the summer of 1938, pro-Nazi agitators in the Sudetenland funded by Germany fomented unrest. Donald Trump Jr. visited Greenland last month to stir up support for American plans. A fundraiser is being planned to foster U.S.-Greenland relations at Mar-a-Lago in April.

Given its potential mining riches, I can understand Trump Sr.'s craving to take over Greenland. He's a property developer at heart. I do wonder what could be in it for the predominately Indigenous inhabitants of Greenland. The United States expanded from coast to coast by seizing territory from Indigenous peoples and breaking treaties with them. The new lands were exploited by settlers to their benefit, not to that of the peoples. Greenlanders today are already well-to-do by world standards with a per capita GDP of around $57,000 per year — ironically enough, around the same as Germans.

Hitler alleged that Sudeten Germans were being massacred in order to justify his claims to the territory. He was lying. Trump has stated that the Greenlanders "want to be with us" to justify his claims. He is lying. According to a recent poll, 85% of Greenlanders say they want nothing to do with joining the U.S.

Hitler wanted Sudetenland and issued threats to get it. Trump wants Greenland and is issuing threats to get it. Hitler didn't care if he flouted international norms, and neither does Trump. Hitler's Lebensraum policy was conducted in a fraught world marked by depression and aggression. A world war ensued.

Trump's expansionist foreign policy is being directed not against a foreign enemy but against a NATO ally. It could prove the end of that alliance. His threat to take over Greenland, which violates the U.N. Charter, is already being used by Russia to justify its attempt to conquer Ukraine. It can only encourage China, too, in its efforts to seize Taiwan.

I believe in a world where peace is kept in large part by the moral leadership and military strength of the United States. I am not sleeping well these days.

Time for Americans to Disbelieve Trump and Believe Their Own Eyes

February 19, 2025

In the 1933 movie farce "Duck Soup," Chico Marx famously asks Margaret Dumont, "Who ya gonna believe, me or your own eyes?"

Trump and members of his team are implicitly asking that same question over and over. They demand to be believed, no matter what Americans themselves see.

Here's the latest instance. Danielle Sassoon, the acting head of the Justice Department's Manhattan office, resigned rather than dismiss bribery and fraud charges against New York Mayor Eric Adams. She explained in a Feb. 12 letter that such a step would be an agreement where Adams made an "offer of immigration enforcement assistance" to federal authorities "in exchange for a dismissal of his case." Acting Deputy Attorney General Emil Bove responded to Sassoon that it was "false" to suggest there was any agreement for such a quid pro quo.

Trump's border czar Tom Homan appeared on Fox News with Adams on Feb. 13 and declared that if the mayor "doesn't come through, I'll be back in New York City, and we won't be sitting on a couch. I'll be up his butt saying where's the agreement we agreed to." Later that day, Adams announced he would sign an executive order giving federal immigration agents access to the city's jail on Riker's Island.

I watched the video of Homan on Fox News. I read a copy of the letter signed by Sassoon, a former law clerk to the late Supreme Court Justice Antonin Scalia. As to whether there's an agreement, I'll believe my own eyes, thank you very much.

From his first day in office, Trump has told Americans what to believe in the face of evidence to the contrary. He claimed on Jan. 20, 2017, that "The overall audience was, I think, the biggest ever to watch an inauguration address, which was a great thing," He had his press secretary Sean Spicer support the claim and accuse the press of manipulation. Only one problem: There were photos showing Trump's inauguration crowd was only about one-third the size of Barack Obama's. (By the way, Spicer later said he "absolutely" regretted what he'd said.)

Unsurprisingly, the claims by acting Deputy AG Bove and press secretary Spicer were right out of their boss's playbook. Trump has called Jan. 6, 2021, "a day of love." On that day, I myself watched live video of marauders beating police with flag poles and spraying them with chemicals. I heard them chant "Hang Mike Pence," the then-vice president, and saw the gallows they'd erected to show the threat was not an empty one.

Were those charged or convicted for their actions "peaceful hostages" as Trump said or members of a violent murderous mob? Who am I going to believe: the president or my own eyes?

More Americans seem to be coming around to Trump's assertions, though. A December 2021 poll indicated 54% of Americans believed the protesters who entered the U.S. Capitol that day were mostly violent. In another poll taken three years later, 46% of Americans believed Jan. 6 was a violent insurrection. The Department of Justice has removed the Jan. 6 page from its website that listed those convicted for their actions that day. "It's been erased," said Sen. Peter Welch, D-Vt. "Winners write history and Trump won. And his version is that it was a peaceful gathering."

The eminent 20th century historian William L. Langer, who taught history to John F. Kennedy in college, wrote a wartime profile of Hitler that cited one of the German dictator's primary rules: "People will believe a big lie sooner than a little one; and if you repeat it frequently enough people will sooner or later believe it." In a video, Trump's former press secretary Stephanie Grisham recalled that Trump used to tell her, "As long as you keep repeating something, it doesn't matter what you say."

I write novels, works of fiction. That means I sometimes find myself in the same business as Trump — trying to make people suspend their disbelief while they're immersed in our made-up stories. But what about when it's time to put the stories aside? How, then, to make certain you're living in the real world and not in Trump's made-up one?

Here's what I try to do. Check what Trump says against trusted sources. Examine credible video, audio and documentary evidence. And most importantly, believe my own eyes and ears, not those of Donald Trump — or Chico Marx.

Trump and Hitler: Too Close for Comfort

February 26, 2025

For years now, I've tried to resist the temptation of writing a side-by-side comparison between Donald Trump and Adolf Hitler. I agreed with Abraham Foxman, the longtime head of the Anti-Defamation League, who said last year, "Comparing him to Hitler is an over-the-top exaggeration which trivializes who Hitler was and the horrors he brought."

Yes, I still agree with Foxman that Trump is no Hitler. But the growing number of similarities in their words and actions can no longer be ignored.

First, there's the claim to serving a divine purpose. Hitler ghost-wrote a biography that deemed him Germany's "messiah." In his victory speech in November, Trump asserted, "God spared my life for a reason."

Even while ostensibly embracing religion, both men declared that some humans are no more than animals. Hitler wrote in "Mein Kampf" of the need to "wipe out this vermin," because "all great cultures of the past perished only because the originally creative race died out from blood poisoning." Trump has said undocumented people living in the United States are "not humans, they're animals" "that live like vermin" and are "poisoning the blood of our country."

The two men have habitually used untruths to win popular support. A U.S. intelligence analysis during World War II said Hitler thought that if you repeated a lie "frequently enough, people will sooner or later believe it." Trump's former press secretary Stephanie Grisham has stated Trump used to tell her, "As you long as you keep repeating something, it doesn't matter what you say."

According to Gen. John Kelly, Trump asked in his first term why U.S. generals couldn't be loyal like Hitler's generals. In his second term, Trump is taking steps to make his wish come true. He says the new designee for chairman of the Joint Chiefs of Staff once told him, "I love you, sir. I think you're great, sir. I'll kill for you, sir."

Like Hitler, Trump is a bully on the international stage. In 1938, Hitler threatened to attack Czechoslovakia in order to annex a piece of it. In the past few months, Trump has set forth an American claim on Greenland. Like Hitler, he's refused to rule out taking the territory by force of arms.

Then there's the shared admiration for the Russian leader of their day. In 1939, Hitler signed a nonaggression pact with Soviet dictator Joseph Stalin whom he regarded as "one of the most extraordinary figures in world history" who "knows his models, Genghis Khan and the others, very well." Trump has called the current Russian dictator Vladimir Putin "very smart" and the Russian invasion of Ukraine "genius."

In 1932, Hitler ran for the German presidency and lost by 6 million votes. His attempts to overturn the results based on voter fraud were dismissed by a court. Hitler did, of course, succeed in coming to power in 1933. Trump, too, sought to retain the American presidency in 2021 despite the election results. He lost over 60 court cases claiming election fraud but nevertheless won back the White House in last November's election.

Twenty-three prominent German industrialists had a secret meeting with Hitler in February 1933 where they agreed to back him with funds in the next month's election. Hitler told them even if he did not win, he would maintain power "by other means." He did win. Trump has Elon Musk, the world's richest individual and his campaign's largest individual contributor, serving as his hatchet man in cutting and undercutting the federal civil service. The world's next two richest persons — Jeff Bezos, founder of Amazon, and Mark Zuckerberg, founder of Meta — were also on display at Trump's inauguration.

In its first year, Hitler's regime passed the "Editor's Law" under which all journalists would answer to the Ministry of Propaganda, not their publications. Non-Aryans and opponents of the regime were dismissed. Trump's nominee to head the Federal Communications Commission, Brendan Carr, wants the commission to punish broadcasters who are unfair to Trump. Investigations into NPR, NBC and PBS have already been launched.

Hitler and Trump both took steps to round up targeted persons in their early days in office. Two months after taking office in January 1933, Hitler's regime opened Dachau as "the first concentration camp for political prisoners" with a capacity of 5,000 people. Less than two weeks after taking office, Trump issued an executive order to expand facilities at the U.S. Navy base at Guantanamo Bay "to provide additional detention space for high-priority criminal aliens." News reports indicate plans are underway for Guantanamo to hold up to 30,000 prisoners.

Hitler called his regime the Third Reich, a successor to the thousand-year Holy Roman Empire founded by Charlemagne. Trump looks backward as well. He wants to make America great again as it was in the days of his privileged childhood in New York City when "we were not pushed around, we were respected by everybody, we had just won a war, we were pretty much doing what we had to do."

There's more, but it's enough to say for now that Trump is no defender of democracy, nor an opponent of aggression, nor a champion of civil rights nor a speaker of the truth. Thank goodness, though, he is a long way from matching the wickedness, murderousness and destructiveness of Hitler. Still, the fact that Trump is so closely tracking the Nazi's playbook should frighten every American.

Once Again, Trump Confirms Putin as His BFF

March 5, 2025

What's more irritating than a columnist saying I told you so?

Forgive me, but I just looked over a full-page opinion piece I wrote for the San Francisco Chronicle in December 2016, the month before Trump took office for his first term. The editors headlined it: "I couldn't write a thriller as strange as a pro-Russia US president."

It holds up pretty well in light of current events. No, no, it holds up *terrifyingly* well.

Trump stopped military aid to Ukraine on March 3. He blames the decision on Ukrainian President Volodymyr Zelenskyy's refusal to agree to a peace settlement that left Russia occupying Ukrainian territory and that offered no true constraints on future Russian behavior. Via social media, Trump accused Zelenskyy of disrespect and told him to come back only "when he is ready" for such an agreement.

Looking back to my 2016 article, it's easy to see how the stoppage jibes with Trump's longstanding pro-Russian, anti-Ukrainian stance. Here are four of the points I mentioned back then:

— In 2007, Trump said on CNN that Russian President Vladimir Putin was "doing a great job in rebuilding the image of Russia and also rebuilding Russia period."

— During the 2016 presidential campaign, Trump declared he would "be friendly with Putin" and not automatically come to the aid of a NATO ally attacked by Russia.

— At the Republican convention in 2016, the Trump campaign eliminated a plank that called for giving Ukraine military aid to defend against invading Russian troops.

— On Oct. 7, 2016, the U.S. director of national intelligence and the secretary of homeland security said the Russians had hacked servers of the Democratic National Committee "to interfere with the U.S. election process" and tilt it toward Trump.

So, after his election victory in 2016, Trump owed President Putin. The Republican-majority Senate Intelligence Committee found that "the Russian government engaged in an aggressive, multi-faceted effort to influence, or attempt to influence, the outcome of the 2016 presidential election." Trump rejected the evidence of this Russian interference uncovered by U.S. intelligence agencies and instead expressed his faith in Putin's "extremely strong and powerful" denial.

In contrast, Trump holds a substantial grudge against President Zelenskyy; David Frum, a former George W. Bush speechwriter, calls it "a highly personal hatred." In a telephone call with Zelenskyy in July 2019, Trump demanded that the Ukrainian president open a baseless investigation into Joe Biden as a quid pro quo for releasing $400 million in military aid. Zelenskyy did not knuckle under. Instead, Trump's demand would form the basis of his first impeachment trial where he was accused of engaging in a "scheme or course of conduct for corrupt purposes in pursuit of personal political benefit." Every Democratic senator and one Republican, Mitt Romney, found him guilty, but the vote fell far short of the two-thirds required to remove Trump from office.

The day after the Trump-Zelenskyy meeting in the White House on Feb. 28, former Russian President Dmitry Medvedev, a close Putin ally, said Zelenskyy had received "a brutal dressing down in the Oval Office" and called for an end to American military aid to Ukraine. Two days later, Trump granted the Russian his wish. So, Trump's latest stoppage can be seen as another thank you to Putin for his past support and another punishment for Zelenskyy's chutzpah in not yielding to threats.

Trump's most recent stoppage of arms sales to Ukraine is the most flagrant in a series of pro-Russian initiatives taken in the weeks since his inauguration. Last month in Saudi Arabia, Secretary of State Marco Rubio met for peace talks on the Ukrainian-Russian War with Russian representatives. No Ukrainian representatives were invited. News reports indicate the White House has already asked the State and Treasury Departments to draft options for easing the sanctions placed on Russia after its invasion of Ukraine. Trump's defense secretary has ordered the Pentagon to stop efforts to counter Russian cyberattacks aimed at influencing American elections, and his attorney general has disbanded a foreign election interference task force.

Back in August 2016, Michael Morell, a career intelligence officer and the former deputy CIA director, said, "In the intelligence business, we would say that Mr. Putin had recruited Mr. Trump as an unwitting agent of the Russian Federation." In 2024, Nikki Haley, then Trump's leading rival for the Republican presidential nomination, said that Trump is siding with Putin, "a thug who's made no bones about the fact that he wants to destroy America."

Here's the ending of that article which ran in the Chronicle just before Trump's first term: "Having won the Cold War, we run the risk now of losing the peace. Trump's intention to tilt toward Russia was public information before election day. The sad thing is millions of American voters just didn't care."

Trump did little to hide his intention to aid and abet Russian aims in his second term either. And again, not enough Americans cared.

Ukraine and Israel: Twin Targets in a Deadly Blame Game

March 12, 2025

On Feb. 24, 2022, 190,000 Russian troops invaded Ukraine. Two years later, Russian President Vladimir Putin said, "We did not start this war in 2022."

On Oct. 7, 2023, Hamas terrorists crossed from Gaza into Israel and murdered over 1,200 civilians, many of whom had been attending a music festival. The Hamas Media Office called the attack "a defensive act."

Russia and Hamas were both guilty of using mirror propaganda to accuse the *victims* of their aggression of being its *perpetrators*.

Three years after the Russian invasion, Donald Trump echoed Putin and declared Ukraine "should have never started" the war against Russia. No surprise. Trump has a long record of expressing sympathy for Russia and admiration for its president. At the same time, he blames Ukrainian President Volodymyr Zelenskyy for his 2019 impeachment and bridles at the "disrespect" he's been shown by Zelenskyy.

Israel has enough enemies and Palestinian Arabs enough champions among media, politicians, influencers and students that Israel is way too often presumed the guilty party in any reaction to the current war. The very day after the Hamas attack, the Harvard Undergraduate Palestine Solidarity Committee and 33 other Harvard student organizations signed a statement that held "the Israeli regime entirely responsible for all unfolding violence." Neither nuance nor truth had any place in the condemnation.

The current Russian regime holds that the U.N.-recognized state of Ukraine is an "artificial" state belonging to Russia. This despite Stalin's genocidal suppression of Ukraine during the 1930s resulting in the death of 3.9 million people and the 92% majority of Ukrainians who voted for independence from Russia in 1991.

Likewise, Hamas claims all the territory of Israel "from the river to the sea." Its 1988 covenant states, "There is no solution for the Palestinian question except through Jihad (Holy War)" and "Israel will exist and will continue to exist until Islam will obliterate it." This despite a Jewish presence in what is now Israel for over 3,000 years, the U.N. recognition of the State of Israel in 1949 and the withdrawal of the Israeli military from Gaza in 2005.

Unfounded charges of Nazism are hallmarks of both Russia's and Hamas' mirror propaganda. The authoritarian Putin charges that the democratic Ukraine is a hotbed of "neo-Nazism." The genocidal Hamas Covenant accuses Israel of "Zionist Nazi activities."

The Russian military has bombed civilian targets including power plants, schools and hospitals. Russia stands accused of abducting almost 20,000 Ukrainian children. A 2023 U.N. report called out the attacks on civilian women: "During Russian armed forces' initial control of localities in Ukraine, many of the... rapes, and sexual violence were committed in the context of house-to-house searches."

In its "narrative" of the Oct. 7 attack, the Hamas Media Office stated, "Avoiding harm to civilians, especially children, women and elderly people is a religious and moral commitment by all the (Hamas) fighters." Over 1,200 civilians were murdered in Hamas's Oct. 7 attack on Israel. A report by Pramila Patten, special representative of the U.N. Secretary-General, described "rape and gang rape" by the attackers. Her investigation "found that several fully naked or partially naked bodies from the waist down were recovered — mostly women — with hands tied and shot multiple times, often in the head."

At the same, too many so-called American "progressives" tilt toward Hamas. I am not certain what is progressive about supporting a gang of murderous, raping terrorists over the Middle East's only democracy. Michigan Rep. Rashida Tlaib refused to vote for a resolution condemning "rape and sexual violence committed by Hamas." Rep. Alexandria Ocasio-Cortez accuses Israel of genocide against the Palestinian people. What does she mean? Since 1948, the number of Israeli non-Jews, overwhelmingly Arab, has grown over 16 times. How is that wiping out a people? Arab citizens voluntarily serve in the Israeli defense forces, and Arab judges have sat on the Israeli Supreme Court.

Israel is imperfect for sure, but so was the U.S. in how it waged World War II. The day after the Japanese attack on Pearl Harbor, President Franklin D. Roosevelt vowed, "No matter how long it may take us to overcome this premeditated invasion, the American people in their righteous might will win through to absolute victory." If the U.S. could not live with the threat of Imperial Japan 4,000 miles across the Pacific from Hawaii, how can Israel be expected to tolerate Hamas on its very border?

So here we are. Trump and his posse disregard American values in tilting their policy toward a ruthless, authoritarian regime bent on subduing Ukraine, a U.N.-recognized democracy. At the same time, many progressive Americans who claim to stand for democracy and multiethnic diversity and to oppose terrorism and religious prejudice take a narrow-minded position against Israel, the only Middle Eastern state that aspires to stand for those same values.

Shakespeare expressed how I feel best: A plague on both your houses.

Corruption Goes Viral in Second Trump Administration

March 19, 2025

A man with a long track record of corruption took office as president in January. In his second term, he's surrounding himself with like-minded cabinet secretaries and agency heads.

It's a fact that Donald J. Trump is a felon, convicted by a unanimous state jury of 34 counts of corruptly falsifying business records. Days before taking office in 2017, he paid $25 million to settle a suit for cheating students who'd enrolled in Trump University. His Trump Foundation was shut down for misusing charitable funds for political gain.

Now back in office, Trump continues to exude the odor of corruption more strongly than ever. Here's one example: his launch of a cryptocurrency product in January. Two days before his inauguration, Trump promoted a meme coin on the social media platform X with a post urging investors to "GET YOUR $TRUMP NOW." Purchase of the coin provides a straightforward way to funnel money to Trump. Last month, the SEC paused its investigation into a businessman after he bought $75 million worth of the coin.

Corruption and conflicts of interest have gone viral in the second Trump administration.

Take Elon Musk, who contributed $288 million to the 2024 Trump presidential campaign and who, according to The New York Times, has signaled his intent to contribute another $100 million to the Trump political operation. Musk's net worth of over $300 billion can be traced primarily to his holdings in Tesla, the electrical vehicle company; SpaceX, the rocket company; xAI, an artificial intelligence company; and Neuralink, a company designing brain implants. He is the CEO of the first three and owner of the fourth. The Washington Post estimates that Musk and his businesses have received at least $38 billion in contracts, loans, subsidies and tax credits from the federal government extending back over 20 years.

After winning the election in November, Trump announced that "the Great Elon Musk" would co-manage the Department of Government Efficient to "pave the way for my Administration to dismantle Government Bureaucracy, slash excess regulations, cut wasteful expenditures, and restructure Federal Agencies." Musk has since become the sole head of DOGE.

According to Bloomberg News, SpaceX engineer Ted Malaska instructed Federal Aviation Administration employees to "immediately start work on a program to deploy thousands of the company's Starlink satellite terminals to support the national airspace system." The Campaign Legal Center has filed a conflict-of-interest complaint with the Department of Transportation citing evidence "that Musk has blatantly and improperly influenced the FAA's decision to work with Starlink" in violation of criminal law. Starlink is a satellite communications company owned by SpaceX.

This past September, the FAA proposed a $633,000 fine for SpaceX's failure to follow its licensing requirements during two 2023 launches. This month, a SpaceX rocket diverted commercial air traffic when it blew up over the Caribbean Sea. According to the company website, SpaceX is working with the FAA "to either close the mishap investigation or receive a flight safety determination, along with working on a license authorization to enable its next flight of Starship." At the same time, the Musk-directed DOGE is laying off FAA employees, over 400 in February.

Dismissing civil servants who are regulating or investigating Musk companies has become standard operating procedure in the current Trump administration. Musk has accused the National Highway Traffic Safety Administration of slowing his company's technological progress. The team regulating autonomous vehicles, which are under development at Tesla, has been cut almost in half. There was no need to lay off any civil servants overseeing former President Joe Biden's executive order regulating artificial intelligence, xAI's business. Trump rescinded the order on his first day in office. The Food and Drug Administration was reviewing the plans of Neuralink for brain implants. Employees doing the review were laid off by DOGE.

Shouldn't federal laws prohibiting federal employees from working on matters where they have a financial interest apply to Musk? Nope, not according to the current administration. Trump has designated Musk "a special government employee," purportedly not subject to conflict-of-interest laws.

On the other hand, there's no doubt Robert F. Kennedy Jr., the secretary of Health and Human Services, is subject to those laws. Prior to his confirmation, Kennedy Jr. was paid over $2.5 million by the law firm Wisner Baum. Under his signed ethics agreement, Kennedy Jr. will continue to receive 10% of fees awarded to the firm as a result of its suit against the pharmaceutical giant Merck. The legal action relates to the Merck vaccine that protects against cervical, vaginal, vulvar and anal cancer. At least Kennedy Jr. promises to "not provide representational services in connection with the cases during my appointment to the position of Secretary." In the Kennedy Jr. confirmation hearing, Massachusetts Sen. Elizabeth Warren said the bottom line was this: "Kennedy can kill off access to vaccines and make millions of dollars while he does it."

Trump has nominated TV celebrity doctor Mehmet Oz to head the Centers for Medicare and Medicaid Services, which has a budget of almost $1.5 trillion that provides coverage for more than 40% of all Americans. According to his filings, Oz's net worth is somewhere between $90 million and $335 million. He holds stock in iHerb, which sells products he has pitched as supplements that stimulate hair growth and "might be able to actually help with Alzheimer's." In office, he could influence Medicare and Medicaid coverage of iHerb products. He has fudged as to whether he would sell his holdings.

There are more examples of potential corruption among Trump's nominees and appointees, but let's stop with Musk, Kennedy Jr. and Oz for now. They remind me of one of my favorite quotes. In Ian Fleming's "Goldfinger," the title character tells 007: "Mr. Bond, they have a saying in Chicago: Once is happenstance, twice is coincidence, the third time it's enemy action."

Chief Justice Roberts Hands Trump the Keys to Power

March 26, 2025

Chief Justice John Roberts recently reprimanded Donald Trump for his irresponsible behavior. That's like a parent scolding their 10-year-old son for reckless driving after tossing him the car keys.

So, what am I accusing Roberts of? Of doing more than just about anyone else in clearing the road for Trump's rise to power and his illegal actions once in the White House. The bill of particulars could be much longer, but let's just look at four counts.

First, there's the Supreme Court's 2010 decision in Citizens United v. Federal Elections Committee. In that case, Roberts cast the deciding vote to reverse a century of precedent by authorizing corporations, other outside groups and wealthy donors to spend unlimited sums on elections. Just days after the decision, President Barack Obama warned the decision "will open the floodgates for special interests — including foreign corporations — to spend without limit in our elections." Unlimited contributions have indeed tilted the American electoral process toward the interests of corporations and the rich. Today, the largest contributor to Trump's 2024 campaign, Elon Musk, is playing an unprecedented role in the current administration.

Second, in 2013, Roberts assigned himself to write the majority opinion in Shelby County v. Holder, which threw out a key section of the Voting Rights Act. A 2024 article in the Journal of Political Economy found evidence that the Shelby County holding decreased turnout of minority voters due to "voter suppression tactics that have occurred in the absence of federal oversight." As two professors wrote in an American Economic Association paper:

"Our findings suggest that perhaps Chief Justice Roberts should be slightly less optimistic about the state of democratic equality in the South."

Third, in 2023, the Colorado Supreme Court ruled that Trump should be taken off the state's ballot because of the 14th Amendment's bar on candidates who have "engaged in insurrection or rebellion" against the United States or "given aid or comfort to its enemies." Upon review, Roberts and four associate justices held that a statute must be passed by Congress for such a disqualification to take effect.

And in the most serious count, Roberts again assigned himself to write for the majority in last summer's United States v. Trump. In his opinion, the chief justice conjured up a right to immunity for the president "from criminal prosecution for conduct within his exclusive sphere of constitutional authority." In a scathing dissent, Justice Sonia Sotomayor says Roberts "invents an atextual, ahistorical, and unjustifiable immunity that puts the President above the law."

Trump agrees wholeheartedly with Sotomayor's analysis. He has said, "I have the right to do whatever I want as president" and "He who saves his country does not violate any law." He appears to know, too, that he owes Roberts a debt of gratitude. On March 4, cameras caught Trump patting Roberts on the arm and saying, "Thank you again. I won't forget."

In his two months in office, Trump has ignored dozens of statutes and constitutional provisions. He's issued executive orders intended to overturn citizenship rights granted by the 14th Amendment, block money appropriated by Congress to the Agency for International Development, blackball an Associated Press reporter from White House briefings, fire civil servants without cause and much more.

Recently, Trump ordered rounding up noncitizens for their alleged membership in a Venezuelan gang and sending them to a prison in El Salvador. He claims the right to do so without a hearing under the Alien Enemies Act of 1798 which applies only in wartime or in case of invasion. Judge James Boasberg, who was first named to a judgeship by President George W. Bush, issued an order temporarily halting these deportations. On social media, Trump called Judge Boasberg, a "Radical Left Lunatic of a Judge" and went on to say, "this judge like many of the Crooked Judges' I am forced to appear before, should be IMPEACHED!!!"

Roberts reacted to the president's post with a statement of his own: "For more than two centuries, it has been established that impeachment is not an appropriate response to disagreement concerning a judicial decision. The normal appellate review process exists for that purpose."

Ah, Mr. Chief Justice, your admonition is too little, too late. You've already played a key role in opening American politics to a corrupting flood of money, restricting the right to vote, ensuring Trump stayed on the 2024 ballot in every state and putting the president above the law. You've put the keys to the kingdom in Trump's hands, and it's not going to be easy to wrest them away.

When It Comes to Trump, It's Time To Choose

April 2, 2025

Go along or stand against?

There's a tendency among Americans to seek compromise, to have a win-win solution for both sides in any controversy, but you cannot compromise with someone like Donald Trump. You either give in or resist.

Since Jan. 20, Trump has issued an executive order violating the 14th Amendment, refused to spend funds appropriated by Congress, called for the impeachment of a judge ruling against him, threatened to invade the sovereign territory of a NATO ally and suggested a run for a third presidential term despite the 22nd Amendment. His appointees have overseen the roundup and deportation of legal residents by masked personnel.

How to react to this second coming of Donald Trump?

Take the prominent law partnership of Paul Weiss in New York City. Trump issued an order attacking the firm for its "diversity, equity, and inclusion" policies and for employing a lawyer who represented clients suing Jan. 6 rioters. He ordered federal agencies to break any contracts with Paul Weiss "to the maximum extent permitted by applicable law." Paul Karp, the firm's chairman, said that even if the firm won a lawsuit against the Trump administration, "clients had told us that they were not going to be able to stay with us." He agreed in a meeting with Trump to "a comprehensive audit" of the firm's employment practices by an outsider and to offer $40 million in free legal services to causes supporting Trumpian views. Trump rescinded the order, and Karp told employees the firm was saved.

Trump also issued an order sanctioning another law firm, WilmerHale, for "obvious partisan representations to achieve political ends." WilmerHale chose a different path than Paul Weiss. They sued the executive office of the president. Pending trial, a federal judge stayed the Trump order, quoting the Supreme Court: "The First Amendment prohibits government officials from subjecting individuals to 'retaliatory actions'... for having engaged in protected speech."

Not only law firms have been targeted by Trump. He canceled $400 million in federal funding for Columbia University allegedly because of the university's failure to combat campus antisemitism. Columbia has tried to appease him by promising to improve its disciplinary process, to expand intellectual diversity among its faculty and, most notably, to appoint a new administrator to review all university programs focused on global regions "starting immediately with the Middle East."

On March 31, the nation's oldest institution of higher learning received a letter from the Trump administration stating its intention to review $8.7 billion in "multi-year grant commitments to Harvard University and its affiliates" in response to "Harvard's failure to protect students on campus from anti-Semitic discrimination." How the administration came up with the $8.7 billion figure is unclear, as is who the Harvard "affiliates" are. If they include Harvard hospitals, is the administration threatening to stop Medicare and Medicaid payments reimbursing patients? Harvard President Alan Garber stated, "If this funding is stopped, it will halt life-saving research and imperil important scientific research and innovation." Harvard, where I am a resident scholar, has already taken numerous steps to combat campus antisemitism. Unlike the Columbia case, no funds have yet been cut off.

I fear Harvard will eventually be placed in a position where it, too, will have to make a wrenching decision between saving lives, preserving jobs, teaching students and extending knowledge versus yielding to governmental bullying and inroads on academic freedom. To avoid the latter, I wonder if the university would dip into its $50 billion-plus endowment.

I wrote my graduate thesis on the end of British appeasement of Nazi Germany before World War II. In it, I focused on the moment in March 1939 when Prime Minister Neville Chamberlain realized appeasement no longer worked against Hitler and he needed to draw a line in the sand.

I don't want to overstate the case, but I believe we are at such a point now. The decision to accede or resist is not just for law firms and universities. It will need to be made by media outlets reporting the facts, by epidemiologists fighting pandemics, by protesters threatened with violence, by Republican officeholders criticizing the administration and by Americans deciding how to vote.

Commit to being loyal to Trump, and we Americans can go about our business without interference from the feds. We can ignore what's going on in Washington and tend to our jobs, children, friends and schoolwork, while enjoying life as best we can.

That choice is defensible. And yet, so is paying attention to the actions of the Trump administration and committing to stand for liberty and justice for all and refusing to abandon the American dream.

The White House has circulated a message from Trump where he refers to himself as a "king" along with an illustration of himself adorned with a golden crown.

On July 4, 1776, the United States declared its independence from a king whose objective was "the establishment of an absolute Tyranny over these States." Those who signed the Declaration of Independence did so to "secure the Blessings of Liberty to ourselves and our Posterity." Above their signatures, they stated: "with a firm reliance on the protection of divine Providence, we mutually pledge to each other our Lives, our Fortunes and our sacred Honor."

I want to stand with those Founders. I want to stand with Lincoln who promised "that government of the people, by the people, for the people, shall not perish from the earth." I want to stand with Ronald Reagan who said, "As long as we remember those first principles and believe in ourselves, the future will always be ours." I want to stand with my dad who fought for freedom in World War II.

It's time to choose sides.

250 Years After Paul Revere's Ride, Boston Still Stands for Liberty

April 9, 2025

In April 1775, Paul Revere set out on horseback from Boston to warn the patriots that the British king in London was sending redcoats to suppress their demands for liberty. When I was a kid, I dreamt I was there.

In April 2025, nearly 100,000 people rallied in front of Boston City Hall to warn the would-be American king in Washington to keep his hands off their democracy. This time, as an adult, I really was there.

In his classic poem, Henry Wadsworth Longfellow wrote that Revere shouted out "a cry of defiance and not of fear" on his ride. There was plenty of defiance in Boston's City Hall Plaza, too. Signs demanded that the Trump Administration keep its "hands off" public health, clean air and water, women's bodies, Medicare, free speech, due process, personal liberty and much more.

Back in 1775, Harvard was the only college in Massachusetts. Harvard's still there, but today in Greater Boston there's also Boston University, MIT, Tufts, Boston College, Wellesley, UMass Boston, Brandeis, Emerson, Lesley and other institutions with a total student enrollment of close to 400,000. It's no surprise, then, that at the rally, signs were also plentiful calling for the administration to keep their "hands off our students, books, education, and science." Cancer survivors waved placards demanding the administration also keep its hands off university cancer research to which they attributed their very lives.

But alas, in addition to the defiance, there was also fear. One protester I spoke to, having no desire to be identified or rounded up, wore a mask, oversized sunglasses and a hoodie. I saw dozens of signs demanding the release of Rumeysa Ozturk, a Turkish national and Ph.D. student at Tufts University who was handcuffed and bundled into a black SUV by masked ICE agents while on her way to meet up with friends. Her only offense was exercising her right to free speech by co-authoring a column in the student paper critical of America's Mideast policy. Over 140 students have had their visas revoked by the Trump administration at last count.

Just what were the patriots fighting for in the Revolutionary War? According to the Declaration of Independence, they wished to win freedom from George III whose "every act" went to "define a Tyrant" and whose character made him "unfit to be the ruler of a free people."

These words resonated among the present-day Boston protesters. They held signs reading, "No kings, no tyranny" and "I thought Schoolhouse Rock said no more kings." Trump has indeed recently referred to himself as a king on social media. In Great Britain, there's been a military parade to celebrate the king or queen's birthday since 1748. Now there are reports Trump wants one for his birthday on June 14. Does he really think that making America great again means a return to monarchy?

In the Declaration of Independence, George III was charged with "a long train of abuses and usurpation" intended to establish "absolute Despotism." Could those same words be used in regard to Trump's actions in his second term? He's issued an executive order violating the 14th Amendment, called for the impeachment of a judge ruling against him, targeted law firms whose partners represented his opponents and disregarded how Congress has appropriated funds by law.

The Declaration of Independence also accused George III of "for cutting off our Trade with all parts of the world" and "for transporting us beyond Seas to be tried for pretended offences." Given Trump's imposition of prohibitive tariffs and the deportation of legal U.S. residents to El Salvador, these words seem eerily spot-on for Trump's actions, too.

There were over 1,400 demonstrations against Trump and his regime in cities besides Boston on April 5. But for me, even after 250 years, Boston stands preeminent as "the cradle of liberty."

A person at the demonstration a few feet away from me held up a sign reading: "Boston: Making Tyrants Nervous Since 1775." I smiled upon the realization that sentiment lives on not only at City Hall Plaza, but also in the names of two local sports teams: for football, the Patriots, and for soccer, the Revolution.

A Depraved Heart Lurks in the White House

April 23, 2025

New York courts have found President Donald J. Trump to be a felon and liar. Colorado courts found him to be an insurrectionist (even though the U.S. Supreme Court blocked attempts to take him off the ballot). I'd like to add one more accusation to his rap sheet: attempted murder.

Now, I don't like to think of myself as an irrational extremist in making such a charge. Of course, I prefer to consider myself a historian and lawyer who comes to the conclusion based on facts and reasoning. Here is my logic in finding the 47th president of these United States has taken actions that will result in foreseeable deaths.

There's a concept in the law known as "depraved heart murder." The classic example is a shooter firing randomly into a crowd and killing a person. Cornell's Legal Information Institute defines depraved heart murder as "killing someone in a way that demonstrates a callous disregard for the value of human life." The Model Penal Code, adopted by many states, restates the concept by deeming it murder when a defendant kills with "extreme indifference to the value of human life."

Isn't that more or less what Trump is doing? Causing deaths with "callous disregard" and "extreme indifference" to human lives? Let me give you some examples.

In 2024, the United States spent roughly $12 billion, about 0.006% of the federal budget for the year, on health programs primarily aimed at poor countries. Trump ordered the cessation of the programs upon taking office. Their future is uncertain. According to modeling done by global health consultants at Avenir Health, a complete end to U.S. funding, not replaced by other sources, would lead to 25 million additional deaths in the next 15 years from AIDS, tuberculosis and other causes. Trump will not be found guilty of these deaths in a court of law but will nonetheless be morally guilty of millions of counts of depraved heart murder.

The coronavirus pandemic cost Trump the presidential election in 2020. Cuts in the Centers for Disease Control and Prevention are undermining the nation's ability to counter the next deadly pandemic, whether that's bird flu or another infectious threat. Trump appointee Robert F. Kennedy Jr. is undercutting support for vaccines across the country. Already there have been at least two deaths from measles this year with more inevitable as the viciously infectious virus spreads among the unvaccinated.

The World Health Organization estimates that in the two decades between 2030 and 2050, climate change will cause "approximately 250,000 additional deaths per year, from undernutrition, malaria, diarrhoea and heat stress alone." The Trump administration's rollback of environmental regulations, retreat from support of clean power sources and advocacy of coal mining and oil drilling will inevitably increase that number.

News reports indicate the Trump administration intends to cut a quarter of the budget of the National Oceanic and Atmospheric Administration. The National Weather Service, part of NOAA, has already curtailed launches of weather balloons required for accurate forecasting. The NOAA cuts are bound to affect its ability to provide life-saving information on impending floods, tornadoes and hurricanes.

Trump is attacking research at American institutions of higher learning. His most prominent target is Harvard, the nation's oldest university. His administration has threatened to take away over $2 billion in federal grants from Harvard in coming years. In its suit to stop him from doing so, Harvard cites "the longstanding collaboration" between the university and federal government that "has enabled researchers at Harvard to develop novel drugs to fight

Parkinson's and Alzheimer's diseases, engineer nanofibers to protect servicemembers and first responders, support American astronauts in space, and design an artificial intelligence system that can be used to diagnose and treat cancer."

Today, such federally funded work at Harvard is slowing or stopping. Professor David R. Walt has received an order to stop work on his research that could result in drugs to treat ALS (aka Lou Gehrig's disease). Research on how to stop future coronavirus epidemics and on a tuberculosis vaccine have also ceased. The next generation of scientists will suffer in their training on how to save lives. The effects of the Trump administration's actions will resound through decades. (I myself am currently a resident scholar at Harvard but receive no federal funding for my work.)

Almost every week, Trump and his appointees take other steps that risk human lives such as reversing bans on toxic chemicals, sending innocent people to horrific foreign prisons, discussing war plans over unsecured channels and revoking security clearances from former officials.

Thousands and even millions of people will die from actions arising from Trump's depraved heart. Trump will not face a jury for these deaths, as he did in the cases finding him a liar and fraudster. Instead, he must stand trial for them in the court of public opinion and in voting booths.

I believe we Americans are a good and compassionate people. I believe we should not, cannot, will not remain passive while a president with a depraved heart causes so many deaths.

If Independent Press Vanishes, So Do First Amendment Protections

April 30, 2025

In addition to guaranteeing freedom of speech and religion, the First Amendment prohibits government action "abridging freedom... of the press."

As President Ronald Reagan declared, "There is no more essential ingredient than a free, strong, and independent press to our continued success in what the Founding Fathers called our 'noble experiment' in self-government."

During the glory days of the American press, newspapers stood up against government pressure. In 1972, Attorney General John Mitchell heard what The Washington Post was going to publish about the Nixon administration's role in the Watergate scandal. He vowed that Post publisher Katharine Graham "is gonna get her tit caught in a big fat wringer if that's published." The paper published, nonetheless.

When the founder of Amazon and its largest shareholder Jeff Bezos bought the Post in 2013, he promised, "While I hope no one ever threatens to put one of my body parts through a wringer, if they do, thanks to Mrs. Graham's example, I'll be ready."

That hifalutin rhetoric came before Trump interfered with a $10 billion contract that Amazon Web Services was seeking with the Defense Department. In a 2019 lawsuit, Amazon accused Trump of seeking to select a competitor in order to hurt Bezos, "his perceived political enemy," because of his ownership of the paper.

Apparently, Bezos learned his lesson. Just before the election last fall, he killed a Post editorial endorsing Trump's opponent for the presidency, Kamala Harris. Two weeks before Trump took office, the paper refused to run a political cartoon by Pulitzer Prize winner Ann Telnaes showing Bezos on bended knee before Trump. A month after the inauguration, Bezos announced: "We are going to be writing every day in support and defense of two pillars: personal liberties and free markets. ... Viewpoints opposing those pillars will be left to be published by others."

Marty Baron, the former editor of the Post, explained, "I don't think that (Bezos) wants an editorial page that's regularly going after Donald Trump" because of the fear "that Trump would take vengeance on his perceived political enemies."

I doubt any part of Bezos' anatomy was put through a wringer as he moved the Post from editorial independence to presidential appeasement. Bezos would not let his ownership of the newspaper harm the source of his own wealth and the livelihood of those who work for the company. When the Post was owned by the Graham family, they treated it as a public trust. For Bezos, it's a side hustle.

Bezos, Amazon and the Post are not alone here. Other news organizations and their owners are yielding to Trump:

— The Los Angeles Times killed an endorsement of Harris last fall, which resulted in the resignation of its editor. The paper's owner, Patrick Soon-Shiong, with an estimated net worth of $10.2 billion, has business interests in pharmaceuticals and biotech that require federal approvals.

Bill Owens, the executive producer of CBS' 60 Minutes newsmagazine recently resigned, saying he was no longer allowed to "make independent decisions based on what was right for 60 Minutes." The controlling shareholder of Paramount, CBS' parent, is seeking government approval for the sale of the company.

Trump has also sued Paramount for $20 billion for the way a 60 Minutes interview with Kamala Harris was edited. To the chagrin of CBS News employees, recent reports indicate Paramount is negotiating a payment with Trump despite the baselessness of Trump's lawsuit.

In the early 19th century, British statesman George Canning declared, "I called the New World into existence to redress the balance of the Old." Relying on the new world of online media to compensate for the concessions of old media is a long shot. In the wake of Trump's 2020 victory, Meta, the parent of Facebook which has over three billion users, announced it would stop fact-checking posts even though, as CEO Mark Zuckerberg admitted, "We're going to catch less bad stuff." Twitter, now known as X, was bought for $44 billion in 2022 by Elon Musk, Trump's largest campaign contributor. In October, Giulio Corsi, a researcher at the University of Cambridge, told NBC News, "We do have a lot of evidence to suspect that X is turning more and more far-right by the day."

Trump himself shows no deference to the First Amendment. During last year's campaign, he called the press "corrupt" and promised to "straighten out our press." He suggested that criticism of federal judge Aileen Cannon for her pro-Trump rulings "should be illegal." As president, he threatened to sue the media for "defamatory fiction" and "blatant dishonesty." He continued, "Who knows, maybe we will create some nice new law!!!."

Back in the glory days of the American press, leading news sources were often family-owned. As noted, Katharine Graham was willing to risk it all for journalistic integrity. The Carters who owned the Delta Democrat Times and the Binghams who owned the Louisville Courier-Journal took unpopular stands in favor of civil rights. The LA Times owned by the Chandlers won a Pulitzer for its reporting on the Watts riots. The coverage of the Vietnam War by CBS News, controlled by the Paley family, helped turn the country against the Nixon administration.

All these traditional news organizations have been sold by the one-time controlling families and have become small parts of larger corporations.

Alas, the First Amendment's guarantee of freedom of the press is an empty promise if there is no independent press to exercise that freedom.

The masthead of The Washington Post's webpage still says, "Democracy Dies in Darkness." If that's the case, American democracy is gasping for breath. It's five minutes before sundown.

Thinking About War and Peace — All 1,224 Pages of It

May 7, 2025

It usually takes me a day to tap out a rough draft of this column, and I spend the next morning wrestling it into publishable form. The other five days of the week I devote to novel-writing. Stephen King says we writers need to read to learn their craft: "If you don't have time to read, you don't have the time (or the tools) to write."

Despite that admonition, for years I'd refused to spend the time reading Leo Tolstoy's novel "War and Peace," published in 1869. A century ago, Nobel Prize winner John Galsworthy, author of "The Forsyte Saga," called it "the best novel that had ever been written." Five years ago, the Economist reported it still "is widely considered the world's greatest novel."

So why hadn't I ever read it? Because it's so daunting, 1,224 pages long in the version I own, almost 600,000 words in English translated from the original Russian. That's about a dozen times longer than "The Great Gatsby."

But in the end, Fate intervened. Casually leafing through the spring course catalog at Harvard where I'm a resident scholar, I came across professor Julie Buckler's course titled simply "Reading Tolstoy's 'War and Peace.'" I checked the student ratings from the last time she'd taught the course — 4.92 out of 5, perhaps the highest score I'd ever seen. I knew it was time. Spread over a semester, I'd only be reading 100 pages a week. No more excuses.

I emailed the professor, who told me I could audit the course — take it but not for a grade — as long as I sat in the back of the classroom. I accepted her terms. (Later I asked if I could move up front to hear student comments better. She acceded to my plea.)

When I turned to page 1, I felt like a marathoner who'd just taken a first step on what was bound to be a grueling challenge.

On the opening day of class, I found myself seated with about 50 students ready to accept the challenge along with me. That in itself restored some of my faith in this generation of undergraduates. These were my people, people who shared my belief in the potential of a college education. Of course, it should teach you how to make a living. But college should also teach you something about how to lead a meaningful life and to make the world a better place. Studying a great novel will not get you a lucrative Wall Street job like an A in econometrics might, but it will teach you about empathy, the human condition, personal relationships and life's purpose. My classmates seemed to understand that.

I don't know about those students, but I doubt I would have had the willpower to read the book on my own. It was professor Buckler's enthusiasm and love for the novel that propelled the ship that carried me through the sea of sentences. Reading the book could be a slog at times, but it was always a fare worth paying to hear the professor's compelling insights delivered with verve and intelligence.

And holy mackerel, the students! So bright, so interested, so engaged, so eager to understand life itself. One student told the class she'd been so focused on her college studies that she hadn't read a novel since high school. The class showed her what she'd missed. She would return to reading fiction, a lost, and now rediscovered, love.

One reason I love to read fiction is to escape from the world we live in, filled as it is with violence, untruths, poverty, racism, inequality, lack of empathy and megalomania. And yet, this book set in Russia during the first two decades of the 19th century echoed present-day events. Russians faced the French Emperor Napoleon whose appetite for power was insatiable. Some were ready to accede to it; others were determined to resist. Sound familiar? On the night before battle, the Russian Prince Andrei is willing to trade the love of "my father, my sister, my wife... for a moment of glory... for love from people I don't know." Is that what soldiers and politicians do today? Where does that impulse come from?

Listening to students grapple with Tolstoy's implicit questions gave me renewed hope for the future. For three years, I co-taught a course on technology and ethics. One student majoring in engineering criticized my teaching by saying, "He asks questions. I want answers." But what is life but questions? There's no one right answer to how to find the right spouse, whether there is a higher power, what is worth dying for and what a person owes their parents and children. Tolstoy gives us insights to help us grapple with these questions ourselves, for what is a great novel but a crash course on life's meaning? In a world where artificial intelligence abounds, what makes us human is all the more important.

Clara Shapiro, a sophomore whose comments in class managed to be simultaneously original, thoughtful, passionate and entertaining, told me, "Reading this book with professor Buckler and the rest of the class helped me feel not just the miracle of reading, but of living even one day on Earth."

What's next? I'm checking the catalog for a course on Marcel Proust's "In Search of Lost Time," a seven-volume novel even longer than Tolstoy's masterpiece. The renowned English author E.M. Forster called it, "Our second greatest novel after 'War and Peace.'" I'm inspired and ready.

The Donald Trump Revenge Tour Is Underway

May 14, 2025

On April 23, 1992, the Rock and Roll Hall of Fame band Kiss started its Revenge Tour in San Francisco.

On Jan. 20, 2025, the Gaming Hall of Fame member Donald J. Trump started his own Revenge Tour in Washington, D.C.

It's dangerous spelunking into the caverns of Trump's mind, but it's clear to me that the motivating factor of his presidency is revenge. And Trump hasn't kept it a secret. On the campaign trail, he repeatedly declared to MAGA crowds, "I am your retribution."

Trump aide Omarosa Manigault warned back in 2016: "Every critic, every detractor, will have to bow down to President Trump. It's everyone who's ever doubted Donald, whoever disagreed, whoever challenged him — it is the ultimate revenge to become the most powerful man in the universe."

So, what are a few examples of pieces Trump has played on his revenge tour?

He removed security protection from his first-term national security adviser John Bolton and Secretary of State Mike Pompeo, who'd both taken actions Trump disliked after leaving their posts. That's despite threats against their lives by Iran. Apparently, any risk to their lives is trumped by a Trumpian thirst for vengeance.

Trump has bullied the media for supposed past offenses, too. He didn't think news platforms such as The Washington Post and Facebook had treated him fairly. Since Trump's reelection, the Post's owner, Jeff Bezos, has constricted what the paper's opinion pages say, and Mark Zuckerberg, CEO of Meta, stopped Facebook from fact-checking posts. When The Associated Press refused to change the 500-year-old name of the Gulf of Mexico to the Gulf of America, Trump had their reporters banned from the White House newsroom.

He considers PBS and NPR hotbeds of liberalism that failed to present "a fair, accurate, or unbiased portrayal of current events" and is trying to end every single dollar of federal funding for them.

State and federal lawyers who worked on cases where Trump was the defendant are especially high priority targets for the current president. He personally ordered the firing of more than a dozen Department of Justice lawyers who worked on special prosecutor Jack Smith's criminal prosecution of him. Pam Bondi, Trump's attorney general, has opened a criminal investigation of New York Attorney General Letitia James, whose office won a judgment against him for fraud. The judgment is now worth more than half a billion dollars. On March 14, Trump issued an order barring lawyers of the New York law firm Paul Weiss from federal office buildings and suspending their security clearances. The firm's primary offense in Trump's eyes was its past employment of one-time Special Assistant District Attorney Mark Pomerantz, who led investigations into Trump.

For Trump, resentment is an unquenchable flame.

In his first term, Trump was impeached for pressuring Ukrainian President Volodymyr Zelenskyy to announce a criminal investigation into rival Joe Biden and his son. Trump blames Zelenskyy for not yielding to his threats and, since returning to office, cut off aid to Ukraine once. He has broached leaving Ukraine to the tender mercies of Vladimir Putin and his North Korean mercenaries.

After Trump lost reelection in 2020, Israeli Prime Minister Benjamin Netanyahu called the winner, Joe Biden, to congratulate him on his victory. Trump has neither forgotten nor forgiven that routine act of diplomacy. Trump bypassed Netanyahu in negotiating the release of Israeli American hostage Edan Alexander, who was being held by the terrorist group Hamas. Trump's team also left Netanyahu out of a deal with the Houthis in Yemen that protected American ships from bombardment but not Israeli territory. Trump is making Netanyahu look like no more than a yapping poodle in the eyes of Israeli voters. It doesn't matter to Trump that an Israel less certain of American support may also be impelled to take riskier actions.

Civil lawsuits are a favored weapon in Trump's arsenal. In one example among many, after winning the 2024 election, he sued respected pollster J. Ann Seltzer and the Des Moines Register for "brazen electoral interference." Why would he undertake such litigation with almost no chance of winning in court? His explanation for suing a business reporter in 2006 applies to the Seltzer case as well: "I spent a couple of bucks on legal fees, and they spent a whole lot more. I did it to make his life miserable, which I'm happy about."

Nothing motivates Trump more than wreaking revenge on those who crossed him, underestimated him, belittled him or told unpleasant truths about him.

Great historical figures are often remembered for a few words that capture what motivated them. For Martin Luther King, they were that "he had a dream" of a country where "all men are created equal." For Lincoln, they were "that government of the people, by the people, for the people, shall not perish from the earth." For Patrick Henry, they were "give me liberty or give me death."

The words that encapsulate Trump's motivation were captured on camera after he beat his opponents in the 2024 New Hampshire primary: "I don't get angry, I get even."

Progressives Anything but When It Comes to Israel

May 21, 2025

Before being accepted to a fraternity or sorority, inductees must take a pledge to uphold its beliefs such as loyalty to fellow members. Similarly, before accepting members to its movement, American progressives are demanding a pledge that they take a stand against Israel.

For example, Rep. Rashida Tlaib, a charter member of the so-called progressive Squad in Congress, says if you don't believe Israel is an "apartheid state," then "it's become clear that you cannot claim to hold progressive values."

Wait a minute. Israel an apartheid state? The Israeli Declaration of Independence calls for a nation that "will ensure complete equality of social and political rights to all its inhabitants irrespective of religion, race or sex." Today, the country is 73% Jewish and 27% non-Jewish. No law restricts non-Jewish citizens to certain neighborhoods. If cities and towns where Arabs live tend to be poorer, that's comparable to the situation in the United States where 17% of Black people live in high-poverty neighborhoods as compared to 4% of white people. Both countries have work to do. Neither is an apartheid state.

Alexandria Ocasio-Cortez, another founding member of the Squad, has accused Israel of genocide, defined by Dictionary.com as "the deliberate and systematic extermination of a national, racial, political, or cultural group." Genocide does indeed underlie the current Hamas-Israel War. But AOC has a topsy-turvy understanding of the conflict. Genocide is the war aim of Hamas, not Israel. The Hamas Covenant calls for Islam to "obliterate" Israel and to "vanquish" all Jews. Hamas does not deny it. When an interviewer on Lebanese TV asked senior Hamas official Ghazi Hamad whether Hamas's war aims include the "annihilation of Israel," Hamad responded, "Yes, of course."

Israel's stated war aims are to free its hostages held by Hamas and put an end to its military and political power. Israel has said it would stop fighting if Hamas releases its hostages. Thousands of Gazans, at great danger to themselves, are now protesting against Hamas with calls for release of the remaining Israeli hostages. At the end of March, Oday al-Rubai was abducted by gunmen in Gaza City and murdered after taking part in such a protest. His family blames Hamas. So, there are protests against Hamas by Gazans but not by American progressives?

The United States Palestinian Community Network attacks "so called" progressives for support of Israel, which it deems "illegitimate" because of its "white settler-colonialism." Illegitimate? The State of Israel was established by a 1947 vote of the United Nations. White? Almost half of Israel's Jews trace their recent ancestry to the Arab and Muslim world and another 3% from Ethiopia. Twenty-one percent of the country are Arabs. Colonialism? If anything, Jews are the indigenous people of the Holy Land, having been there for over 3,000 years.

Another member of the progressive Squad, Rep. Ilhan Omar, has attributed support of Israel to the "Benjamins, baby." She's referring to political contributions by pro-Israel Americans — hundred-dollar bills bear a picture of Benjamin Franklin. If Omar were going to follow the byword of the Watergate scandal — "follow the money" — she'd find a foreign country trying to suborn American democracy with "Benjamins."

In their recent article "How Qatar Bought America," Frannie Block and Jay Solomon outline how the small Persian Gulf nation spent almost $100 billion over the last two decades "aiming to shape U.S. policy — or shield themselves from it." Qatar spent "three times more in the U.S. than Israel did on lobbyists, public-relations advisers, and other foreign agents in 2021." It also supported Hamas with over $1.8 billion over the years. Recently visited by President Donald Trump, Qatar offered him a 747 jet as a gift and is the prospective site of a new Trump luxury golf resort.

A key plank in any progressive platform is support for LGBT rights. Tel Aviv, Israel's largest city, holds Asia's largest gay pride parade each year with up to 250,000 participants. (It was canceled last year, though, in respect to the hostages still held by Hamas.) In Equaldex's LGBT Equality Index, Israel is ranked 39th, seven slots behind the U.S. Palestine, including Gaza and the West Bank, is ranked 158th. Which country should progressives be supporting?

Even if progressives believe what they are saying about Israel, why have they singled it out when more outrageous behavior exists elsewhere in this world of ours? Actual settler colonials from China are today taking over Tibet, which was invaded and conquered by China in 1950. The United States has also found China guilty of genocide for subjecting Uyghurs to imprisonment, forced labor, torture, rape and sterilization. What about Russia, which launched an unprovoked attack on Ukraine and abducted Ukrainian children? What about Myanmar, where, according to the State Department, the government "launched a brutal campaign against Rohingya — razing villages, raping, torturing, and perpetrating large-scale violence that killed thousands."

Why are progressives protesting only against a multiethnic democracy, fighting in a war started by a terrorist group bent on genocide? Because they don't think Jews, 0.2% of the world population, deserve their own nation? The French do, the Russians do, the Americans do, but not the Jews whose roots in Israel go back three millennia? There can be an Islamic Republic of Iran and an Islamic Republic of Pakistan, but not a Jewish State of Israel?

Does a strain of antisemitism run through so-called progressives in this country?

I do not support Trump's policies attacking education, undermining due process, ignoring court orders and embracing authoritarian regimes. Nevertheless, I am a proud American patriot.

I am no fan of Benjamin Netanyahu's government and fervently wish it did better in feeding the hungry and avoiding deaths of noncombatants. Still, I support the State of Israel in defending its right to exist against its genocidal, terroristic neighbor.

And most of all, I support what ought to be the most important plank in any progressive agenda — a lasting peace.

Hey, Harvard! Pick Up the Phone and Call Canada

May 28, 2025

Harvard is the oldest American university. Its faculty has won more Nobel Prizes and educated more U.S. presidents than any other school. It's endured the Salem witch trials in the 1690s, occupation by British troops in the 1770s and the McCarthy Red Scare in the 1950s.

But will it survive Donald Trump in the 2020s?

In a letter sent on April 11, the Trump administration demanded control of which students Harvard admits and who teaches them and what they're taught. Until Harvard accedes, the administration has ordered the stoppage of over $3 billion in federal support for Harvard, mainly support of lifesaving medical research.

Why has the man who paid a $25 million fine for running the fraudulent Trump University turned his guns on Harvard University? Because if he can intimidate Harvard, what choice will universities less rich and less renowned have but to follow suit?

The Trump administration fired another shot at Harvard on May 22, when Trump's Secretary of Homeland Security Kristi Noem revoked the visas of all international students enrolled at Harvard under the Student Exchange and Visitor Program, thereby barring almost all international students from attending the university.

Taking on Harvard is popular with the Trumpian base. It's seen as an avatar of elitism. Even the future monarch of Belgium, a student at Harvard's Kennedy School of Government, was caught up in the ban. But Harvard is not just for the royal and rich. Over half of Harvard undergraduates receive financial aid. During the academic year, I live on the Harvard campus with undergraduates whose parents work as waitstaff in restaurants and who run small bodegas.

Their families pay nothing for their education if their income is under $100K and no tuition if under $200K. Harvard opens the door of opportunity for these students.

Even as Trump decries the American balance of payments deficit, the over 1.1 million international students in the United States contributed an estimated $44 billion to the economy during the 2023-2024 school. His right-hand man Elon Musk was born in South Africa but received his undergraduate degree from the University of Pennsylvania, Trump's own alma mater.

But international students benefit the United States for reasons beyond mere economics. The loss of international students will diminish both the education that they receive and the one that their American classmates receive. I have taught, advised and conversed at length with these students. Differing perspectives broaden horizons and catalyze learning. As Harvard President Alan Garber told Harvard's international students: "If we are to maintain our leading position in science, business and the arts, we must cherish our status as a magnet for talent the world over. To undermine this is to undermine America itself."

Garber moved beyond mere rhetoric and had Harvard sue the administration for its attempt to expel Harvard's international students. He is standing up for his university and every university. Already, a federal judge has issued a temporary order to stop the administration from taking away the visas.

However, Trump and his team have the visa stamp. Even if Harvard wins its case, new visas for new students will have to be issued, and Secretary of State Marco Rubio can deny and delay their issuance. What students, what professors will want to come to Harvard with such a threat hanging over them? Even now, many of Harvard's current international students are in a state of panic and fear coming back this fall.

Fighting the Trump administration in court is the right thing to do, but Harvard needs a contingency plan.

Harvard ought to take steps to open a second campus. Toronto is only 400 miles from Harvard's main campus in Cambridge, Massachusetts. Students admitted to the university but not to the United States can pursue their studies at a second campus there. Some classes will be attended via videoconference from classrooms in Toronto. Professors from Massachusetts can whisk there in less than two hours by plane to teach classes onsite. Others can be based in Toronto for a semester or longer, and it will be students in Cambridge who attend via the internet. Jet aviation and electronic technology can unite the two campuses.

Harvard undergraduates live in a dozen undergraduate houses, each with a dining hall, library, classrooms and gym. Let's open one more in Toronto. Students on the main campus could rotate there for a semester, and students in Toronto could rotate or transfer to the U.S.

Harvard can move fast when it must. During the Revolutionary War when the British occupied Harvard Yard, classes were moved to Concord, 20 miles away. After World War II, when the university was inundated by returning veterans, Harvard bought the Brunswick Hotel in Boston to house them. When the pandemic closed down the campus in March 2020, neither I nor any other instructor paused in our teaching — we pivoted and taught via videoconference.

Setting up a campus in Toronto won't be easy. There'll be red tape, work permits for professors and deans and visas for students. Garber needs to work with the government of Canadian Prime Minister Mark Carney, Harvard College Class of 1987, to come up with a plan to open a Harvard campus in Toronto, ideally this fall.

Nicolas Dominguez Carrero, a graduating senior elected to Phi Beta Kappa and with family from both Texas and Colombia, told the Harvard Gazette: "I think Harvard's doing an amazing job standing up for academic freedom and democracy, writ large. It is a time of crisis, but if there's an institution that can weather this storm, it's Harvard."

Carrero is correct in his analysis. And to increase the odds that it does indeed weather the storm, Harvard must move with speed, force and decisiveness.

President Garber, pick up the phone and call the prime minister. Today.

Antisemitism Raises Its Ugly, Un-American Head

June 4, 2025

Jews who came to the United States from Eastern Europe in the late 19th and early 20th centuries celebrated the country as the "Goldene Medina," Yiddish for the "Golden Land." And by comparison to life in Czarist Russia with its pogroms, conscription of Jewish men for 25 years and restrictions on professions and owning land, so it was.

Jews have certainly flourished in the United States. While only a little over 2% of Americans are Jewish, over 30% all the Nobel Prizes won by Americans have been won by Jews, ranging from Bob Dylan's for literature to Paul Samuelson's for economics. The founders of iconic American companies such as Facebook, Estee Lauder, the Home Depot, Oracle and Warner Brothers were all Jewish.

In fact, a March 2023 Pew Research poll found Americans felt more positive about Jews than mainline Protestants, evangelicals, Catholics or atheists. And yet by March 2024, an article in The Atlantic declared the golden age of American Jews is ending. Another article in The New York Times this month reported "a sense that simply existing in public as a Jewish person is increasingly dangerous."

What changed in those 12 months? On Oct. 7, 2023, Hamas attacked Israel. The subsequent war between the terrorist group and the Jewish state awakened the slumbering dragon of American antisemitism, prejudice against Jews. Three recent assaults on Jews in this country dramatically illustrate the point:

— In April, a man set fire to the residence of Pennsylvania Gov. Josh Shapiro, who is Jewish, on the first night of Passover. The accused called Shapiro a monster "for what he wants to do to the Palestinian people." As a state governor, Shapiro has no role in formulating U.S. policy toward the Middle East.

— In an incident last month, a man who murdered a young couple he did not know as they left the Capital Jewish Museum in Washington, D.C., told police, "I did it for Palestine, I did it for Gaza."

— This month, a man yelled out "Free Palestine!" as he set fire to demonstrators in Boulder, Colorado, who were calling for the release of Israeli hostages held by Hamas.

In all three cases, the motivation for the attack was opposition to Israel. In all three cases, the intended targets were presumed to be Jewish. The attackers' reasoning must have gone something like this: I am against Israel, Israel is a majority-Jewish state, therefore I should attack Jews wherever I find them. The assailants then targeted Jews not because of their individual beliefs, which they did not know, but because they are Jews.

Blaming a Jew who is an American resident and citizen for what happens elsewhere in the world is not a pro-Hamas, pro-Arab or pro-Palestinian stance; it is an antisemitic one. It is antisemitism when American citizens who are Jewish are held responsible for the actions of the state of Israel, a foreign country over 6,000 miles away.

Americans of Russian descent whose families have been in the U.S. for generations are seldom if ever blamed for the bloodshed resulting from the Russian invasion of Ukraine. Why then do so many who oppose Israeli actions in the Middle East blame American Jews whose roots in this country often go back a century or more? The obvious answer is antisemitism, a prejudice against Jews that can be traced back from ancient times through the Holocaust when 6 million Jews were murdered because of their religious ancestry.

The renewal of widespread antisemitism in this country is like a biblical plague of locusts that lay buried for years, only to reemerge and devastate society. In 2022, the Anti-Defamation League counted 3,697 antisemitic incidents in the United States. Two years later, the number was 9,354, up over 2.5 times. Swastikas were painted near a Holocaust memorial in Philadelphia and on a synagogue in Minneapolis. Jews were excluded from an anti-Nazi rally in Cincinnati and a march supporting lesbians in New York City.

I live on the Harvard campus during the school year. There are Jewish students and faculty here who support Israel's efforts to free the hostages and defeat Hamas, and there are Jews who oppose the very existence of the state of Israel. One Jewish student told me over a meal in the dining hall that he feared for his physical safety if he spoke out in favor of Israel. Since the Oct. 7 attack, many students now hide their identity as Jews. There have been chants on campus to "globalize the intifada" — which seems to call for exporting Middle Eastern violence to the U.S. A report on antisemitism at Harvard found, "We are not aware of any other group on campus that is subject to social exclusion as part of an intentional campaign by political organizers."

Rabbi David Wolpe, a visiting professor at Harvard Divinity School in 2023-24, said a Jewish student told him: "They don't just hate what I believe. They hate me." Sheila Katz, chief executive of the National Council of Jewish Women, wrote: "Our position on this war, or on Israel, does not affect how extremists perceive us. To them, we are all Jews, and that alone makes us targets for hate and violence."

Antisemitism is anti-American. It is now and always has been. In 1790, George Washington wrote to a synagogue in Rhode Island: "May the Children of the Stock of Abraham, who dwell in this land, continue to merit and enjoy the good will of the other Inhabitants; while every one shall sit in safety under his own vine and figtree, and there shall be none to make him afraid."

Amen.

Is King Donald Pushing California Toward Independence?

June 11, 2025

In the spring of 1775, the royal governor of Massachusetts, appointed by King George III, commanded 700 Redcoats to march to Lexington to suppress the colony's Patriots. Almost exactly 250 years later, the American president ordered 700 Marines to Los Angeles to suppress California demonstrators.

The royal governor's action set off a chain reaction that led to American independence. It's certainly a long shot, but I wonder if Donald Trump's action will lead to California's.

The British troops came to Lexington seeking to arrest Patriot leaders John Hancock and Sam Adams, both future governors of Massachusetts. Trump recently said, "I think it would be a great thing" if current California Gov. Gavin Newsom were arrested.

The year after the British march on Lexington, the Declaration of Independence accused George III of being "a Prince, whose character is thus marked by every act which may define a Tyrant." Referring to himself, Trump has posted, "LONG LIVE THE KING!" He has declared, "I have the right to do whatever I want as president." Trump acts accordingly even as the courts play Whac-A-Mole in attempting to block his executive orders.

The Declaration of Independence also accused George III of obstructing "the Laws for Naturalization of Foreigners; refusing to ... encourage their migrations hither." California has the largest number of immigrants of any state, and 57% of its voters believe they are a net positive for California. Roughly the same percentage support providing state health care to eligible low-income Californians, no matter their immigration status, "even if the Trump administration threatens to withhold significant federal funding." Clearly Trump's roundups and troop dispatches are not intended to win over a majority of the California electorate.

The Declaration of Independence goes on to cite King George's "cutting off our Trade with all parts of the world." Los Angeles's port is the largest in the United States. The director of the port expects volume to plummet in the wake of Trump's tariffs.

California represents a future that Trump disdains, even as 1 in 8 Americans call the state their home. Its Silicon Valley is ground zero for technology. Hollywood is the capital of world culture. Residents of Latino heritage constitute 40% of California's population with 34% white, 16% Asian American or Pacific Islander, 6% Black and 3% multiracial. The United States as a whole is 75% white, but the trend is clear: White people are a minority among American K-12 students.

Trump doesn't like that future. He looks backward to a mythical 1950s when America was overwhelmingly white, Jim Crow flourished, wives stayed at home, TVs were tuned to "Gunsmoke" and "Leave It to Beaver" and America's largest companies included General Motors and U.S. Steel, not Apple and Nvidia. He is attacking California because of its leading position among the states, just as he has targeted Harvard as the nation's most prominent institution of higher learning. He has threatened to cut off federal funding to both. If California and Harvard buckle under his authoritarian assaults, others might meekly follow.

In 1775, the Patriots were fed up with King George III. In 2025, Californians are fed up with Trump. A poll this year shows a clear majority of all Californians believe they'd better off if their state could peacefully leave the Union. Perhaps the departure would even be welcomed by Trump supporters. About half of the nation's Republicans believe California is "not really American." Florida GOP Gov. Ron DeSantis has implored, "Don't allow Florida to become San Francisco."

California accounts for 14% of the U.S.' output of goods and services. If it were an independent nation, it would be the world's fourth largest economy, trailing only the rest of the U.S., China and Germany. In 2024, California grew faster than any of them. At a time when the overall federal deficit is massive, California pays $83 billion more in federal taxes than it receives in federal funds. Without California, the other states would have a larger deficit to deal with, while an independent California would run a substantial surplus.

To Californians, that sure looks like taxation without representation. In 2000 and 2016, they supplied the votes that provided Al Gore and Hillary Clinton with an edge in the nation's popular vote. But thanks to the arcane Electoral College, which provides more weight to voters in small states, George W. Bush and Donald Trump were awarded the presidency in those elections.

Trump believes in "the art of the deal." From a transactional perspective, Californians may have struck a bad one in joining the Union.

I myself am a Californian, a proud product of its public schools, a fan of its weather, beaches, music, diversity and athletic teams. I worked in Silicon Valley. I am married to a native Californian who traces her roots in the state back to when it was a Spanish colony. But even with all that, my loyalty to the United States trumps my Californian roots. I owe so much to this country that has provided a life of freedom and bounty to my forebears and me. My father felt the same when he fought against fascism in World War II.

Trump and his MAGA followers need to be careful, though, in their war on California.

Mark Twain is one of many reputed to have said, "It is difficult to make predictions, particularly about the future." In fact, I am not going to predict that California's departure from the Union is imminent. Still, Donald Trump ought to bear in mind that George III didn't figure on the loss of Massachusetts from his empire when those troops were sent to Lexington.

Russian and Iranian Threats Dim in Summer Brightness

June 18, 2025

Way back in 1919, the poet William Butler Yeats wrote of a time when the "centre cannot hold," and "mere anarchy" and "the blood-dimmed tide" spread throughout the world. Sounds like today, doesn't it?

And yet, as the summer of 2025 begins, I see signs that the center is making a comeback and that those fighting to spread blood and anarchy are being beaten back.

Two of the nations in the world that most aggressively oppose freedom and democracy, Russia and Iran, are at war with countries that aspire to them.

In 2005, Russian President Vladimir Putin declared the Soviet Empire's collapse "was the greatest geopolitical catastrophe of the century." He set out to begin rectifying it nine years later when he sent troops to seize Crimea, which constituted about 4% of the former Soviet republic of Ukraine. Given the relatively weak response of the Obama administration, which relied on economic sanctions, and Germany, which was dependent on Russian natural gas, it was inevitable Putin would come back for seconds. He did so in 2022 when he ordered his army to invade the rest of now-independent Ukraine.

While Putin expected Russia to occupy the Ukrainian capital of Kyiv within days, the war grinds on three years later. The Center for Strategic and International Studies, a nonprofit think tank, estimates up to 250,000 Russian soldiers have died in the war against Ukraine, with overall Russian casualties approaching a million.

What has Putin gained in return for a sea of spilt Russian blood? He has spurred the historically neutral nations Finland and

Sweden to join NATO and exposed Russia as something less than an irresistible force. The United Kingdom, Germany, Poland and France are bolstering their support for Ukraine as they modernize and enlarge their own defense capabilities. The combined size of those four countries' economies is over five times larger than Russia's. Even taking into account the Trump administration's fluctuating American support for Ukraine, Putin's attempt to take over that country may be the worst foreign policy blunder by a major power since World War II.

Hamas took over rule of Gaza in 2007. In July 2012, then-Iranian President Mahmoud Ahmadinejad said that "any freedom lover and justice seeker in the world must do its best for the annihilation of the Zionist regime (Israel)." Iran armed Hamas as well as Hezbollah in Lebanon and the Assad regime in Syria as a less expensive and safer alternative to direct confrontation with Israel.

On Oct. 3, 2023, Iran's Supreme Leader Ali Khameini posted a message on social media promising that "the usurper Zionist regime is coming to an end." A Hamas terrorist attack followed four days later. Since then, Israel's forces have drastically diminished the fighting capability of both Hamas and Hezbollah, and Syria has undergone a regime change, leaving Iran to stand virtually alone against Israel.

In 2021, Israeli Prime Minister Benjamin Netanyahu vowed to the U.S. defense secretary, "I will never allow Iran to obtain the nuclear capability to carry out its genocidal goal of eliminating Israel." On June 12 of this year, the International Atomic Energy Agency declared Iran was breaking the rules against developing nuclear weapons. On June 12, too, the 60 days that President Donald Trump had given Iran to negotiate an end to its development of such weapons lapsed.

The next day, June 13, Israel attacked Iranian sites and personnel involved with nuclear weapons development. Trump publicly endorsed the Israeli move once its success was clear. Now the specter of a nuclear-armed Iran is far closer to disappearing. Without a looming Iranian threat, Saudi Arabia might well resume moving toward normalization of relations with Israel, an event former Secretary of State Antony J. Blinken in 2023 called a potentially "transformative event in the Middle East and well beyond."

There is a risk that Israel will overreach. The clerics who run Iran are far from popular. In fact, in its attack on Iranian nuclear sites, Israel received assistance from their opponents within Iran. But it's not up to Israel to force regime change. It must be a groundswell of Iranians.

Israel should keep in mind Churchill's aphorism — "In War: Resolution, In Defeat: Defiance, In Victory: Magnanimity, In Peace: Good Will." The country has shown resolution and defiance in the wake of the Hamas terrorist attack on Oct. 7, 2023. For lasting peace, it must show the magnanimity and goodwill that are required for lasting peace.

Despite all, planet Earth remains a dangerous place. The slaughter continues on the Ukrainian-Russian border. Nation-building in Lebanon and Syria remains a work in progress. Hamas has not been utterly defeated. Noncombatant Gazans need to be protected, fed and sheltered. The Israel-Palestinian Arab deadlock festers. Outside of Europe and the Middle East, China still claims Taiwan and the rogue state of North Korea, unlike Iran, already possesses nuclear weapons.

Still, a more peaceful world is within reach. With summer comes hope.

Iranian Regime Remains No Friend to Peace in Middle East

June 25, 2025

The proverb "the enemy of my enemy is my friend" goes back to Roman times. But being repeated through the centuries doesn't mean it's always true.

Recently, Israeli Prime Minister Benjamin Netanyahu and U.S. President Donald Trump ordered warplanes to bomb Iranian nuclear development sites. If you regard either or both of them as enemies, does that mean the Iranian regime is your friend?

Reader, do not fall into that trap. You can criticize, disdain or even despise the American and Israeli heads of government and still abhor the Iranian regime and everything it stands for.

In 1979, the Iranian Revolution led to the replacement of the country's monarchy by a dictatorship headed by clerics. By 1986, the U.S. State Department had already deemed the Iranian regime "the world's leading exporter of terrorism." And no wonder. There's little doubt the Iranian theocracy instigated and supported a 1983 bombing in Beirut that killed 241 American Marines and other service members.

The Iranian regime also targeted Jews wherever they might be found. In the most notorious incident, 85 people were killed and more than 300 injured in a 1994 explosion at a Jewish community center in Buenos Aires. Prosecutors placed the blame on Iranian president Hashemi Rafsanjani and other officials.

The export of terrorism, of indiscriminate attacks aimed at the United States, Israel and Jews, has continued over the past three decades. During the first Trump administration, the State Department held: "The Iranian regime is responsible for the deaths of at least 603 American service members in Iraq since 2003. This...

is in addition to the many thousands of Iraqis killed by the IRGC's (Islamic Revolutionary Guard Corps) proxies."

Trump has a well-deserved reputation for taking any action personally. His Secretary of State Marco Rubio has declared, "The Iranian regime has been trying to murder President Trump and other American officials for years." The Biden Justice Department charged an Iranian agent of also "plotting to assassinate former President Donald Trump's national security advisor John Bolton."

The Iranian regime has supplied Russia with weapons including drones and ballistic missiles for its use in its aggression against Ukraine, an American ally. In 2024, the Pentagon reported, "The United States has confirmed reports that Iran has transferred shipments of Fath 360 close-range ballistic missiles to Russia, which we assess could employ them within weeks against Ukraine, leading to the deaths of even more Ukrainian civilians."

The longstanding claims by the Iranian regime that it was developing enriching uranium for peaceful purposes is belied by its actions. Uranium enriched to around 4% is adequate to generate electrical power. Before the recent Israeli and American bombings, Iran had reached purity levels of 60% from which it's relatively quick to reach the 90% level required for nuclear bombs. Moreover, the key installation where the enrichment process would take place was Fordow. This installation was guarded by 300 feet of concrete and anti-aircraft missiles, protection hardly required for a plant devoted to peaceful uses of uranium. The International Atomic Energy Agency reported this spring that Iran had violated its rules intended to stop the proliferation of nuclear weapons.

For years, the Iranian supreme leader Ali Khameini has threatened the end of Israel. In 2014, he called in a tweet for its "annihilation." In 2015, he said, "Israel will not exist in another quarter century." A digital clock in Tehran was even erected counting down the days until 2040 when Israel would supposedly disappear. (Israel reported its warplanes blew up the clock on June 23.)

Threats of annihilation together with clandestine development of nuclear weapons could only lead Israel to regard the current Iranian regime as an existential threat to its people.

Of course, Iran and Israel share no border. It's about 1,000 miles from the Israeli capital of Jerusalem to Tehran. The Iranian regime has long embraced a strategy of using militias and armed terrorist groups neighboring Israel, such as Hamas in Gaza and Hezbollah in Lebanon, to foment terrorism and missile attacks. As the U.S. State Department found in 2019, Iran is an "outlaw regime" using the Islamic Revolutionary Guard Corps, part of Iran's official military, "to provide financial and other material support, training, technology transfer, advanced conventional weapons, guidance, or direction to a broad range of terrorist organizations."

In the 18th century, French diplomat Honore Gabriel Riqueti suggested, in regard to the militaristic forerunner of Germany, that "Prussia is not a state which rules over an army, but an army which rules over a state." Similarly, today Iran is not a state which rules over a policy of aggression and terrorism, but a policy of terror and aggression which rules over a state.

A policy of aggression and terror directed against the "Great Satan" (the United States) and the "Little Satan" (Israel) certainly appears to be more important to Iran's rulers than the economy. From 1978 to 2023, the per capita GDP of Iran grew about two times in constant dollars, while Israel's grew over 11 times. The Iranian regime has squandered the prosperity of two generations and for what? No wonder the Iranian people have shouted for regime change in thousands of street protests.

I myself am no friend of Trump nor of Netanyahu. But I still abhor the evil, murderous regime in Iran.

Democracy Strikes Out

July 2, 2025

In Chief Justice John Roberts's opening statement at his confirmation hearing, he explained that judges are like baseball umpires. "Umpires don't make the rules," he said. Their job is "to call balls and strikes."

In the case of Trump v. Casa decided on June 27, it appears a majority of the Supreme Court called three strikes and you're out for American democracy.

Strike one: Chief Umpire Roberts cast the Supreme Court's deciding vote in the 2010 Citizens United case which allowed corporations and wealthy donors to spend unlimited sums on elections. President Barack Obama did not kick dust on Roberts' shoes to protest this blown call, but he did warn the decision "will open the floodgates for special interests — including foreign corporations — to spend without limit in our elections." So, it's proven. The largest contributor to President Donald Trump's 2024 campaign, Elon Musk, was given access to confidential government records and led the administration's efforts to shut down agencies in violation of the law.

Strike two: Roberts wrote the opinion for 2024's Trump v. United States case in which the president was granted absolute immunity "from criminal prosecution for conduct within his exclusive sphere of constitutional authority." In her scathing dissent, Justice Sonia Sotomayor notes that Alexander Hamilton made "an important distinction between 'the king of Great Britain,' who was 'sacred and inviolable,' and the 'President of the United States,' who 'would be amenable to personal punishment and disgrace.'" Sotomayor points out that under Roberts' ruling, a president who orders the Navy's Seal Team 6 to assassinate a political rival would be immune to prosecution. Ominously, she also suggests the president might be immune if they organize a military coup to hold on to power. If only President Richard Nixon could have had Roberts calling the balls and strikes in the Watergate Scandal.

Strike three: The 14th Amendment, adopted in 1868, ensures citizenship to "all persons born... in the United States, and subject to the jurisdiction thereof." In the 1898 case of United States v. Wong Kim Ark, the Supreme Court held the amendment meant just what it said: Babies born in the United States are citizens whether or not their parents are. On his first day in office this year, Trump ordered that citizenship be denied if the baby's mother is in the country unlawfully or temporarily and if the baby's father is not a citizen or lawful permanent resident.

Federal district courts in Massachusetts, Maryland and Washington state issued injunctions against enforcement of Trump's order pending a decision on the merits. Appellate courts upheld the injunctions. Trump's Department of Justice appealed those decisions to the Supreme Court. Roberts appointed Justice Amy Coney Barrett to write the court's opinion. She in essence held that the lower court rulings delaying enforcement of the Trump order until the Supreme Court could rule ought not apply nationwide but only to the parties bringing suits.

Twenty-two states and two cities had sued to have Trump's order ruled unconstitutional. Presumably, the Supreme Court will make a ruling that applies in all 50 states some time in the indeterminate future. In the meantime, there could be cases where a baby born in one of the 22 states is a citizen, while another newborn with the same status in one of the other 28 states is not and can be deported. That's like saying the same pitch is a strike in Wrigley Field and a ball in Fenway Park.

In her dissent, Sotomayor warns that, even though birthright citizenship is guaranteed by the Constitution, "no right is safe in the new legal regime the Court creates." Justice Ketanji Brown Jackson writes in her concurring dissent, "When the Government says 'do not allow the lower courts to enjoin executive action universally as a remedy for unconstitutional conduct,' what it is actually saying is that the Executive wants to continue doing something that a court has determined violates the Constitution — please allow this."

All this means, as Sotomayor points out, that some future administration "may try to seize firearms from lawabiding citizens or prevent people of certain faiths from gathering to worship." The majority of the court holds "absent cumbersome class-action litigation" that in many cases courts will be powerless to provide relief even for flagrantly unconstitutional governmental acts. Thus, Bill of Rights guarantees such as freedom of speech and freedom from unreasonable searches are "meaningful in name only for any individuals who are not parties to a lawsuit."

Major League Baseball is testing a system using artificial intelligence to call balls and strikes rather than human umpires. Perhaps American democracy would be better served by using AI programmed to support our constitutional rights and democracy rather than the human justices now making the calls.

But, come on, that's not going to happen. So, where are we then? Unlimited amounts of money flow into federal election campaigns and undermine American democracy. Presidents can do whatever they want while in office with little fear of prosecution for breaking the law up to and including assassinating political opponents. And presidents can issue illegal orders overruling constitutional rights that will not be completely stopped unless and until the Supreme Court gets around to ruling on them.

What's left of our Constitution? Not much. Put those three calls together and, American democracy, you're outta here.

No Defense for the Indefensible — but Trump Team Tries Anyway

July 9, 2025

President Donald Trump and his acolytes need to learn that the days of falsely blaming the deep state, government inefficiency or DEI hires for their own bungling are over. They, not Joe Biden and his team, are now running the country.

Three days before the deadly July 4 flood in Texas, Republican Sen. Ted Cruz inserted language in the "One Big Beautiful Bill Act" that eliminated $150 million aimed at improving weather forecasting, modeling and warnings. Twenty-four hours after the Guadalupe River crested at record levels, reporters found the Texas senator on vacation touring the Parthenon in Athens. Not a good look.

It's not clear how much the Trump administration's cut of over 600 National Weather Service employees contributed to the disaster, but Trump signed the bill even as young campers and others were perishing in the flood. Since then, the Federal Emergency Management Agency's response has been feeble at best. That's no surprise; just last month Trump declared his intention to begin "phasing out" FEMA, and the number of FEMA personnel ready to deploy to disaster sites had already been cut by two-thirds.

White House press secretary Karoline Leavitt declared that the flood was an "act of God" and that blaming Trump "serves no purpose during this time of national mourning." Leavitt needs to stop defending the administration's acts with empty rhetoric. Cruz, too. About all he could offer was an accusation of "partisan finger pointing."

The flood in Texas will prove the first of many natural disasters in the next four years. As meteorologist Dr. Jeff Masters wrote in Yale Climate Connections, "We're pushing our luck if we think the cuts to NOAA, which oversees the weather service, won't cause a breakdown in our ability to get people out of harm's way in the future." The gutting of FEMA won't help in the aftermath of the disasters either.

The Trump administration shows few signs of getting its act together as it deals with crises and challenges whether natural or manmade.

Trump crowed that his decision to drop "bunker buster" bombs on Iranian nuclear sites obliterated them. And yet, a preliminary report from the Defense Department suggested Iranian development of nuclear weapons would be delayed only by a few months. Leavitt responded by saying, "The leaking of this alleged assessment is a clear attempt to demean President Trump." Maybe, but if wrong, who will be blamed when Iran joins the nuclear club? God? Genies?

Trump's sporadic military support of Ukraine and his loosening of sanctions directed against Russia have made a victory of the latter over the former more likely. If President Vladimir Putin should fulfill his war aims and turn Ukraine into a satellite state, what will Trump say? Any attempt to blame NATO, Biden or Ukrainian President Volodymyr Zelenskyy will ring flat, indeed.

The Trump administration has dismantled teams in the FBI and Department of Homeland Security that protected against foreign interference in American elections. Arizona's secretary of state, Adrian Fontes, warned in a letter to the president, "This decision undermines Arizona's election security at a time when our enemies around the world are using online tools to push their agendas and ideologies into our very homes." What excuse might the Trump team come up with for unfettered interference by China, Russia, North Korea and Iran in the 2026 and 2028 elections?

The tariffs imposed by Trump raise the prices on foreign imports. The dollar has lost about 10% of its value since Trump took office in January, which will also increase the price of imports to American consumers. Who will there be but Trump for Americans to hold responsible for the increased costs of purchasing cars, cellphones and coffee?

As of July 8, 1,288 confirmed measles cases were reported by 39 states. That's four times more than in all of 2024 and about 20 times more than in 2023. A measles epidemic looms, aggravated by the anti-vaccination policies of Trump's secretary of Health and Human Services, Robert F. Kennedy Jr. Children will die unnecessarily in 1 to 3 of every 1,000 cases. What will Trump and RFK Jr. have to say to their parents?

A recent study in the highly regarded medical journal Lancet estimates American aid to less-developed countries, especially in Africa, has saved over 90 million lives over the past two decades. The article goes on to estimate that the Trump administration's cuts in these programs will cost 14 million lives in the next five years. Secretary of State Marco Rubio denied in congressional testimony that the cuts had cost lives. In response, reporter Nicholas Kristoff wrote about 5-year-old Evan Anzoo from South Sudan who was kept alive by American-supplied medicine costing less than 12 cents a day. Evan died after the administration froze most humanitarian aid. I wonder how Trump or Rubio will argue that makes America great again.

According to a PBS News/NPR/Marist poll released on July 1, 54% of Americans describe the actions of Immigration and Customs Enforcement in enforcing immigration laws as having gone too far — that's triple the number who believe ICE has not gone far enough. Nevertheless, the OBBBA allocated about $75 billion to build detention centers and expand ICE staff. How will Trump and Homeland Security Secretary Kristi Noem defend mass roundups and building what appear to be concentration camps in the United States?

I do have a word of advice to the Trump team. Yes, Americans were willing to elect a candidate who'd been found by the courts to be a felon, insurrectionist and sexual assaulter. And yet, I suspect they will show far less tolerance for a president who cannot protect them from Mother Nature, Vladimir Putin, pathogenetic viruses, inflation and the deaths of innocent children. You're going to have to do a better job defending your policies than mere denials, irreligious appeals to the Almighty and empty attempts to shift blame onto political opponents.

As the owner of a china shop told a clumsy customer, "You break it, you own it."

NYC Democratic Candidate Mirrors Trump's Campaign Strategy

July 16, 2025

The Democratic nominee's campaign for New York City mayor is a mirror image of Donald Trump's first presidential campaign. Their political images might be reversed, but their campaign tactics are awfully similar.

New York City Democrats nominated state assemblyman Zohran Mamdani as their candidate for mayor in a primary on June 25. While the office of mayor has little to do with foreign policy, Mamdani has made pro-Palestinian Arab and anti-Israel pronouncements a centerpiece of his campaign and, as he himself says, of his political identity.

Before ever running for office, Mamdani sent his "love to the Holy Land Five," five Americans convicted of illegally donating to the terrorist group Hamas. His posting on social media the day after the Hamas attack on Oct. 7, 2023, which killed over 1,200 Israeli civilians, did not mention Hamas by name at all. Instead, he wrote that a lasting peace would come only after Israel ended its "occupation" of Gaza. Only one problem: There were no Israeli troops in Gaza on Oct. 7. They only entered Gaza in response to the attack on Oct. 13. Mamdani was spreading untruths that fit his political views.

Trump used the issue of immigration in a similar way. Announcing his candidacy in 2015, he declared, "When Mexico sends its people, they're not sending their best... They're bringing drugs. They're bringing crime. They're rapists." Of course, the country of Mexico wasn't itself sending any people, let alone drug dealers, criminals and rapists. More recently, Trump has deceitfully accused the country of Venezuela of invading the U.S. He's modeling political behavior for Mamdani.

Mamdani has defended calls for "a global intifada," which implies attacks on Israel and Jews around the world, as a call for "Palestinian human rights." In the wake of Oct. 7, 2023, there have been a firebombing at a Melbourne synagogue, hit-and-run assaults on Israeli soccer fans in Amsterdam, the murder of two attendees at the Capital Jewish Museum in Washington, D.C., and countless more incidents. No matter. Mamdani is appealing to his core supporters who regard condemning Israel and downplaying attacks on Jews as a prerequisite to being a true progressive.

In his first campaign, Trump did concede some of the immigrants from Mexico are "good people." In last fall's, he even shouted out, "I love Hispanics." During his primary campaign, Mamdani proclaimed he "loves Jewish New Yorkers." In a post-primary meeting with New York City business leaders, Mamdani said he would discourage use of the phrase "globalize the intifada." No matter in either case. The followers of Trump and Mamdani heard the dog whistles and know where they stand.

Bob Dylan sang "You don't need a weatherman to know which way the wind blows." Trump certainly didn't need a political meteorologist to detect the winds of change sweeping across the country in regard to immigration. Likewise, Mamdani sensed a gale in regard to American views on Israel. Nationally, the number of Democrats with a negative view of Israel has increased from 53% to 69% in the last three years.

While the Democratic leaders of both the Senate and the House, New York's Chuck Schumer and Hakim Jeffries, remain steadfast in their support of the Israeli state, Mamdani understands that the future of the Democratic Party is to stand four-square against the Middle East's only democracy. He is proving himself by opposing PEPs, a leftist term of derision for those who are "progressive except for Palestine."

Mamdami mimes Trump's tactics in another way, by promising much more than he could ever deliver. In 2016, Trump promised to build a "great, great wall" along the southern border, paid for by Mexico. Mexico paid nothing, and the wall that was built was both short and easily breached. He also pledged to end Obamacare and set up a half-trillion-dollar infrastructure fund — neither of which happened.

Mamdani's list of promises that will never be kept might even be longer than Trump's. He has promised free child care, higher taxes on the rich, borrowing $70 billion to build 200,000 units of affordable housing, free fares on buses and nearly doubling the minimum wage to $30 per hour in the next five years. The state legislature would have to go along with most of these initiatives, and the chances of that are zero.

Otto von Bismarck, the 19th century German chancellor, famously said, "Politics is the art of the possible." Trump and Mamdani are proving Bismarck's aphorism to be outmoded. Instead, for them politics is promising the impossible.

Once nominated in 2016, Republicans rallied around Trump. In March of that year, then-Sen. Marco Rubio warned, "For years to come, there are many people on the right, in the media, and voters at large, that are going to be having to explain and justify how they fell into this trap of supporting Donald Trump." Six months later, Rubio endorsed Trump and today serves as his secretary of state.

A similar dynamic is at work with Mamdani's candidacy. New York City Democratic Rep. Jerry Nadler, former chair of the House Judiciary Committee and a longtime supporter of Israel, endorsed Mamdani after his primary victory, as have Democratic Rep. Adriano Epsaillat, Lt. Gov. Antonio Delgado and Attorney General Letisha James. Epsaillat explained his decision, saying that "If there is a common denominator in every decision that I've made since I began to represent this district, in terms of supporting someone, it's called the Democratic Party."

If there is indeed a common denominator among politicians of both parties that Trump and Mamdani can rely on, it's an unprincipled thirst for power.

In Robert Louis Stevenson's classic story, the respectable Dr. Jekyll looks into a mirror and sees himself as the hideous and deformed Mr. Hyde. If Mamdani could peer into that same mirror, he might well see an image of Donald Trump.

Superman, Not MAGA, Stands For the American Way

July 23, 2025

When I was a kid, I read "Superman" comics at the corner drugstore and watched reruns of the 1950s TV show starring George Reeves as the Man of Steel. Even now, I recall the intro to the show announcing Superman fought for "Truth, Justice and the American Way."

How could I not, then, head to the local multiplex and catch the latest screen version of "Superman," this summer's top blockbuster? The criticism of the movie from the MAGA folks made it even more of a must-see.

In regard to the film, former Trump campaign manager Kellyanne Conway declared, "We don't go to the movie theater to be lectured to and to have somebody throw their ideology onto us." Fox News labeled the movie "Superwoke," and its host Laura Ingraham pledged this was "another film we won't be seeing."

My verdict on the movie? Enjoyable enough with its high-res color and flash-bang special effects, but it really couldn't capture the simple magic of those comic books and black-and-white TV episodes. I did watch intently, though, wondering the whole 129 minutes what Conway and her band were criticizing.

Was it a hero who stands for truth? Last year their own hero, President Donald J. Trump, was found guilty on 34 counts of corruptly falsifying business records and, in another case, liable for $83 million for lying about journalist E. Jean Carroll. The Washington Post's Fact Checker column found Trump had made 30,573 false or misleading claims in his first term as president. By contrast, the only deception made by Superman in his latest multiplex adventure was disguising himself as Clark Kent, the mild-mannered reporter for the Daily Planet.

Perhaps MAGA's problem with the movie was a hero who advocates justice, who resists uncalled for aggression and brutal arrests. The current Trump administration has deported American citizens, legal residents and undocumented immigrants alike without even a pretense of due process. Career lawyers who actually work for a government department with Justice in its name are fired for doing their jobs prosecuting insurrectionists and enforcing ethics guidelines.

Could it be that Trump and MAGA stand against the American Way? The Superman film's writer/director James Gunn said it's the story of "an immigrant that came from other places." So are Trump and his allies against the movie because Superman himself is not a native-born American, but an immigrant from Krypton?

Really? Could a president whose mother was born in Scotland, whose wife was born in Slovenia, whose biggest campaign contributor was born in South Africa and whose secretary of state's parents were born in Cuba stand against an immigrant seeking the American dream? Do he and his MAGA followers reject the underlying premise of what President Ronald Reagan called "this land of opportunity" for new arrivals?

Apparently. Fox News host Jesse Watters snidely suggested that "MS-13," the name of a criminal gang most powerful in El Salvador, Honduras and Guatemala, was emblazoned on Superman's cape.

And what can be a more integral part of the American Way than loyalty to a pet dog? Comic relief is provided throughout the Superman film by the superdog Krypto who ignores Superman's commands and bowls him over at every opportunity. In contrast, when the 14-month-old dog belonging to Kristi Noem, Trump's current secretary of homeland security, displayed an "aggressive personality," she shot Cricket dead. Perhaps she should have shipped the pooch to a dog pound in El Salvador instead.

With the release of the blockbuster movie, the White House tweeted a poster of Trump in a Superman costume with the slogan "Truth, Justice and the American Way" inscribed across the bottom. Yeah, right. They might as well have posted him dressed as Mother Teresa.

In another poster, from way back in 1949, Superman tells a bunch of kids that if they "hear anybody talk against a schoolmate or anyone else because of his race, religion, or national origin, don't wait: tell him that kind of talk is un-American." What does that make Trump? He has claimed that Mexico is sending rapists across the borders, that the United States's first Black president was not born in this country, that a white supremacist rally contained "very fine people," that Muslims should be banned from entering the United States, that "thousands and thousands" of Arab Americans in New Jersey celebrated on 9/11 and that any Jew who votes for a Democrat shows "either a total lack of knowledge or great disloyalty."

At the "Superman" premiere, Gunn said, "I think this is a movie about kindness and I think that's something everyone can relate to." No, not everyone, Mr. Gunn.

The Senate Kisses Trump's Ring

July 30, 2025

Evidence was offered in recent Senate hearings that judicial nominee Emil Bove told subordinates the federal courts might need to be told "f**k you" if they opposed the administration. Nevertheless, in a display of their complete, utter and abject submission to President Donald Trump, Republican senators voted on July 29 to confirm the former Justice Department official as a judge on the U.S. Court of Appeals.

This result ought not be viewed as a surprise but as proof of the Senate's surrender to the power of Trump. He's already shown he could bully the Senate into passing a bill to cut Medicare payments by close to a trillion dollars, into acquitting him of leading an insurrection and into confirming a vaccine-denier to head federal health programs. Now, in their latest profile in cowardice, 50 Republican senators showed beyond any doubt that loyalty and obedience to Trump counts for more than the loyalty and obedience to the Constitution.

In addition to this column, I write novels. I would be hard-pressed to make up a believable character less suited for a federal judgeship than Emil Bove.

Senators heard testimony in confirmation hearings that Bove, a senior official in the Department of Justice, accentuated with an obscenity that the DOJ might have to ignore court rulings if they blocked Trump's deportation program. Bose claimed he had "no recollection" of such a statement despite corroborating evidence from other whistleblowers. In a July 21 article, The Washington Post reported that the Trump administration stood accused of defying or frustrating court oversight in over one-third of the cases where the courts had ruled against them.

Only 11 days after Trump's inauguration last January, Bove had overseen the dismissal of more than a dozen federal prosecutors who'd worked on cases arising from the Jan. 6 insurrection. He explained he would not "tolerate subversive personnel actions."

In February, Bove ordered that corruption charges against New York City Mayor Eric Adams be dropped in an apparent quid pro quo for his support of Trump administration immigration roundups. Hagan Scotten, a highly regarded federal prosecutor in New York and a former clerk to Chief Justice John Roberts, refused to be the one who dropped charges against Adams. He wrote to Bove, "No system of ordered liberty can allow the Government to use the carrot of dismissing charges, or the stick of threatening to bring them again, to induce an elected official to support its policy objectives.... I expect you will eventually find someone who is enough of a fool, or enough of a coward, to file your motion." The charges were eventually dropped by another official per Bove's orders.

Over 900 former Justice Department lawyers signed a letter to the Senate Judiciary Committee opposing Bove's confirmation as a federal appellate judge. "It is intolerable to us," they wrote, "that anyone who disgraces the Justice Department would be promoted to one of the highest courts in the land, as it should be intolerable to anyone committed to maintaining our ordered system of justice."

Chair of the Senate Judiciary Committee Charles Grassley abandoned decades of support for whistleblowers by supporting the Bove nomination. He offered this excuse: "My Democratic colleagues made no effort to support whistleblowers who raised alarms about the Biden family."

Bove's nomination was in the end confirmed by a 50-49 majority of the Republican-majority Senate.

Trump has demonstrated his untrammeled power over the Senate and the federal judiciary. He nominated a manifestly unfit candidate to an appellate court to show he could force what was once known as "the world's greatest deliberate body" to kiss his ring. His Justice Department defies court rulings to show judicial power relies on nothing more than nonexistent good faith. If a seat opens on the Supreme Court while Trump is in office and the Republicans still have a Senate majority, I'd bet on Bove as his nominee.

On Dec. 23, 1776, the patriot Thomas Paine wrote, "THESE are the times that try men's souls.... He that stands by (his country) now, deserves the love and thanks of man and woman. Tyranny, like hell, is not easily conquered; yet we have this consolation with us, that the harder the conflict, the more glorious the triumph."

We Americans need to heed Paine by waking up and standing up — for our country, for our Constitution and for the institutions meant to protect them.

For America, It's Time To Count What Really Counts

August 13, 2025

Donald Trump fired the head of the Bureau of Labor Statistics because he didn't like the numbers announced in her monthly jobs report.

The bureau reports not only on jobs, but also on inflation and compensation. All those numbers affect policy and politics. Slowing job growth might encourage the Federal Reserve to lower interest rates. Higher inflation might call into question the Trump administration's tariff policy. Compensation growth rates might affect voters' choices in next year's midterm elections.

And yet, there's more to making the United States the kind of country we want to live in than can be found in economic indicators alone. Of course, it's vital that Americans have enough to eat, a place to live and a job. But there are other vitally important numbers that should also affect our national policies.

Back in 1968, one of my political heroes made a speech at the University of Kansas during his campaign for the presidency. Then-Sen. Robert F. Kennedy spoke first of the national shame when Americans, especially children, were not adequately nourished. Even after poverty is wiped out, though, he believed, "Too much and for too long, we seemed to have surrendered personal excellence and community values in the mere accumulation of material things." He goes on to point out that building prisons, manufacturing bombs and guns, running cigarette ads and cutting down redwood forests all count toward the gross national product. Measuring economic output alone does not account for:

"The health of our children, the quality of their education or the joy of their play. It does not include the beauty of our poetry or the strength of our marriages, the intelligence of our public debate or the integrity of our public officials. It measures neither our wit nor our courage, neither our wisdom nor our learning, neither our compassion nor our devotion to our country, it measures everything in short, except that which makes life worthwhile. And it can tell us everything about America except why we are proud that we are Americans."

Robert F. Kennedy, the brother of the slain president and the father of the current secretary of Health and Human Services, was no naive, airheaded politician. The adjective most associated with him was "ruthless." He took on Fidel Castro, the Communist dictator of Cuba, and Jimmy Hoffa, the boss of the Teamsters Union, as well as Lyndon B. Johnson, the formidable vice president and then president of the United States.

So, 57 years after RFK spoke out, shouldn't we put the government's statistics people to work on measuring what makes life worthwhile? If we did, we might have a different country. One that values educating children over mining coal. One that cherishes its novelists, poets, musicians and painters. One that looks to public figures for integrity. One that cares for the unfortunate. One whose citizens empathize with their political opponents rather than demonize them.

If ranked by gross domestic product per capita alone, the United States is in fourth place among the world's nations. But the World Happiness Report adds five more criteria to the ratings: social support, healthy life expectancy, freedom to make one's own life choices, generosity of the general population and perceptions of internal and external corruption levels. With those criteria included, the U.S falls to 23rd place, while the top five slots are held by Finland, Denmark, Iceland, Sweden and Israel.

It's time to listen to what Robert F. Kennedy told us.

Hanging on my office wall is a quote from the ancient sage Ben Zoma. He asks, "Who is wealthy?" and answers this way:

"Those who are happy with what they have." Seeking to measure what makes life worthwhile is no easy task, nor is adjusting government policies to foster that goal. But these are challenges we Americans should undertake.

Trump may not like the numbers that are being reported by the Bureau of Labor Statistics, but he's not even looking at so many of the most important ones.

Acknowledgments

Without the inspiration, teaching, and urging of friends, family, and teachers, there would be no *The Raffel Ticket*. But they should not be blamed for the content of my columns. For better or worse, the opinions are mine.

Having said that, I would like to thank the teachers of my youth who cultivated my interest in this world we inhabit: from Palo Alto High, Patrick Presto and Shirley Griffin; from Harvard, Ernest May, Stephen Schuker, H.J. Hanham and Philip Heymann; and from Oxford, R.A.C. Parker.

The genesis of this column was sparked by a class on political writing taught at the Kennedy School of Government by Gregory Harris. Thank you, Lauren States, for twisting my arm and insisting I take it.

I so appreciate Creators for providing a forum for my column each week. In this era of "cancel culture," they let me say what I want and need to say. And I am especially indebted to Creators' Megan Leberknight for her expert editing, suggestions and counsel.

Lee Child, Ty Cobb, Andrew Heyward, Judy Perry Martinez, Jamie Raskin, Susan Samuelson, and James Slusher have done much to make this a better world, and I am so fortunate they have provided generous comments on this collection.

I care deeply about those who will inherit the Earth from me and my generation — especially my children, sons-in-law and grandchildren who inspire me every day.

While writing most of these columns, I lived among the undergraduates of Mather House. Thank you, Matherites, for granting me passage to Shangri-La.

Dear readers, thank *you* so much. Without you I would only be spitting into the wind. Even if you disagree with one or 10 or all of my opinions, I hope they provoke your thinking on the issues of the day, both trivial and momentous. One thing we cannot do is remain passive in this world where neglect, injustice, violence and authoritarianism abound even as joy, learning, righteousness and the quest for peace endure.

Finally, I owe much to my son Harry for ensuring I'm not too far off base in my historical or legal judgments and to my wife Teri, who pores over every rough draft of my columns and provides her own invaluable take on them, sharpening and improving what I submit. I care what she thinks of them most of all.

About the Author

Photo: Doug Peck

As senior counsel to the Senate Intelligence Committee, Keith Raffel worked to monitor the activities of the CIA, NSA and other three-letter agencies. Keith left the Intelligence Committee to return home to California and run for Congress. Although losing that race is still a painful memory, he counts himself lucky for escaping the morass of congressional politics when he did.

With an engineer father and hometown of Palo Alto, Keith then followed the path Fate had laid out and embarked on a tech career. He founded and then sold Silicon Valley's first cloud-computing company. For the past eight years, he's been a lecturer and resident scholar at Harvard. While there, he developed and co-taught a course on technology, ethics and society.

Keith writes a weekly column for Creators Syndicate that appears in newspapers and on websites across the country. In addition, he has established a career as a bestselling novelist. *The New York Times* deemed his first work of fiction, *Dot Dead*, "worthy of a Steve Jobs keynote presentation." All told, he has five published novels: two Silicon Valley mysteries, an archeological thriller, a spy story and a historical thriller.

A long-time denizen of Palo Alto in the heart of California's Silicon Valley, Keith now spends the academic year as a resident scholar at Harvard where he lives in an apartment in the same 400-student dorm as he did when an undergraduate himself.

The Raffel Ticket: Betting on America is also available as an e-book for Kindle, Amazon Fire, iPad, Nook and Android e-readers. Visit creatorspublishing.com to learn more.

CREATORS PUBLISHING

We find compelling storytellers and help them craft their narrative, distributing their novels and collections worldwide.

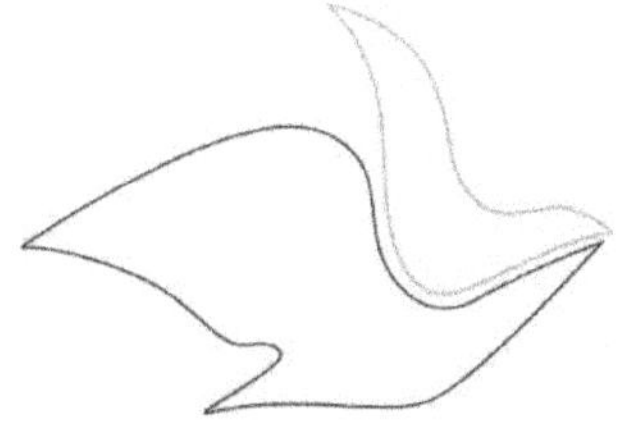